PUPILS
AS PERSONS

The Intext Series in Guidance and Counseling

Consulting Editor, Philip A. Perrone
University of Wisconsin—Madison

PUPILS AS PERSONS

Case Studies in Pupil Personnel Work

BRUCE R. AMBLE

RICHARD W. BRADLEY

Southern Illinois University

Foreword by John W. M. Rothney

INTEXT EDUCATIONAL PUBLISHERS
NEW YORK AND LONDON

To all teachers who are dedicated to their profession and discipline, and distinguished by genuine concern for, and understanding of, individual students, as exemplified by James L. Gordon, long time Band Director of Waterloo, Iowa.

Library of Congress Cataloging in Publication Data

Amble, Bruce R
  Pupils as persons.

(The Intext series in guidance and counseling)
1. Personnel service in education—Case studies.
I. Bradley, Richard W., joint author. II. Title.
LB1027.5.A54   371.4'07'22   73–6532
ISBN 0–7002–2439–4

Intext Educational Publishers, 257 Park Avenue South, New York, New York 10010

Text design by Paula Wiener

Contents

vi   *Contents*

Foreword

The time must come in all phases of pupil personnel services when theory needs to be focused by getting down to cases. Statistical studies, valuable as they may be for some purposes, can produce general laws, but when one looks at the individual, the laws must be modified. That statement should become perfectly clear to the student or practitioner who has read the material and done the exercises presented in this volume.

Employing an approach that has never previously been described in print, the authors demonstrate that case work is the heart of pupil personnel work and emphasize the fact that doing it is a difficult, demanding, but always an interesting activity. The reader will be challenged to think as he sees the various approaches to pupil problems used by others as they try to assist each pupil to make the most of his personal assets and environmental opportunities and to improve them. After reviewing what others have done, the reader is required to come to grips with real situations and to think hard about his own recommendations and the reasons for them.

The value of personnel services is being questioned very seriously at this time. The response to the questioning can best be made by providing evidence that effective action on the part of educators to assist particular pupils to help themselves is stimulated by personnel services, and by demonstrating that the personnel worker himself can provide assistance that no one else is in a position to offer. Study of this volume should assist those who would attempt such tasks, through providing evidence that pupil personnel work is an essential aspect of any effective educational offering.

JOHN W. M. ROTHNEY
Emeritus Professor of Counseling and Guidance
University of Wisconsin—Madison

Preface

The purpose of this book is to help interested readers gain a closer understanding of the practices by which pupil personnel services can become an integral part of the educational process. Originally the book was intended for use with graduate students in school psychology and school counseling interested in pupil personnel services. However, as a wide range of responses to the case studies from school personnel was accumulated, it soon became apparent that the book should be equally useful to teachers and school administrators. Concern for pupil adjustment and educational planning is not the sole province of the personnel specialist. Student welfare is a shared responsibility because the effectiveness of pupil personnel services rests upon all school personnel working to create better learning environments and programs for students.

Since it is in school settings that pupil personnel specialists must make their educational contributions, the book is directed toward examining pupil personnel services—in their total context—by using actual case study information. The case study approach not only highlights the involvement of the entire school staff—as well as parents and other family members, peers, and friends, and indeed the entire community—in pupil personnel matters, but also emphasizes the uniqueness of every child, thus persuading the reader to see the pupil as a person and not merely as a type, a subject, or a statistical phenomenon tending toward, or deviating from, some mean or norm.

This book is divided into three basic sections. The initial three chapters in Part One introduce the need for the case study approach, present a professional model of pupil personnel services, and orient readers to the use of student case information with the aid of responder participation. Part Two presents six cases based on information taken from actual student records. Each of these cases is then elaborated with a wide range of responder analyses, syntheses, and educational recommendations. The responders' reactions are accompanied by the authors' comments and questions. The responders were selected from persons involved in education, with varied backgrounds and professional orientations. Consideration of the responder reactions will help to present a realistic view of the complexity of pupil personnel services in schools. Part Three presents six cases without responders' or authors' comments, for use in individual evaluations or class discussions.

The twelve cases in Parts Two and Three are concerned with pupils at all school grade levels, from kindergarten through high school. The children discussed in the case histories have a wide range of problems, from mild to severe. Full information about the children represented in the cases, including their grade levels and the nature of their problems, is given at the beginning of each case, which also identifies the type of material presented for each case.

Chapter 3 of Part One contains a list of 11 questions which the reader is urged to answer *in writing* for each case, as the responders did. Problems for Discussion appear throughout the text. These two forms of questions should be considered an integral part of the training strategy presented here. They are designed to involve readers in the case materials. Readers are asked to respond to questions related to the case materials in terms of individual school problems, overall educational planning, and the related assumptions of pupil personnel services. By assuming individual responsibility for the evaluation of pupil case information, the reader will then become a participant in the evaluation-judgmental aspects of the pupil personnel process.

In personnel services work few generalized statements can be made, and in education the task is infinitely more complex. The reader will need to think through the responders' arguments and consider their logic carefully; then, employing the same criteria, examine his own interpretation. Complex problems can benefit from multiple approaches and strategies for solutions. Perhaps the reader's methods of educational planning will prove best in his particular school setting. It is vital to understand that one's assumptions may not be true for another person, because in each case a different set of school conditions and personal biases operates.

PART ONE

Introduction to Case Study

CHAPTER 1 The Meaningful Use of Pupil Case Study Information

All school personnel—teachers, administrators, and specialists—should work toward the same goals: to help children progress successfully toward designated educational objectives and to help them prepare for the responsibilities they will assume in adult life. There have been numerous statements of educational goals, which reflect the unique needs of individual school districts as well as broader national priorities. They often have a familiar sound, and the shift in emphasis over time is subtle and is in the process of change. This shift is readily evidenced by the well-known statement made in 1955 by the Committee for the White House Conference on Education, whose objectives continue to reflect the central educational commitments of our country.

1. A general education as good or better than that offered in the past, with increased emphasis on the physical and social sciences.
2. Programs designed to develop patriotism and good citizenship.
3. Programs designed to foster moral, ethical, and spiritual values.
4. Vocational education tailored to the abilities of each pupil and to the needs of the community and nation.
5. Courses designed to teach domestic skills.
6. Training in leisure-time activities, such as music, dancing, avocational reading, and hobbies.
7. A variety of health services for all children, including both physi-

3

cal and dental inspection, aimed at bettering health knowledge
and habits.
8. Special treatment for children with speech or reading difficulties
    and other handicaps.
9. Physical education, ranging from systematic exercises, physical
    therapy, and intramural sports, to interscholastic competition.
10. Instruction to meet the needs of the abler students.
11. Programs designed to acquaint students with countries other
    than their own in an effort to help them understand the problems
    America faces in international relations.
12. Programs designed to foster mental health.
13. Programs designed to foster wholesome family life.
14. Organized recreational and social activities.
15. Courses designed to promote safety. These include instruction in
    automobile driving, swimming, and civil defense.

If responsible educational personnel can work *together* toward similar
goals, this cooperation should result in an increased opportunity for students to acquire the broad ranges of skills, knowledges, and attitudes
stated as the purpose of education.

Education as an Agent of Change

In thinking about pupil personnel services, it is necessary to view
education as a *process committed to change,* in order to understand the
student in the social institution called the school. "When we speak of
learning, we are talking about how behavior is changed through experience," as May Seagoe has written.[1] After summarizing all that a child has
learned before starting school, Dr. Seagoe enumerates the main accomplishments that the pupil learns in his classes: "When he enters school, he
learns to associate the words he uses in talking with words that are written
or printed, and to reproduce them—that is, to read, write, and spell. He
observes quantitative relationships and represents them as symbols—that
is, he does arithmetic. He learns many facts and attitudes in social studies,
in science, and in the arts." Clearly, even the child's formal classroom
work has a social as well as an individual side, an emotive (or affective)
together with a rational (or cognitive) aspect. Yet the child learns far more
from his school experience than prescribed subject matter. To quote Dr.
Seagoe again: "Most important of all, he learns to exercise self-control
without frustration; to work systematically, yet tolerate interruption; to
evolve ideas of his own to which he is committed, yet tolerate different
ideas in others; to play as a member of a team or be content to play alone;
to take a lead in a class play or be a stagehand in the wings."

[1]May V. Seagoe, *The Learning Process and School Practice* [New York and London: Chandler
Publishing Company, 1970], p. 3.

Finally, the schoolchild's learning about many vital matters, especially in the social domain, continues outside the school through his experiences in the larger world. As Dr. Seagoe describes it, "Outside school he learns how to earn and spend money, to live with people his own age who give him none of the special privileges that families allow, to adopt a religious belief which may differ from that of his fellows, to plan life beyond school in terms of work and a family of his own, and to relate in a useful fashion to his community and country."

As soon as any professional person in education begins to assume responsibilities for the educational welfare of a child, personal factors come into play. This is as true with a teacher planning a daily lesson as with a guidance specialist helping in career planning. A dialogue between any two professional faculty members to benefit the child also involves personal factors. Inescapably, every professional employee must be responsible for understanding both children and other adults, since such understanding is needed in educational planning—whether for an entire school, a class, or an individual pupil. Thus teachers and administrators, as well as pupil personnel specialists, must be able to evaluate pupil case information effectively, since they share in the responsibility for the student's educational welfare. Pupil personnel specialists differ from other school personnel only in that they possess special skills for gathering case information and providing supportive services.

A classroom teacher sometimes may be in a better position to help a pupil with personal, "nonacademic" problems than is the personnel specialist. This is so because of the teacher's closer familiarity with the child's everyday behavior and because of his relationships with significant peers, family, other teachers, and the community at large. The teacher may happen to be more perceptive and sympathetic than the specialist—just as he may not be. The teacher's *technical proficiency* in some aspects of the helping relationship may actually be superior to that of the professional personnel worker. John W. M. Rothney cites one instance of the possible superiority of some teachers in pupil personnel work:

> It is often amusing to note the naïveté of many workers in elementary school counseling. They propose, for example, to add courses and units in occupational information to the curriculum. In doing so they seem to ignore the inability of small children to grasp the complex concepts involved, and fail to realize that good teachers have always done some work in this area at a level that children can understand.[2]

Similar instances could be cited of the effectiveness of others, such as the principal, the subject matter specialist, the coach or club advisor, or the child's minister, priest, or rabbi—or even of amateurs such as the

[2]John W. M. Rothney, "Who Gets Counseled and for What?" in Vernon F. Haubrich, ed., *Freedom, Bureaucracy, and Schooling* (Washington: Association for Supervision and Curriculum Development, NEA, 1971), p. 176.

parent, an older child, or the scout leader. The point here is not to build up the amateur or semiprofessional, let alone to tear down the professional personnel worker. Rather, the point is to emphasize the mutual, nonexclusive nature of the helping enterprise.

One responsibility of the pupil personnel specialist, then, is to enlist the cooperation of everyone involved with a child's welfare. Classroom teachers, in particular, must be encouraged to see that pupil personnel matters offer a challenge and an opportunity which they cannot shirk. If they fail to meet this challenge, they are left without an adequate way to meet student needs.

The authors recently provided information to an elementary school teacher, Mr. Smith. about a student, Geoff, who was not progressing satisfactorily in school. The situation of Geoff was not an unusual one to find in school settings; the reader will have an opportunity later, in Case No. 1, to evaluate the information provided to this teacher. The teacher was also not unusual. Mr. Smith was 28, and after graduation from college had served three and one-half years as an officer in the armed forces. Following his military obligation, he began his public school work and was in his second year of teaching sixth grade mathematics, social studies, and science, and seventh grade geography. To the case information on Geoff, Mr. Smith wrote:

After a thorough reading of the case information and the questions following, I find it *unfair* and impossible to answer any of the questions. Most of the material presented in the case means nothing to me. I have had no training in this area; therefore, I am unable to correlate any of the given information. Even to make a "good guess," it would have taken additional hours of careful study and research, time I could not afford to give. I found it very difficult to keep my mind on the task at hand. In this situation I feel that any attempt to answer the questions would have done nothing to advance the cause of Geoff.

Judging by his responses, Mr. Smith demonstrates little individual capacity as a teacher to help Geoff in school or to assist other education personnel to develop a more effective school environment for students. If his evaluation of the case is typical, as a teacher he probably has little to offer students who do not fit model educational patterns. What might be the educational experience for Geoff if he were in Mr. Smith's sixth grade class and were unable to understand the assigned tasks because of low reading skill?

As an entering child becomes involved in the educational process, he becomes a product of the kind of personal involvement he has experienced in the encounter. What are the personal consequences to a child if the experiential requirements are beyond his ability and skills to deal with successfully? The educational process is an interactive experience. The pupil responds to his peers and teachers within a curriculum and program context. What kind of experiences in education would Mr.

Smith be likely to provide Geoff in their encounters? What would be the predicted outcomes of Geoff's experiences in social studies if the teacher were insensitive to, or unable to comprehend, the student's experience in the learning process?

When attempting to understand the student in the educational setting, attention must of necessity be given to *all* aspects of the educational environment. It is impossible to assay Geoff's performance in his school program without also understanding the kind of program he is in and the characteristics of the key persons responsible for his development. What are their perceptions and expectations?

The Case Study Approach

The focus of this book, therefore, is upon understanding the process of analysis and synthesis of pupil personnel materials and the steps that can be taken for furthering student development. A book with this basic purpose could be perceived as a second step, so that some attention needs to be given to the first step. The first step, or grasping the case study method, has been given considerable attention by other authors who assume that some actions (that is, the processes emphasized in this book) will be undertaken. A good brief description of the case study is given by Nancy C. Ralston and G. Patience Thomas:

> The case study is a highly concentrated, specific approach to the process of understanding human growth and development, involving an in-depth study of one individual. Other approaches employ large numbers of subjects and may eventually result in the production of norms, principles, and generalizations which one can understand and appreciate more fully when they are applied to an individual with whom one is familiar. The case-study method, by comparison, permits the application of general knowledge within a very personal frame of reference, and in turn generates an understanding which has broad applications to all individuals. Using the case-study method, we move from specific to broad applications, in contrast to other methods which operate in the opposite direction.[3]

Doctors Ralston and Thomas go on to point out that the "scope of the case study is virtually limitless, as long as the detailed information contributes to an understanding of the unique organization of the particular personality involved." The professional personnel specialist applies his expertise on both the "input" and the "output" sides of the case study. On the input side, or on the first step, he may play such roles as deciding what persons to approach for information about a pupil, designing and conducting interviews with the child himself and with others, and selecting standardized tests to be administered to the pupil. On the output side, or the second step, he applies his knowledge of developmental, educational, social, and clinical psychology, as well as the principles and practices of

[3]Nancy C. Ralston and G. Patience Thomas, *The Child: Case Studies for Analysis* [New York and London: Intext Educational Publishers, 1972], p. 1.

guidance and counseling, to the analysis and synthesis of the case information.

There are important and different approaches to the *initial* development of the pupil case study method. Individual inventories, interviews, family-social-school histories, medical and mentalistic data, self-reports are but a few methods utilized by practitioners. The reader can consider procedural differences for the case study method by consulting some of the following sources. Note, however, that case study is an ongoing process, and as illustrated in Part Two, is often as much an amplification of the person who utilizes the information as it is of the referred student.

Suggestions for Additional Reading

DEVELOPING CASES.   The actual development of case studies is beyond the scope of this book but needs to be considered somewhere in the training of pupil personnel specialists. Some of the key works on the "how to" aspect of collecting and compiling case studies follow.

ALLPORT, G. W. *The Use of Personal Documents in Psychological Science.* New York: Social Science Research Council, Bulletin No. 49, 1942.

This book and the one that follows are classics for considering what materials to use in case studies.

DOLLARD, J. *Criteria for the Life History.* New Haven, Conn.: Yale University Press, 1935.

Seven criteria of the life history method are laid down and then applied to the evaluation of six histories:

ROTHNEY, J. W. M. *Methods of Studying the Individual Child: The Psychological Case Study.* New York: Blaisdell Publishing Company, 1968.

For persons who plan to write case studies, this book is suggested for its concise, yet thorough, coverage of the clinical approach:

WHITE V. *Studying the Individual Pupil.* New York: Harper & Row, Publishers, Inc., 1958.

White clearly demonstrates that alert and concerned classroom teachers can gain an understanding of children that contributes significantly to the pupil personnel process.

GROWTH, DEVELOPMENT, AND PERSONALITY STUDIES VIA CASES.   Once students begin the development of their own case studies, the need to have an understanding of child or adolescent development and personality becomes apparent.

Case studies have been extensively used as a research method for documenting and studying developmental processes. A few of the works that illustrate this method follow:

GINZBERG, E., and YOHALEM, A. M. *Educated Women: Self Portraits.* New York: Columbia University Press, 1966.
GOETHALS, G. W., and KLOS, D. S. *Experiencing Youth: First Person Accounts.* Boston: Little, Brown and Company, 1970.
PIAGET, J. *The Origins of Intelligence in Children.* New York: W. W. Norton & Company, Inc., 1963.

Piaget has made extensive use of the observation method in his research; this work is included as only an example of many, as is Wadsworth's book listed below. There are many secondary sources reporting on Piaget's work.

WADSWORTH, B. J. *Piaget's Theory of Cognitive Development.* New York: David McKay Company, 1971.
WHITE, R. W. *Lives in Progress.* New York: Holt, Rinehart and Winston, Inc., 1952.

CASE BOOKS. The following are books that present case approaches or case studies extensively used in pupil personnel training.

ADAMS, J. H. *Problems in Counseling: A Case Study Approach.* New York: The Macmillian Company, 1962.
CALLIS, R., POLMANTIER, P. C. and ROEBER, E. C. *A Casebook of Counseling.* New York: Appleton Century Crofts, 1955.
MILLARD, C. V., and ROTHNEY, J. W. M. *The Elementary School Child— A Book of Cases.* New York: Holt, Rinehart and Winston Inc., 1957.
ROTHNEY, J. W. M. *The High School Student—A Book of Cases.* New York: Holt, Rinehart and Winston, Inc. 1953.
SEARS, P. S., and SHERMAN, V. S. *In Pursuit of Self-Esteem—Case Studies of Eight Elementary School Children.* Belmont, Calif. Wadsworth Publishing Company, Inc., 1964.

STUDIES IN DEPTH. The following three books are particularly recommended because of their penetrating insights and their intriguing styles. Each is a book-length work centered around one subject.

ALLPORT, G. W. *Letters from Jenny.* New York: Harcourt, Brace Jovanovich, Inc., 1965.

A series of 301 letters written over an 11-year period from Jenny to a young, married couple provided Allport with a rich picture of a life beset by frustration and defeat.

AXLINE, VIRGINIA M. *Dibs: In Search of Self.* Boston: Houghton, Mifflin Company, 1964. (Ballantine Books edition, 1967.)

This book, which reads like a novel, is the story of the emergence of a strong, healthy personality in a previously deeply disturbed child.

GREEN, H. *I Never Promised You a Rose Garden.* New York: Holt, Rinehart and Winston, Inc., 1964.

Green tells the story of a young girl's three years in a mental hospital and her journey back from madness to reality.

CHAPTER 2 Providing Pupil Personnel Services

The primary responsibility of pupil personnel specialists is to help the schools operate effectively to benefit students in learning programs. They share this responsibility with school administrators, teachers, and other specialists, who also work to help students to achieve the goals of education and to prepare for adult life. Therefore, pupil personnel work is discussed here not only for those who aspire to enter the profession, but also for the orientation of teachers and administrators who will work with specialists.

Pupil Personnel Specialists in Schools

Let us now move to the next step, that of assaying pupil personnel specialists. What kind of professional people are we? What do we bring to our jobs that should add to the educational process? What kind of assumptions do we make? Around what theories do we operate?

WHAT IS A PUPIL PERSONNEL SPECIALIST? Pupil personnel specialists are as varied as the rest of the population; however, the majority of them have some characteristics in common. Most of them firmly believe in the goals and programs of education and have been employed in education as teachers. They have continued their training by specializing in specific nonteaching programs. They develop a unique core of knowledge and skills that define their expertise. These include advanced training in child and adolescent psychology, which emphasize developmental aspects of social, emotional, and physical growth. Usually there is some training in individual and group testing procedures, counseling techniques and test interpretation. Historically, individual testing has been associated most closely with the development of special education programs, while group testing is usually associated with the broader scope of education.

From this basic knowledge, the pupil personnel specialist develops a method of operation. The knowledge and skills are functional; they permeate most aspects of his role. The case information on a student is replete with individual descriptive and quantitative information. The pupil personnel specialist obtains information by testing, observation, and interview procedures. Teacher reports are obtained; often family and other community data are included in the educational assessment. With older student cases, information gathering and planning can take place with their teachers; direct work with the students is also possible. Ideally, the method of operation will be so effective that many potential problems will be forestalled because of early educational and vocational planning. Pupil personnel specialists should be answering significant questions regarding the basic procedures needed to make educational programs more effective for the students and they should be helping students to operate more effectively in the designated programs.

WHY USE PUPIL PERSONNEL SERVICES?   The assumptions made by school superintendents in hiring pupil personnel specialists are that they can help schools operate more effectively for the welfare of students. The number of pupil personnel services has increased dramatically during the last two decades because leaders in the communities and the government have become increasingly aware that schools must assume a broader range of educational responsibilities for all students. Literally thousands of children and young adults have not had suitable learning experiences in their school programs because education was too often geared to serve only the college-bound student. Dropout rates of 50 to 60 percent were no longer considered acceptable after World War II. Educational retardation and poor employment potential were no longer acceptable in our industrial and technological society. Schools were encouraged to reassess their models of education by community and governmental pressures.

Reassessment in education during the last decades brought with it a new group of personnel experts to provide individual student information and consultation for program development. There was a need to bridge the gap between instructional practices and the psychological needs of the school population. The pupil personnel specialist found himself attempting to help the educational establishment translate objectives into more meaningful programs for more students, with the emphasis on the development of new programs to meet the student's immediate and future needs. In this regard many people in education contributed to the curriculum development because special concerns for student welfare were a responsibility shared by all professional groups. Teacher training institutions and school officials had little trouble in offering many new programs once financial support was available to deal with problems they had long recognized were in existence.

WHO MEETS EDUCATIONAL DEMANDS?   The pupil personnel specialist is *not* employed by the school board to conduct psychotherapeutic work irrespective of its application to school goals and student progress. The school psychologist who has a special procedure that intrigues him contributes little to the articulation of school programs if he applies his techniques indiscriminately to every referred student. The expectations of employers, therefore, center on the assumption that once employed, the pupil personnel specialist can indeed alter the educational environment and indirectly the social environment of the student.

The focus of personnel services, *all* personnel services, is to develop a day-by-day learning condition that will maximize each student's growth potential in all basic areas of his life. This is a developmental and a continual growth process, not a remedial or "therapeutic" one. The pupil case study approach in education is designed to help make appropriate and necessary corrections to match student educational needs with student potentials.

Broadly speaking, the pupil personnel specialist can approach his task of assaying the student's condition of learning by reassessing (1) the educational objectives of the school, (2) the translation of educational objectives into various programs and curriculums, (3) the procedures utilized to implement programs, (4) the degree to which individual differences are being considered in these processes, and (5) the social behavior and attitudes of students, teachers, and other significant persons related to the questions that have been raised.

At the beginning of Chapter 1, we discussed briefly the broad range of educational objectives recommended by the Committee for the White House Conference on Education. Have *you* examined these recommendations as they relate to your school? Have these objectives all been translated in viable programs in your model of (public) school education? Are your programs variegated to meet student needs for health services, wholesome family life, and safety education? Do more able, as well as disadvantaged, students have programmatic opportunities at *all* levels of education in your school system? Do you train for domestic skills, leisure time activities, and social activities? Do your programs effectively promote patriotism, good citizenship, *and* international relations? Are courses in physical and social sciences tailored to meet needs of students in the vocational training programs?

Given appropriate goals and programs, the pupil personnel specialist must then closely inspect the procedures of program development and the unique characteristics of the significant people involved: the teachers and the students. This is the daily focus of most personnel efforts in education; it is no longer sufficient to view the activities of the pupil personnel specialist as simply an adjunct to instructional procedures and program operations. Teachers who want to be more effective in their instruction keep raising the question, "What can I do to help this student?" Understanding each student is only a starting point; the availability of suitable educational programs requires the transference of this understanding into the moment-by-moment activities of the classroom. Pupil personnel workers are being asked for advice on matters of instruction when teachers feel they have failed to accomplish their objectives. Fortunately, former teachers are in the majority among those training for pupil personnel roles. They usually bring to their job responsibilities an experienced sensitivity and know-how that is evidence of learning far beyond their academic training. In the conference between the teachers and a pupil personnel specialist, even without an expertise in teaching methodology, there are numerous occasions when discussion can clarify problems and clear up frustration by providing an avenue to constructive planning. Attention to teachers' concern creates a supportive atmosphere for developing educational alternatives. Where broad program changes are not indicated, changes in attitudes about how to deal with students may help create more favorable conditions for learning in the classrooms.

The dialogue between the pupil personnel specialist and other school personnel is one in which information is shared. Teachers can report on all types of information, including their feelings about what observed behaviors mean in classrooms. Pupil personnel specialists might also have information obtained by observation, testing, and interviews. Cumulative information provides a basis for an historical perspective. Family reports, medical reports, and other sources of information become grist for the preliminary planning evaluation. The different perceptions of the professional school staff are also significant points of information. Relevant and consistent observations are noted. Prejudice, bias, and hearsay reports are dealt with. Discrepancies in information are noted—and explanations are offered. "If these are the main findings, then we should proceed with this plan of action." It is as important in educational planning to understand the student as it is to understand the condition of the student: his teachers, his programs, and his activities.

Several points need to be reemphasized here: the first is that individual analyses of students involve the accumulation of *related* information on them. The second is that these analyses are appropriate and relevant to the student's best educational interests. By defining activities in this manner, a proper and useful professional posture is maintained. Gossip, the fostering of student or teacher dependency, and inquiries about extraneous information are but a few of the nonprofessional behaviors referred to in this statement. A third point, a combination of the first two, is the need for consistent vigilance to make sure that student information is not misinterpreted. Although in the schools we operate a psychosocial environment, a great many demands of the day often impel our colleagues to take literally many statements that are not so intended. Abstract ideas are given concrete relevance. For example, an IQ score of 90 might be interpreted as meaning that the student cannot do well in the classroom, so therefore the teacher must not expect so much of him. Surely this would be a serious misperception of the available information, since the expectations must remain high for all students as appropriate learning experiences are designed for their development. Thus one of the major tasks of personnel specialists is to be sensitive to the understanding of other school personnel and, when misperceptions exist, to provide the necessary consultation to alter errors in judgment.

CAN THERE BE TEAMWORK?   For pupil personnel services to operate effectively in schools, *a good working relationship between all school staff members is of paramount importance.* Effective working relationships among the professional staff are a necessary condition for implementing educational changes that will benefit students. The pupil personnel specialist must understand the workings of teachers in their classrooms; conversely, the teachers must have an understanding of how the pupil personnel specialist can help them. In a sense, a pupil personnel specialist cannot be more effective in providing services than he can be effective in communicating ideas and understanding to the people he is working with and the community that employs him. The same is true of the relationship between pupil personnel specialists and school administrators. School board members and the school superintendent delegate responsibility for the operation of each school to a principal. He is responsible for what goes on in his building. Therefore, if pupil personnel services are to be implemented effectively, support and endorsement from the administration becomes a condition of success.

Many experienced pupil personnel specialists find a great deal of their professional efforts geared to developing effective relationships with their teaching colleagues. They find that to accomplish their objectives they must know and understand the school staff affected by these services. They must be able to communicate in a manner that is understood and thus will be useful in the educational process. Basically, the same conditions apply to situations where the student is the prime person with whom a relationship must be established. As a result, the student can assimilate new ideas into his own perceptual patterns so that he can act more effectively and be better able to participate in educational programs. A good deal of this book will be devoted to understanding the meaning of school-related information about individual students, and the attitudes and perceptions of professional people and students of education.

The authors take the position that in pupil personnel services, the providing of information on the student's mental and personality characteristics is not a sufficient contribution of the educational process. *It is not sufficient just to counsel a student; one must be able to determine if this encounter has any substantive educational outcomes.* The personnel worker becomes a school specialist when mentalistic information and interpersonal encounters have meaningful carry-over in terms of educational planning and student success in school programs. This is why it is so necessary to translate theories of counseling and theories of personality development very carefully into the educational setting.

Theoretical ideas and procedures have to be examined and tested against the basic goals established for the schools. This is the school objective toward which all school employees work. In this chapter, we have reviewed relevant assumptions and behaviors of pupil personnel specialists. The many unique and complex characteristics of the school process make singular individual theories of development or simple personal technologies obsolete when indiscriminately applied. A counselor who is always a Rogerian or a psychologist who is singularly a Freudian or a behaviorist has about as strong a professional position in education as the teacher who says there is one method of instruction or one technique of learning.

Questions of Professional Judgment

In practice, most people who provide pupil personnel services operate from several theoretical frameworks be they teachers, administrators, or pupil personnel specialists. They react to given student situations on the basis of certain assumptions, which can be overtly stated or are implicit in their judgment. In a sense, the assumptions of the pupil personnel specialist permeate almost every professional judgment and every formulation of how, where, and with whom he spends his time. Implicit in the observable behavior of the pupil personnel specialist must be a process of "selecting-in" the performance of certain activities and "selecting-out" others. Eventually, there develops a model of how pupil personnel services can best be utilized in the school to make them more effective for students in programs. Time and other limiting factors prevent the implementation of every conceivable personnel service. There are usually far too many students to allow for the full spectrum of specialist participation.

The school psychologist cannot provide 100 individual examinations per year; observe in all classrooms; consult extensively with all teachers who have referred students; maintain a sensitive relationship with a wide range of special education teachers, school administrators, and community agencies; provide individual and group therapy; provide special instruction in perceptual training; conduct research; work with the curriculum specialists; and offer inservice training and individual assistance to teachers who need instruction in behavioral management for students with social and classroom learning problems.

Similar arguments can be presented for the school counselor who cannot counsel the student body and staff, provide family counseling and group therapy, serve as a liaison person to the community, teach vocational selection procedures, and be of service to every normal child as a group tester and confidant.

Initially, professional judgment appears to develop as a function of one's background training and personal experiences prior to taking a pupil personnel specialist position. Once on the job, the specialist's capacity to improve his initial abilities depends on these predisposing conditions and other individual characteristics. The type, quality, and amount of training will be important in defining the initial position of the specialist. To argue that training experiences are unrelated to job performance would be an enormous indictment of our academic programs. In fact, such a position would be untenable in light of feedback to the contrary by school boards that encourage graduate training of their staff and by professional organizations that help to define and upgrade their professions. One should be wary of the critic who overgeneralizes the faults of the professional group until he has carried their responsibilities.

On-the-job experience built upon background experiences will shape the type of professional activities actually provided for students. The weighty responsibilities involved in pupil personnel services often result in the specialist's adopting a fairly mechanical application of whatever theoretical position his professors espoused. It should not take a psychologist long to realize that a diagnosis of "ego dysfunctioning with regressive features" does *not* help teachers with behavior problems in classrooms. They do not need anyone to tell them what they have been living with all year—they need to know what to do about the students. If a student deviates too much from the mores of the school community, the counselor can respond with only so many "reflections of feelings" while waiting for the student to become self-actualized. Therefore, the real test of one's professional judgment as a personnel specialist begins with employment. Once on the job, the specialist offers recommendations and other professional services. Follow-through procedures to assay their effectiveness provide a fertile opportunity for his judgment to mature.

THE COLLECTING OF PUPIL INFORMATION.   The pupil personnel specialist utilizes at least three kinds of procedures to almost every situation requiring his professional judgment: (1) he attempts to withhold interpretation until he has gathered information from as many related sources as necessary; (2) he must analyze this information; and (3) he has to synthesize the information meaningfully in relation to the educational question. In personnel matters, there is little clinical evidence that limited amounts of student data will be more satisfactory than a more comprehensive report, but it is important that whatever information is obtainable be pertinent to the question being raised. A careful analysis of the presenting conditions will probably increase the likelihood of planning alternatives that will facilitate student educational attainment.

This may seem to be an obvious point, but numerous errors in personnel services occur because a careful inspection of student information was curtailed. This happens occasionally when the specialist gets caught up in a theoretical position that restricts rather than facilitates his perception of available information. An overcommitment to a given view of student behavior can take on an almost religious significance. While such zeal may comfort the disciple, it also can create nonadaptive attitudes. Such rigidity of thinking can result in perceptual distortions, halo effect, overgeneralizations, and poor reality testing. The personnel specialist who assumes that his hunches (hypotheses) are more than testable questions becomes a victim of his own biases.

There are numerous and obvious examples of this fallacy in the day-to-day activities of almost every school district. School districts are known to exist that have no programs for mentally retarded children, hence no retarded children. Some districts have many educable, mentally handicapped classes but none for children with specific learning disabilities, and for some districts almost the reverse is true. Some personnel specialists find a high proportion of students with neurological damage and others have had many youngsters with emotional problems. Some specialists report that anxiety behaviors are caused by unresolved Oedipus complexes *or* poor social skills; likewise, educational failures might unjustifiably be labeled as the sole product of poor instruction *or* broken homes. Dependency problems in children may as often be attributed to overprotective mothers as to those mothers who neglect their children. Some specialists counsel for self-actualization and others emphasize information procedures and on-the-job training. Some errors in personnel judgment are associated with decisions arrived at too early in the evaluation processes. Errors occur when appropriate student information is not collected or when inconsistent or contradictory information is available but remains unexplored. Poor judgment in student personnel services is more often obvious after the fact, and sometimes irretrievable.

Perhaps the majority of student personnel errors are made in education because it is socially inconvenient for a staff member to admit an error or because new information is rejected when it would entail revising premature formulations. An example of this is a student who, while in high school, was specifically advised by the assistant principal not to pursue college training because he could not handle the academic requirements. He was advised instead to seek industrial employment at one of the local factories. Today this person is completing a master's degree and has a half-dozen creditable years of professional experience as an elementary school teacher and part-time school principal. Evidently, because of some test score (probably incomplete data without adequate analysis and synthesis), inappropriate advice was rendered. How much human potential might have been reduced under these conditions?

A BEHAVIORAL POINT OF VIEW.   Behavioral specialists in education are primarily interested in the conditions of learning, *after* vital judgment has been made as to what type of curriculum is needed for a given student and the program of instruction has been established. They are interested in maximizing learning conditions in the classroom that will encourage desired student behavior. Thus, at a behavioral level, they would want to increase the frequency of students' attending to assigned work, completing assigned tasks, remaining in the assigned work area, not interfering with other students' learning, and increasing measurable skill outcomes. The behavior specialists have tried to analyze quantitatively the conditions of learning in the classroom. Using these data, they attempt to determine procedures that the teacher might employ to deal more effectively with students. Often the focus of the behavioral specialist has been on disruptive student behavior, although this is not an inherent limitation of their capacity to participate effectively in the educational process. Finding the appropriate student motivators (reinforcers) becomes the essential task in manipulating and shaping student behavior.

Somewhat regrettably, the zeal of this group in applying the behavioral approach to a wide range of classroom and school related problems has tended to impede the use of professional judgment. In the authors' experience with students in the behavioral specialty, they seem too often unwilling to utilize other procedures and approaches in problem solving and student management. In fact, carried to its logical conclusion, college teachers would only need to train student teachers in behavior modification procedures so that learning and behavioral management problems could be eliminated in the educational process. Then there would be little need for pupil personnel specialists because referral problems would be negligible.

Fortunately, it is implicit in the behavioralistic approach that a careful analysis of the child's observable behavior should be completed. The behavioral modifier focuses special attention on what teacher actions can be used in the classroom to help students function better socially and in learning applications. This can often give teachers novel alternatives and encourage them to establish new teaching procedures. The consultative relationship with the teacher is supportive, and there is a sharing of responsibility for student management problems. This condition of consultation offers a positive and constructive alternative to her feelings of teaching frustration. Very often, this approach can lead to immediate teaching alternatives with procedures that may help the students to participate at a more effective level in their program. In this sense, the teacher's behavior can be changed by formulating alternative approaches to the immediate demands of teaching responsibilities.

Furthermore, the more careful behavioral analysis often extends to an understanding of the motivational needs of children. Taking motivational factors into account is implicit in data gathering, analyzing, and making behavioral predictions. The behavioral approach is empirical in application and does not require a complex and detailed theoretical formulation. The approach is simple, direct, and immediate. There will be cases with given students in which such behavioral approaches will have merit. Among older students it may be more difficult to develop much rationale for such behavioral control if the educational goals are for more autonomous development and independence. For example, little would be accomplished in counseling if reinforcing smiles and nods of encouragement resulted in the students' making educational or vocational choices without respect to their unique, personal characteristics and aspirations.

An additional example took place in a learning disabilities class, where the staff decided to manipulate a student's lunch period in an effort to foster more effective involvement in the program. Certain specific tasks were outlined, and the lunch period was postponed unless agreed-upon work was completed. This behavioral modification approach was starting to work, but after several days the student failed to bring his lunch to school. After the second day of no lunch the mother reassured the school that her boy had left on the bus with his lunch. He had beaten the system.

There is little disagreement in education about our commitments to change student behavior and attitudes. Even a cursory review of the educational objectives offered by the White House Conference (see Chapter 1) would give strong evidence of this commitment. There seems to be a good rationale for behavioral management, since it represents a significant refinement in personnel approaches to the daily activities of the teachers. But it is just a refinement, not a panacea. Token reinforcers do not differ much from the rewards of stars and teacher praise. Providing food reinforcers to foster the reoccurrence of certain kinds of student behavior does not differ conceptually from making sure that the child in your classroom is not so hungry he cannot concentrate on assigned tasks.

The behavioral approaches are not a new phenomenon so much as they represent a more systematic observational approach to classroom activity, without concomitant individual diagnoses and planning procedures. Counting instances of teacher behavior and student behavior must be viewed only as the very beginning of a much more complicated and demanding process. Counting instances of behavior may make it empirical, and perhaps even scientific, but teachers have been smiling, praising, and encouraging the student in the learning process prior to this more systematic endeavor. On the other hand, systematically assaying student and teacher behavior is a significant start to understanding the conditions of classroom learning. Behavioral approaches have challenged pupil personnel specialists lost in intrapsychic analysis and too often ignorant of ongoing classroom and social processes. For the "testing psychologist," it is about time to take a detailed view of the student-teacher encounter.

When planning procedures for the educational benefit of the student, behavioral psychology should be considered as one available tool; it is often not the only technique that can be employed. Approaches should not be considered mutually exclusive and combinations are often appropriate. Fostering attention behavior *in conjunction with* an understanding of a student's reading skills, the need for providing appropriate materials, and the need for appropriate teaching methodology are compatible alternatives. In fact, maybe if the student had had the appropriate materials in the first place, the "attention problem" would not have become the focus of a classroom management problem.

EDUCATIONAL ALTERNATIVES.   Educational planning is the process of developing strategies for the implementation of specified goals. The majority of personnel services and consequent strategies remain within the boundaries of the school setting. For some students, however, it is a community problem that shows up in the school. In such cases, the school planning alone may not be sufficient to help the student. Planning may need to be extended to resources in the community, as with the seven-year-old child who remains extremely dependent and immature in his social behaviors. Such behaviors were *probably* learned at home, and the parents might be advised to seek child guidance services. Knowledge of, and working relationships with, community agencies is a viable alternative when pupil personnel specialist's services extend into the community.

Alternatives for educational planning become the focus of the personnel services, once there is sufficient information available related to the problem. It would be a mistake to assume that for the pupil personnel specialist this is always a long and laborious job. It may be that the information is immediately available in dialogues with teachers or students. If views of the problem are shared, the specialist may only need to provide the reassurance that goes along with shared understanding and concern for the future. Further clarification may be obtained if needed, namely, "Tell me more about it" or "How do you view this situation?"

In personnel services, it is probably at this point that many errors are made. Often, the crucial consideration is not that the pupil personnel specialist must be able to solve the problem at hand, but rather that he be able to deal effectively with others so that they can be more effective in dealing with the problem. If there can be shared information on what the problem is and the conditions associated with its existence, then alternatives need to be developed within the functional range of the people involved and the educational resources available. It might surprise the reader to find how many different answers will be offered to the question, "What are some of the things that can be done to work this out?" Altering classroom procedures, redefining classroom objectives, seeking additional help, defining strategies that include program changes, obtaining more information, selecting alternative approaches to the goals established, defining or redefining educational and vocational goals, and getting public commitment, are but a few of the possible communications that will be forthcoming.

The pupil personnel specialist should be in a key position to act as the consultant he was trained to be. When performing on the job, he can provide information to other persons about the perceptions of both students and staff. He can help clarify perceptions and feed in new information as people are able to assimilate it. These activities often become the moments of truth for the pupil personnel specialist. The effectiveness with which these activities are carried out determine the quality of his services. The reference person can just as well be a high school football player, his eight-year-old sister, the new junior high school principal, or the president of the school board.

As mentioned earlier, a good working relationship with other school personnel (especially with the students) and the professional skills necessary to assess the validity of obtained information are the necessary substructure for the development of effective personnel services in the schools. Once a strategy or series of strategies have been developed in educational planning, the stage is set for their implementation. Ordinarily, at this point, implementation is not a problem, since there is already substantial involvement by the key people. The analysis, synthesis, and planning have already been completed; the ground work has been done. The pupil personnel specialist then finds his role to be that of following up on the case to determine if the student's situation is improving. Supportive contacts and direct involvement may help to assure that the educational plans are being tried out. This does not guarantee that the strategies will be successful, however; follow-up procedures need to be included in order to evaluate and reassess the plans. Thus there has to be an opportunity to reformulate the plans and make necessary adjustments as the case indicates. In microcosm, this is the process of the counselor-client relationship, in which the counselor is using client responses to guide his personnel activities *for the benefit of the client.*

There are times when the student, the teacher, or some other person does not carry out certain agreed-upon activities. This event represents an immediate signal to the specialist that the strategy is not working well. The problem may then need to be redefined by the parties involved in order to focus on alternative procedures to get the plan underway. A school principal who neglects the transfer of a student from one class to another, as was decided upon, may be prodded about his procedures and the timetable for implementation of the plan. The student who makes a time-study commitment to the counselor and fails to follow through with it may need an opportunity to reassess his own position, because this activity may in turn be related to many of his other personal and vocational goals.

One technique of planning implementation that works rather well is to clarify agreements by written communication. This makes a public contract out of the agreement, even if between two people. Later there is no hazy misunderstanding about what was to be accomplished and how, and where the responsibility lies. This strategy of implementation works with both the students and the school staff. Activities and responsibilities are clearly defined. Placing a copy of a school staffing report in the student's cumulative record, with carbons to those who have assumed task responsibilities, establishes the commitment as a professional responsibility. This creates a situation in which few of us are willing to take too great a risk of public exposure by failing to follow through.

Although there is not just one way of establishing a "truly correct" model of pupil personnel services because of the many variables in the educational process, in the final analysis the model for the personnel specialist must fit both the school's needs for pupil personnel services and the person employed to provide them. The authors do not agree with intuitive arguments that the school is just a convenient place for the student to become self-actualized. Favorable attitudes of mental health and the prevention of emotional problems are personal conditions influenced by the student's school experience. Understandings, skill competencies, and healthy self-concepts result from effective participation in school programs. We must have schools with culturally relevant goals. In turn, the programs must be designed to help mold the student so that he can become a contributing member of his community.

Summary

Student needs for pupil personnel services are not the sole province of the specialist. The normal encounter of daily student activity requires all school staff members to share in the responsibility of planning and change. The pupil personnel specialist helps to bridge the gap between instructional practices and the specific educational needs of students. Therefore, the specialist and all professionals in education must develop their ability to meet changing student and community needs. Students will show evidence of progressing successfully toward the goals of education as a result of both the nature of the curriculum and the conditions of classroom learning.

All student personnel services are designed to maximize each student's growth potential, so that the focus of these activities is developmental and not simply remedial. This condition is established by close cooperation, communication, and mutual respect among members of the educational team. The dialogue among school personnel is one of shared information and planning.

Participants in student planning must withhold *judgment* until all relevant information is obtained. In an open and professional manner that avoids an air of secrecy, the unique set of pupil information is analyzed and then synthesized as it applies to the referral questions. Alternative procedures are reviewed in the light of pupil needs and the available resources. Action is taken, based upon professional judgment; finally, a follow-up is needed to assay the effectiveness of the formulated plans.

At all times the pupil personnel specialist must work within the limits of his particular training and competence, turning to other specialists, such as a physician, psychiatrist, licensed psychologist, vocational counselor, social worker, or subject matter specialist, as the need arises. However, this implies that student personnel specialists must become involved in a sharing of relevant information about students. The faculty team members who affect the social adjustment pattern of students and are responsible for their educational development must also be included. Too often an air of secrecy develops in and around pupil personnel offices so that neither students nor teachers perceive it as a usable place for student growth and professional dialogue. Neither students nor teachers can benefit from a communication system clouded by mistrust and misunderstanding. It must necessarily follow, then, that much of the thinking on the issue of confidentiality be revised. If pupil personnel specialists are to do the job they are supposed to do, it will often be necessary for them to speak frankly and openly with all members of the team who have an influence on the life and experiences of students.

CHAPTER 3 Introduction to Pupil Case Information

The 12 cases in Parts Two and Three are representative of a wide range of student types from various levels of public school education. In reviewing these cases, the reader may feel these pupils are not typical or that they present unique and sometimes difficult problems in the educational setting. The reader will be right about the latter part of the statement, but not the former. Each student is unique with respect to family history, personality, and mental characteristics. It is with the uniqueness of each student that we become more aware of the complexities of educational planning. Combine these idiosyncratic characteristics with the multiple learning experiences and available social encounters in the setting, and the picture is even more diffuse. In this sense, every student case involving personnel services is typical of the ones presented in the text.

The reader should note that the authors use the term *problem* in reference to pupil personnel services to cover almost any type of professional involvement requiring judgment or services. Thus a gifted student may have problems even if he functions well in school. It could be that the school has not provided a sufficient curriculum for him. As another example, a teacher may want assistance on the evaluation of a new supplementary program in phrase reading development and will ask the school psychologist to help design a study to assess the value of the new procedure. Therefore, the term problem has been used to refer to *pupil personnel services requiring involvement beyond the usual classroom setting.*

An attempt was made to select cases covering a variety of school-age pupils (see Figure 1) and situations. Teacher-initiated referrals, parent referrals and cumulative student information have been included for con-

24

sideration. From the viewpoint of educational planning, the cases cover a wide range of school conditions associated with such problems as social adjustment, learning disabilities, educational retardation, and racial biases. Often, information in the case materials provides related information for several years preceding the referral, and the epilogues provide the reader with actual outcomes in given cases.

Each of the six cases in Part Two was referred to a group of *responders* —professional workers, who will be discussed in more detail later—for their answers to the following questions:

A. *From the available information, what in your opinion are the most significant aspects of the case?*

B. *What, if any, do you perceive as the main problems in the educational setting?*

C. *What, if any, do you view as related problems?*

D. *How would you likely feel about this situation?*

E. *How would the student likely feel about this situation?*

F. *What would be your suggestions or alternatives for solving or improving the problem situations you identified?*

G. *How would you go about implementing your suggestions?*

H. *What additional information would help you in developing possible solutions to these problems?*

I. *When reviewing the information available on this student, what assumptions did you have to make?*

J. *What assumptions were necessary to make when defining the problem(s) as you did?*

K. *In order for your recommendations to be successfully implemented, what assumptions would be necessary?*

The reader is urged to write out his answers to the above questions for each case in Part Two, then to consider the responders' answers and the authors' comments, and finally to discuss the cases with classmates or colleagues. This procedure is suggested to provide an opportunity to examine one's own judgments by comparing them with those of other persons—persons with varying experiences in education and varying points of view. Most important, the reader will have the opportunity to examine more closely the assumptions and perceptions upon which his decisions are based.

When the reader comes to Part Three, he will be completely on his own, for no responders' answers or authors' comments are given with the six cases presented there, except for a brief introductory note and an epilogue to Cases 11 and 12. In Part Three, again, the reader is urged to

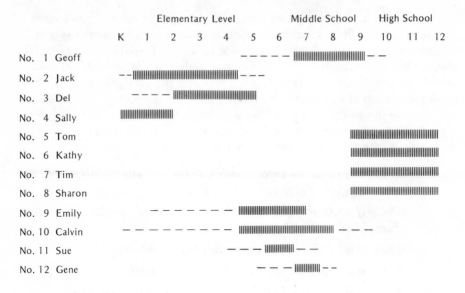

Figure 1. Grade Levels of Pupil Personnel Cases

write out his answers to the questions given above. The reader or his instructor (if the reader is a student) may want to intersperse the study of cases in Part Three with those in Part Two.

The use of this textbook will require active participation on the part of the reader; active participation in itself is a valuable tool that will be helpful in developing the sensitivity and good judgment necessary for discriminating decisions in pupil personnel work. There are few precise rules that can simply be memorized and applied in general to questions about educational planning for individual students. In reality, there are too many unique individual characteristics associated with each student's personal, school, and learning history *and* too many variables within the context of the educational setting to rely on simple general assumptions and procedures.

The process of "acquiring good judgment" in matters of pupil personnel services requires the reader to become more aware of himself or herself as a part of this judgmental process. The social-educational world of the school culture is one of people interacting with one another while attempts are being made to develop effective programs of instruction and favorable conditions for student learning. Students are not cold statistical facts or numbers but are persons with feelings and emotional strengths and weaknesses. Thus what the teacher-specialist can bring to matters of personal judgment are the qualities of his or her training and experience, and his or her unique views of educational goals and people in the educational process.

The judgmental process in school personnel services is not scientific but is a matter of shared responsibility by professional people in education. So, in writing this manuscript, we have considered responder reports as professional opinion that represents their best judgment in matters related to pupil personnel services. One major premise of this book is that pupil personnel services combine the use of student case information with professional judgment within the interpersonal and social context of education.

The authors have tried to communicate the logical development of the responders' judgments in these cases; however, the responders' judgment as well as ours is clinical, not scientific. Our opinions do not represent some kind of unvarnished truth. In fact, we encourage the reader to question every assumption and every position suggested. We encourage the attitude of open inquiry and the development of alternative models of pupil personnel services based on logical and defensible premises. These are favorable habits for the pupil personnel worker to cultivate, since open review and a questioning attitude will more likely facilitate the educational process for the benefit of students than will defensive attitudes, categorical denials, stereotyped thinking, and panacea solutions.

Responder Information

Early in the planning for this text it was found that people responded to case materials in terms of a set. The reader, in order to become more aware of factors that may influence his professional judgments should complete the Personal Information Form at the end of this chapter. Approximately 300 persons completed this form for the authors, and about 100 of them were included in the discussion of Cases 1 through 6. These persons are called responders throughout this text. The responders were given these instructions prior to reviewing the student case information and the related questions:

We are interested in learning how people of various disciplines and various levels of training understand and utilize student case information on students available in the schools.

Please complete personal data information so that we can learn something about your background experience and training.

Next, review the case study information and answer the questions to the case. All personal data information and case information answers will be dealt with as confidential reports.

On the following pages student case information is provided which should require pupil personnel assistance in educational planning. The information included is based on an authentic school referral for services. Confidentiality is maintained by changing names and state and by slightly altering the individual student social-family data. An attempt has been made to present the referral materials as they appeared in the student's cumulative folder.

Please review the case information and respond to the questions following the report.

In reading through the cases, the reader may notice abbreviated sentences, conflicting statements, and the accumulation of related information over a period of time, sometimes years. By encountering the information in this manner, the reader has almost the same opportunity for giving advice and consultation as did the school people who formulated educational plans when the cases were processed.

The personal information collected from the responders covered their professional experiences, training, role perceptions, and related data. When the reader completes the Personal Information Form, he will place himself in the same perspective as the responders whose comments are included in the book. Thus the reader will share with each of them the unique educational and personal background experiences that shape every personnel worker's approach to student case information.

It was pointed out in the last chapter that the students do not function in a vacuum in school settings. Their experiences are dynamic and personal. It is in this sense that we must also learn to understand how significant people in school situations view students. Given student information, how do significant others react to it personally? What would they do to help students? By understanding responders, the reader is also in a better position to understand students. It will soon become apparent that, even among professionals, not every one sees an individual student in quite the same way. Often, different sets of assumptions are used by different professional groups. Differences in evaluating the student's problems result in even more substantive differences in the recommendations to resolve the educational problems. The reader will recall that, in Chapter 1, Mr. Smith took the no-commitment approach to Geoff's referral problems. Before the end of this book the reader may consider Mr. Smith's position somewhat safer for the student than some of the suggestions of responders who have become committed to alternatives the reader may find totally unacceptable.

Thus it is through the responders that we learn about the thinking processes of professional people in education. We learn how they attempt to deal at an effective level with student personnel problems. The focus of this inquiry, therefore, is as much on the problem-solving process employed by people in education as on students with identified problems.

Case Information Evaluation

In beginning the case information evaluations, the reader will be entering the arena of pupil personnel services, charged with the responsibilities for establishing the best possible program in education that will benefit the student. He will share in the delegated responsibility to provide programs and learning experiences in education that will meet the objectives outlined by the Committee for the White House Conference on Education at the beginning of Chapter 1.

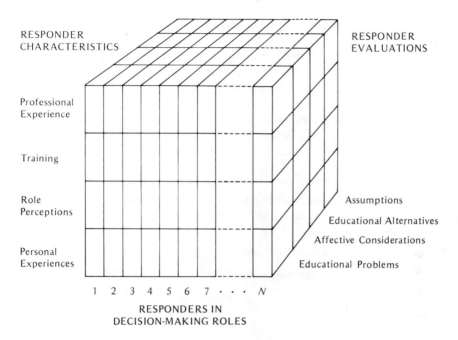

RESPONDER
CHARACTERISTICS

RESPONDER
EVALUATIONS

Professional
Experience

Training

Role
Perceptions

Assumptions

Educational Alternatives

Affective Considerations

Personal
Experiences

Educational Problems

1 2 3 4 5 6 7 · · · N

RESPONDERS IN
DECISION-MAKING ROLES

Figure 2. Responder Variables in the Evaluation of Student Case Information

As diagrammed in Figure 2, the reader will become part of the educational process of planning for the future for each student discussed in this book. To meet his responsibilities successfully, the personnel worker must be cognizant of the complexity of the task. As a responder, the reader will share each case with colleagues from widely differing backgrounds and role perceptions. The readers' approaches to the student will differ one from the other, but by the processes of sharing in the responsibility for the student's progress in education, the best-known climate for pupil personnel services is created.

In Figure 2, the logic of these points is graphically presented. Multiply the four areas of student information assessment* and the four sources of the reader-responder information (4 × 4 = 16) with two additional dimensions for the authors (16 × 3 = 48) to establish the complex position the reader is in simply upon beginning Case No. 1. If the reader is in a discussion class of 31 students, the complexity rapidly increases to over 500 combinations, *not* including the interaction among responder participants. Multiply these figures by the 12 cases in Sections 2 and 3 of Figure 1, and by the differences *within* the responder information slots, and the numericalization of the case information begins to approach an astronomical figure. Fortunately, the task is delimited to some degree by some

*School history, social-family reports, health data, and psychoeducational data.

similarity in responses and some limitation in terms of educational alternatives.

This point should now be emphatically clear: With regard to an individual case few singular answers or alternatives will be available. There are virtually no computerized answers to student problems in education, since the applications are to noncomputerized contingencies in the real world. The authors are not able to simply provide the reader with a few selected generalizations or a few discriminative cues that will readily solve the problems. Now is the time for the reader to pool his judgment with others to seek better ways in education.

Educational plans for the student are hammered out in open discussion with the student and with others charged with the responsibility for seeing to it that each student has the best opportunity to reach the maximum of his potentialities.

Personal Information Form

The data requested on a personal information form may vary from one school to another. A sample form follows.

Name.   *Age.*

Address.

Phone.

Professional Work Experience:

    1. *Current position.*

       Years of experience.

       Describe duties briefly.

    2. *Previous position.*

       Years of experience.

       Describe duties briefly.

    3. *Other types of work experience. Describe duties and years of experience.*

Educational Background:

    1. *Undergraduate education*

       School(s).

       Year of graduation.

       Describe program emphasis and related information.

2. *Graduate background*

    M.A. or equivalent school.

    Year obtained or expected.

    Ph.D. or equivalent school.

    Year obtained or expected.

    Describe program emphasis and related information for most recent degree.

What do you perceive as your main job role?

What would you like your main occupational role to be?

What do you think you will be doing in five years?

What would you like to be doing in five years?

Please provide additional information about yourself that would help a reviewer of your responses to understand in a general way the kind of experiences you bring to the case study task. This might include additional work or educational experience, professional certifications, and social and family information.

PART TWO
Individual Case Studies

CASE NO. 1 Geoff
(Grades 8 and 9)

The transition and adjustment period is often hectic at the junior high level. Special arrangements that can be worked out in the elementary program are often prohibitive for the entering freshman. Geoff's situation is complicated by a recent move from another state and the resentment by his parents of the expectations established by school personnel. Communication patterns seem disturbingly poor all the way around.

The case study of Geoff begins with a collection of materials about this student which is reported in slightly disguised form from the student's actual cumulative folder. As will be seen, the case of Geoff is a school-parent referral for assistance in educational planning. The reader interested in developing his skills in pupil personnel work will answer the questions on page 25 of Chapter 3 after he has read the case study materials. The next section in the case study of Geoff, headed "Information about Responders," summarizes data from the personal information questionnaires completed by the seven professionals who were invited by the authors to express their views. The responders' perceptions and recommendations, with a running commentary by the authors, follow these biographical sketches. Finally, an epilogue recounts what happened to Geoff in the year following the referral of his case. Throughout the presentation of responders' and authors' views are Problems for Discussion, which the reader is urged to consider and later discuss with fellow students or co-workers.

CASE STUDY MATERIALS ON GEOFF

Parents' Statement

In a Southwestern state, Nazoneth, we were aware that Geoff was placed in some slower classes but still at grade level. Because of personal acquaintance with the teachers and the principal, we felt there was excellent communication between the home and the school. Never did the school indicate that Geoff had a major problem at his grade level. He attained goals set for himself, such as scouts (he is currently a Life Scout), music, and sports. Geoff was in a junior high school (seven-eight-ninth grades) in eighth grade in Nazoneth. When we moved to a Midwestern state, Minowa, in March 1969, he was enrolled in the eighth grade at Watertown School. About the beginning of May, we were advised that Geoff was failing all his academic subjects (excelling in Physical Education) and that retention was being considered. As a result of some nationwide test ratings, we were informed that he possessed only fifth grade abilities. This seemed incredible to us, and naturally we were dumbfounded, since Nazoneth schools gave no indication that he had a major problem such as that described.

As Geoff's parents, we feel we cannot overemphasize the importance of the right decisions, the need for complete diagnostical testing—achievement and psychological (motivation, attitudes, ability, interests, skills, and so forth) in order to evaluate and take proper action. Decisions made now, as a result of this testing will affect Geoff's *entire future life* in a major way.

We value greatly the high professional skills of your staff and will be extremely grateful for the evaluation and recommendations that are certain to influence greatly, if not determine completely, the future of this fine young boy.

(Father's signature and date)

Remarks by Parents on Family Information Form

Home and family history. Parents married 15 years, with three children younger than Geoff. The next youngest child was slowed down and repeated grades because of severe head injuries. The father is a college graduate, mechanical engineer; the mother attended college and is listed as a homemaker.

Family social contacts. Sports, neighborhood, church, and music.

When did the problems first begin? Some academic lack of achievement in Grades 5 and 6; seemed to progress in Grades 7 and 8 in Nazoneth. In Minowa, in April 1969, the school notified the parents of extremely poor achievement, ability, and/or motivation to a degree that seemed impossible to the parents.

Has this child ever been examined or received treatment for this problem before? No.

Is this child sociable or does he prefer to be alone? Sociable.

How does this child get along with: Mother. Resents authority. *Father.* Resists authority. *Brothers and sister.* Bossy, aggressive, antagonistic, generous, and inconsiderate.

How does this child behave in adult company? Very well, unless other children are present, particularly his brothers—acts immature.

How does this child get along with friends his own age? Mischievous but well liked and popular.

With whom does this child prefer to be? His peers.

Developmental history. No reported difficulties, except slow to talk—poor word sounds in early speech.

What are this child's main interests? Scouting (Life Scout), music, water skiing, swimming, and hiking.

What recreational activities are enjoyed most? Camping, water skiing, swimming, and horseback riding.

Are there work responsibilities? Yes. *What kind?* Lawn mowing (regular basis); miscellaneous jobs—house painting. Cleans room; has held paying jobs well.

Attitude toward work. Materialistic—good attitude if employed for pay outside family. Work as a responsible member of the family without pay—poor attitude.

Speech development. Lacks ability of self-expression. Attempts to get brothers to relate experiences and events they share together. Had speech correction from school therapist K through Grade 4. Private therapist for summer sessions.

School Reports

GRADE 6

Iowa Test of Basic Skills

V	Vocabulary	G.E.	47	P.R.	18
R	Reading	G.E.	53	P.R.	24
L-1	Spelling	G.E.	59	P.R.	40
L-2	Capitalization	G.E.	33	P.R.	3
L-3	Punctuation	G.E.	26	P.R.	1
L-4	Usage	G.E.	37	P.R.	9
L	Total Language	G.E.	39	P.R.	6
W-1	Maps	G.E.	40	P.R.	9
W-2	Graphs	G.E.	47	P.R.	17
W-3	References	G.E.	52	P.R.	22
W	Total Work Study	G.E.	46	P.R.	10
A-1	Concepts	G.E.	66	P.R.	54
A-2	Problems	G.E.	50	P.R.	19
A	Total Arithmetic	G.E.	58	P.R.	34
C	Composite	G.E.	49	P.R.	16

GRADE 7

Subject	Grade	Citizenship
Arithmetic 7	C−	S
Social Science 7	C+	E
Physical Education 7—Boys	C	S
Metals	B+	S
Woods	B−	S−
Graphic Arts	B	E
Drafting	B	E
Lunch & Reading Improvement	C	S
English 7	D+	S−
Intermediate Band	A−	E

GRADE 8

Nazoneth Junior High School

9/68–2/69
Grades to date of leaving
        2-24-69

	Units	Grade	Citizenship
Physical Education	5	C	S
English 8	5	C	S
Social Science 8	5	B	E
General Science 8	5	D	S
Advance Band	5	A	E
Arithmetic 8	5	B	S

10/23/68	Lorge-Thorndike Int		Verbal	Nonverbal	Average
Ca 167	Level-E	MA	122	140	131
Gr 8	Form-1	IQ	76	87	82
		IQ%	07%	21%	13%

School Report—Watertown

Academic Adjustment:

Grade Marks

Subject	Present Mark	Indicates Improvement or Deterioration	Comments
Reading	C—Seventh grade level	Neither	
Language	F—Eighth grade level		
Spelling	D—Fifth grade level		
Social Studies	D—Seventh grade level		
Science	C—Sixth grade level		

Attendance record. Regular attendance.

Special academic interests (please list). None.

Special academic difficulties. Grammar, Spelling, Mathematics, Social Studies.

Classroom participation. Seldom—daydreams much of the time.

Social Adjustment:

Describe this child's relationship with peers. He seems to relate well to the other students, especially the girls.

How does this child participate in groups? He seems to follow rather than lead.

What roles does he usually assume (leader, follower; passive, aggressive, and so forth)? Follower.

What is the child's response to authority? Usually he obeys for a few minutes and then ignores authority.

What is this child's general physical appearance? He seems to be in good physical shape, neat, nice looking.

Are any particular health problems apparent? (Describe.) No.

Please discuss briefly any problems (social or academic) that have been observed in this child's siblings. Geoff's brother entered fourth grade at Watertown and was sent back to third where work was more nearly on his level. He will repeat third grade during the coming school year.

What is the relationship between the school and this child's parents? Good communication.

(Teacher signature)

Current Diagnostic Reading Examination Report

On April 23, 1969, SRA Achievement Test was administered. The results were:

Social Studies	5.1
Science	4.7
Language Arts	4.4
Arithmetic	5.7
Reading	4.4

Specific Analysis of Reading Strengths and Weaknesses:

On May 12, 1969, Geoff was administered a Gates-MacGinitie Reading Test (no form given). His scores were:

Vocabulary	5.5
Composite	4.1

The results of these tests, administered during Geoff's eighth grade school year, indicate his instructional reading level (4.2–4.3) to be nearly five years below his present grade level (9.0).

1. *Word discrimination.* The test score on the Huelsman Word Discrimination Test indicates that Geoff's visual word discrimination skills are approximately four years below his actual reading grade placement.

2. *Oral reading.* On the Gray Oral Reading Test (GORT), Geoff scored at the 3.7 grade level. Weakness in comprehension of literal recall was somewhat evident at the fourth grade level. On the sixth grade passage, the comprehension score was 50 percent. On the seventh grade passage the comprehension score was 25 percent, and at the eighth grade passage the frustration level had been reached and there appeared to be no comprehension.

   Geoff's apparent lack of word attack skills and techniques was demonstrated on this test, as he showed a strong tendency simply to substitute or mispronounce a word rather than attempt to unlock one he did not instantly recognize.

3. *Auditory discrimination.* His score on the Wepman Auditory Discrimination Test indicated that he apparently has no auditory problems which would hinder him from making progress in learning the necessary reading skills.

4. *Silent reading vocabulary.* On the O'Rourke Survey Test of Vocabulary, Geoff achieved below the 2nd percentile according to the standardized norms for his age group.

5. *Rate of comprehension.* On the Van Wagenen Rate of Comprehension, the score indicated that Geoff was reading 42 words per minute with understanding. This is somewhat below the third grade reading level.

6. *Sight vocabulary.* On the Dolch List of Basic Sight Vocabulary Words, Geoff made only a few errors. His main error on the list was in substitution of words that look somewhat alike. The basic analysis errors seemed to stem from the attempt to use configuration and to guess at words he did not know.

Psychological Report

Parent Interview:

Geoff's mother came alone to the parent interview. What she had to say was consistent with the parent application form and statement. It was apparent that she felt it was a mistake to retain Geoff for social reasons and was quite disturbed with the Watertown school system. She also pointed out that the principal's report to the parents concerning Geoff's test scores and prognosis for success were reported to the parents by phone and was overheard by Geoff. In her estimation this has been quite damaging to Geoff's motivation and self-concept.

The mother is not ready to accept the principal's diagnosis and is ready to do almost anything to help Geoff complete high school and prepare for college. School placement where Geoff can receive the most help is the top priority with her.

Wechsler Intelligence Scale for Children (WISC):

Verbal IQ	99
Performance IQ	103
Full Scale IQ	101

Wide Range Achievement Test (WRAT):

Reading Grade Equivalent   5.4
Thematic Apperception Test (TAT), Selected Cards
Bender Motor Gestalt Test (BMGT)
Draw-A-Person Test (D-A-P)

Test Results:

Geoff was a 15½ year old boy, accompanied by his mother to the pupil personnel offices for the examination. His general appearance was average for a boy his age. During the examination, he talked spontaneously of his summer activities and was friendly. There was no affective disturbance during the examination. Speech was clear and articulate. There were no apparent physical problems, and no health problems were reported. Geoff was cooperative and might be described as mildly dependent.

The results of the WISC would indicate that Geoff has normal intelligence when compared to the norms for his age group. The differences between the verbal and performance areas of functioning were negligible, and the subtests were relatively unscattered. The highest subtests were Block Design and Arithmetic. The findings of the WRAT indicated functional reading skill at the fifth grade level. This evaluation is comparable to the findings reported earlier. His work on the perceptual motor tasks did not indicate problems of development. Planning and organization were adequate on the Bender Test. The human figure drawing was a side view, male, including basic features but few elaborated details. Responses to the TAT indicated a loss of self-esteem, anxiety about school achievement, and some problems of dependency and emotional separation from his parents.

The results of the examination were discussed at some length with the mother. She and her husband were obviously very upset by the telephone call informing them that their son was to be retained in the eighth grade and the principal's report that Geoff could never be successful at the college level. They feel that retention in the current program and grade would not be satisfactory, since this approach would not resolve the basic problems of educational retardation and might create another situation of failure for Geoff, as he would be removed from his supportive peer group.

INFORMATION ABOUT RESPONDERS

For his first case, the backgrounds of seven responders will be presented. In addition, brief descriptive statements of other responder participants will be included where such information will add to the understanding of case material interpretation. From time to time, the authors will raise questions for discussion about responder comments and summarize various approaches utilized by the responders in the evaluative process. It will soon become apparent to the reader that the responders selected represent different segments of education, ranging from the inexperienced graduate student to the seasoned school teacher and administrator.

THE BEHAVIORAL SCIENTIST. This responder reports the following personal data information. He is 27 years old and a Ph.D student in educational psychology on a research assistantship. His work experience includes animal behavior research, behavior modification therapy with children and with adult psychotics, and college instruction. He describes his doctoral program as operant conditioning and behavior modification in the school settings. His self-identified occupational role is that of teacher and researcher dealing with the technology of teaching. The behavioral scientist comes from a family of four children and has maintained close family ties. He describes himself as having been a poor student in grade school and high school. After three years of military service, he married and began his college career. He has not been a paid employee in the public schools.

THE SUPERINTENDENT.   Personal data information about the superintendent indicates that he has had 11 years of public school experience, 6 as a classroom teacher and 5 as a teaching superintendent. His teaching experience has been at the upper elementary-junior high level in mathematics, social studies, and coaching. A college graduate, he perceives his main job role as administering his district with as few problems as possible and giving the children the best education possible. He has not had any major problems in his role as superintendent. He stated he was raised as a Christian in a Christian home. "My father is a minister. I have taught in Bible School classes for a period of years."

THE COUNSELING PSYCHOLOGIST.   This responder has had three years of school experience as a psychologist in the high school district and previously was a rehabilitation counselor for eight years. He has had approximately 100 hours of graduate work from two major universities. His job role is that of a school psychologist, but "counseling happens to be my felt area of effectiveness, and the needs for counseling are great for today's youth." He sees his future in counseling or teaching counseling. The psychologist stated that adults with problems are available too late for the counselor who wishes to employ *preventive* measures. He believes that there is a greater need for utilizing community resources as an alternative to adult institutions for psychiatric and prison populations.

THE READING SPECIALIST.   This specialist is a 28-year-old woman, an advanced doctoral assistant in a college reading clinic with administrative and clinical responsibilities. She supervises practicum students and provides direct clinical services in diagnosis and correction of referral reading cases. Previously, she taught first grade for two years and worked as a remedial reading instructor and teacher consultant for another year. Her undergraduate degree was in elementary education; the doctorate emphasis is on curriculum and instruction. The reading specialist sees her main job role as "helping teachers learn to vary their teaching methods and materials to better meet the varying abilities and needs of students —to get the emphasis on reading to learn rather than on learning to read." She is married and her husband is pursuing graduate work in English.

THE TEACHER.   This female teacher has had 17 years of classroom teaching experience and an additional 3 years of employment as a remedial reading teacher. Among her school experiences is listed the teaching of rural school, Grades 1 to 8. Academically, the teacher has 20 hours beyond a master's degree with training in both the humanities and the sciences. She finds that "helping children to learn within the limits of *my** ability . . . suits me very well." She would consider an administrative position in education only if it would do more toward helping the children. She is married to a mechanical engineer and has a son who is a college graduate.

THE PRINCIPAL.   This responder has been employed in the public schools for 19 years as a supervising principal and 17 years as a classroom teacher, in Grades 1 to 8 in various positions and schools. He is state certified in administration and elementary education. His college training includes elementary education, social studies, psychology, and English. He perceives his main job role as that of (1) improving teaching by using the proper techniques in leading teachers and (2) innovating new programs which will improve the learning process. "I was the principal for 15 years in a school in an economically deprived neighborhood. The ratio of black to white is now about 60:40. Integration took place under my administration with no serious problems. . . . I am trying to point out that I have worked with people from various economic levels. Their problems are different, so they have to be treated differently."

THE TEACHER-COUNSELOR.   This responder has had four years of teaching experience, Grades 6 to 12, in mathematics, science, and sociology. He was director of his school district's gifted program. He has also been a clothing salesman, a swimming instructor, and a bartender. He is now working on his doctorate in guidance and counseling, secondary level; as an undergraduate, he studied mathematics, physics, and sociology. Now 27 years old, the counselor sees his future occupational role as that of a consultant to the directors of school guidance programs and as a college statistics teacher. His parents are both college graduates; his father has a master's degree in chemistry. "I have always taken a great interest in the affairs of other people. I enjoy working with and helping them. . . . My experiences in graduate work in sociology and guidance have given me some insight into the case study approach."

Responders' Perceptions and Recommendations, with Authors' Comments

A.   *From the available information, what in your opinion are the most significant aspects of the case?*

The behavioral scientist begins his comments by referring to Geoff as a *subject** and continued with this reference throughout his discussion. The term "subject" is usually the reference term in experiments; "client" in personnel services; "student" in school learning situations. Thus, at the

*Italics added.

outset, he appears to approach Geoff as an object of scientific or experimental inquiry. What then is significant to the scientist? The subject has normal intelligence. He does not participate much in the classroom and what was formerly acceptable behavior is now considered failing except in physical education. Geoff "works hard . . . for money . . . and has done well in the scouts."

The principal notes four major aspects to the case materials, with some interpretation as to cause-and-effect relationships. Geoff apparently has average ability but is working in most academic areas at the fifth grade level. He does better in activities that do not require academic skills. Evidently, as a result of these conditions "Geoff has developed an inferiority complex concerning his school work and has developed somewhat of a rebellious attitude, finding it easier to be a follower than a leader."

The superintendent simplifies the question of significant aspects to the single statement that Geoff does average or better in activites that interest him.

Geoff's problems are of long standing, according to his teacher, and the academic difficulty is mostly associated with reading problems. Poor work and study habits are indicated by the 10th percentile rank of the Iowa Test, and Geoff ranks at only the 50th percentile rank of the Gray Oral Reading Test for the sixth grade level although he is in the eighth grade. She also notes that his average potential for learning is average at his grade level.

It is interesting that the reading specialist directs three of her five comments to Geoff's family constellation. The parents have overly high aspirations for him and are concerned about his present school situation and their overall relationship with him. (The reading specialist comments on Geoff's resistance to his parents' authority and his problems of emotional separation from his parents, as shown on the TAT.) Low reading ability with attendant academic difficulties and success in nonacademic pursuits are noted, too.

The counseling psychologist approaches the case by pointing out that Geoff is rather typical of many students entering the high school program. Geoff has a discrepancy between achievement levels and IQ score that reflects deterioration of motivation and/or comprehension, starting in the fifth grade and continuing to the present. "The absence of success, peer acceptance (especially male), and reward will thwart any attempts at retention or the like." He points out that at the community high school a program for students like Geoff already exists, the school officials evidently having recognized the high frequency of similar students at the secondary level.

The teacher-counselor pinpoints several other significant aspects of the case: the move from Nazoneth; Geoff's need to get attention in many ways, being the oldest of four children; the phone call to the parents, which Geoff overheard; and the change in grade-point averages from 3.25 in Nazoneth to 2.20 in Minowa. The counselor noted that the current adjustment problems are made worse by Geoff's negative school history in Grades 5 to 9.

In reviewing the responder information to the first question, there is a general consensus that Geoff is not learning at an effective rate in school. However, beyond this fact, the embellishment of significant aspects to the case becomes quite divergent. The professionals in education do not define "significant aspects" of the case in the same manner. Interpretations ranged from the "money reinforcer" of the behavioral scientist to the possible "birth order effects" of the teacher-counselor to the reinterpretation of an interpreted TAT protocol. Based on these initial findings it is probably evident that different points of emphasis are likely to generate more differences as the case materials are further refined and synthesized.

Problems for Discussion:

1. How do you account for responder differences in their descriptions of the significant aspects of the case?
2. In what manner do these case interpretations reflect the particular perceptions of the responder?

B. **What, if any, do you perceive as the main problems in the educational setting?**

The purpose of this question was to help the responder to qualify further the student case information with reference to the school setting, thus encouraging a closer inspection of the school aspects of the case materials from the more general focus of Question A. Occasionally, students are referred by outside agencies, which report that the student has presented no particular learning or management problems in the school setting. In fact, the personal school experiences of the student may be contributing to his social and personal developement. With the case at hand, however, other considerations are more evident.

The behavioral scientist defines the main school problem in this way: "The educational setting *in league with** the parents has not produced a system to motivate the subject." He is joined by the superintendent, who states bluntly that the school must "get him interested." The teacher-counselor also alludes to motivational factors by noting Geoff's *resistance to the recent change** and to the new *principal's attitudes** concerning him.

The reading specialist shifts from a child-family emphasis to an *educational, functional level assessment* approach.

*Italics added.

The major problem in the educational setting seems to be the result of Geoff's apparent lack of reading skills. If Geoff is functioning approximately four to five years below his present grade level in an individual diagnostic reading situation, it can be assumed that he is virtually unable to read any of the material that students are usually required to read in typical eighth and ninth grade academic classes. This problem is magnified when no curricular provisions are made for students with such difficulties.

The teacher and the psychologist tend to emphasize Geoff's educational problems in an historic or developmental sense. Hence his teacher reports that Geoff's early school experience did not include help in orientation for reading, even though he was slow to talk and had poor word sounds. He received early speech correction K-4 . . . yet the "reading problems did not develop until the sixth grade and have never been examined or received treatment before, according to the parents." Even though Geoff's ITBS composite was only the 16th percentile in the sixth grade, his parents were ignorant of more than a slight need for help.

The psychologist states that individual counseling and family help should have been instituted in the fifth grade. He considers the IQ information not comprehensive enough to have been reported to classroom teachers, and he notes that the successful areas of interest were not continued in Geoff's program.

After reemphasizing the reading difficulty only, the principal clearly defines the main problem in the present context: "At this time, just what procedures should be recommended for Geoff to improve the situation in which he has been placed?" The principal seems to approach the problem as one that needs to be solved, here and now.

Problems for Discussion:
3. When, if ever, should information on parental expectations enter into educational planning?
4. What would be Geoff's status in school if the eighth grade teachers had simply given him passing grades as did his teachers in Nazoneth? Based on the case information, what would you have estimated Geoff's educational level to have been while in the fifth grade?

C. *What, if any, do you view as the related problems?*

The behavioral scientist takes a rather cautious approach to this question: "I do not care to speculate as to what the related problems may be." In contrast, the principal first raises the question about what school procedures should be recommended to assist Geoff now; he then seeks to define more closely the substrata of related problems: age and grade placement, academic achievement, the ability to succeed, parental opinion and concern, and the Watertown school policy. He now begins to see some value in trying to understand and consider Geoff's current desires and motivations.

The reader may have noticed the authors' more favorable reaction to the principal's approach to the case material. In Chapter 2, it was stated that one of the first priorities in school personnel work is to establish what question or questions need amplification. This characterizes the principal's approach: grasping the overall problem, deciding what the major questions are, and then establishing the need for related information.

In a rather vague manner, the superintendent sees the related problems as Geoff's being "a below-average student who needs a lot of personal help; the school must try to find something that he can excel in or get interested in enough to want to be successful at school." So far the superintendent has described Geoff as "doing average or better in activities" and as a "below-average student." It will be interesting to see what the superintendent recommends later to stimulate Geoff to succeed in school.

The teacher and the reading specialist look to the family constellation to assay related problems in Geoff's lack of educational progress. The reading specialist summarizes:

> The relationship between Geoff and his parents seems to have direct bearing on Geoff's educational problems. The parents seem to have set up very high goals for Geoff, goals that are seemingly out of his reach. They appear to be placing so much emphasis on academic accomplishments that they may not even recognize Geoff's actual strengths in other areas. In addition, the relationship between the parents and the new school seems to be far from ideal; it almost appears that the parents are using the school as a scapegoat to explain away Geoff's problems.

The teacher attempts to juxtapose Geoff's reading problems and the mother's relationship to the brain-injured child. "The mother may have had to give unusual time and attention to the child who was injured in the head and who is younger than Geoff.

Problem for Discussion:
5. How do you react to this kind of cause-and-effect thinking by the teacher responder?

The teacher also notes the change in school standards and suggests that the parent-teacher relationship in Nazoneth may have kept the faculty from viewing Geoff objectively. She also suggests that Geoff may need corrective glasses as an aid to word discrimination at near-point.

The two remaining respondents add several related problem topics, most of which have been mentioned by others in this discussion. The teacher-counselor points out areas for consideration, such as Geoff's early troubled speech pattern and an aversion to failure. (Is this a cause-and-effect situation from his preschool and early school years?) The move from

Nazoneth resulted in Geoff's loss of enjoyable friendships and shared activities.

The counseling psychologist alludes to Geoff's problem in school with reference to available educational facilities and programs. Geoff's personal interests, as well as the parent-sibling, parent-school relationships need to be explored. He requests more information than is available to "enhance the prospects of my contributing substantially in effective recommendations." Later on, he will define this need more specifically.

Problems for Discussion:
  6. How significant is it that Geoff's college-educated parents establish for him college education as a goal?
  7. Select several related problem comments and attempt to explain why the responder may have selected them. Are these problem areas more likely to be the result of some other problem, the cause of some other problem, *or* both?

D. How would you be likely to feel about this situation?

The responders' different "feelings" about the case information on Geoff reflect their broad range of personal and professional reactions. This question calls for more evaluative and affective reactions on the part of the responder. So far, the responders have tended to define their own feelings about Geoff from the various perspectives they had already established in the earlier analysis-synthesis process. The focus of their answers to this question will shift from the student to the school—past, present, and future in reference.

The behavioral scientist's response to the questions of feelings should not be surprising: "I do not know how to respond to this question."

Problem for Discussion:
  8. Does the behaviorial scientist's response suggest that his own personal feelings are not relevant to the case? Does he negate affective-type inquiries in his view of education as a technology?

The reading specialist refocuses her attention on Geoff's past experiences in the Nazoneth educational setting. She feels it is "too bad that Geoff's academic problems have been allowed to progress to the extent that they have without some earlier attempts to help the boy. Using the words 'too bad' is a gross understatement." She sees the problems of reading and the discrepancy between the parents' view of their son's education progress and his actual progress emanating from the earlier school experiences:

> Although provisions seem to have been made for slow learners in the Nazoneth schools, little or nothing seems to have been done about Geoff's reading problem. In addition, it appears that the school did not adequately explain to the parents the grades that were given in the slower groups. Thus, since Geoff's parents saw satisfactory grades on his report cards, they seem to have assumed that he was having no academic difficulty and would have no trouble completing high school and college.

The principal emphasizes three aspects of the case, empathizing with the parents, rebuking the Nazoneth schools, and justifying the need to get the problem out in the open. He states that as a parent "I would be very unhappy," thus recognizing the parents' emotional reaction to their son's school status. With reference to the earlier school experiences, he points out that as an administrator he would feel the Nazoneth schools were "150 years behind the times." In his self-identified role as administrator, he would "feel justified in doing what was done." The failure of Geoff to make satisfactory educational progress "should have been recognized several years before it was and appropriate steps taken to correct the situation."

From among the available information, the specific problems of the transition period from the Nazoneth school to the new program in Minowa seem most important to the teacher-counselor. He feels that the change in community and school location was "very detrimental, especially at this stage of Geoff's development, approximately 14½ years. This is the period of time when children seem to be most critical of themselves."

Looking at Geoff's current placement in school, the superintendent anticipates that Geoff will rebel toward school in general; that is, he will probably be a rebel. Evidently, the superintendent anticipates that Geoff will be a behavioral and management problem in the school and/or community.

The remaining two responders suggest alternative educational procedures for Geoff as they react to his condition in school on a personal basis. The teacher offers an alternative of retention in the eighth grade with remedial help in reading. She describes this condition as "crucial." Her rationale for this procedure is that she feels that it will allow Geoff to enter the high school environment with the expectation of some productivty. "Since he seems to respond to reward (works for pay), he may find the remedial work so rewarding that it will offset social drawbacks to retention." Otherwise, Geoff indeed seems to be a potential high school dropout.

Since the counseling psychologist is in a school system that already offers a program for students like Geoff, he looks with a positive view toward Geoff's matriculation into his program. He asks that Geoff be sent to the ninth grade, where he will participate in vocational courses, on-the-job experience, and counseling services to enhance his self-concept.

The reader will note the wide range of "personal" ways of viewing and reacting to Geoff's individual condition in school. The responders are beginning to establish their own stylistic form as they reveal how they begin to understand and deal with the same pupil personnel information. The principal approaches the case material by raising relevant questions, dealing directly with the parents and the school-related problems. Another administrator, the superintendent, is almost nondescript in his analysis and synthesis of the case materials: vague inferences and simplistic reactions are recorded.

Problem for Discussion:
9. As a third party in dialogue with the above school administrators, your understanding of them would be critical to the interpretation and planning you might wish to pursue in the case of Geoff. Consider also the following responders, the teacher, who *feels* that retention in Grade 8 is indicated, and the psychologist, who favors a substantial change in program and curriculum in the ninth grade with indivdiual counseling as a more viable alternative for Geoff. How much do you think the feelings of these administrators are influenced by their roles in education and their experiences in education?

E.   How would the student be likely to feel about the situation?

There was a general consensus regarding the feelings that Geoff might be experiencing in his school situation, although the responses ranged from telescopically brief ones to more elaborate and interpretative reactions. The single exception to this condition was the response of the behaviorial scientist, who stated, "I am in no position to say." It is difficult to determine from his answer whether he does not feel empathy with Geoff and his condition, chooses to ignore information related to Geoff's affective behavior, or does not believe that it is a significant area of concern with regard to Geoff's future situation in the school. If the last interpretation is correct, it would follow the earlier position of the behavioral scientist of not moving into the affective domain other than to note that the educational setting in league with the parents has not produced a system to motivate the subject.

The reading specialist again attempts to summarize the condition of the student and establish a basis for making the case information consistent and interrelated.

Geoff's reading problem did not develop overnight. His reading grade level has probably been lower than his actual grade placement during most, if not all, of his school career. Geoff, therefore, has probably faced failure in the classroom for a number of years. When this "failure" is covered with his parents' apparent motivation for academic success, it is no wonder that the TAT indicated lack of self-esteem and anxiety about school achievement. Geoff probably views the classroom as an extremely frustrating situation. In fact, Geoff appears to withdraw from it by spending his time "daydreaming" (as indicated on the school report).

The sense of frustration alluded to by the reading specialist is elaborated and interpreted in different ways by the other responders. For example, the psychologist simply described Geoff's feelings as "discouraged," while the superintendent saw "frustration leading to aggression." He felt that Geoff would get more attention from misconduct with his peers than he could by doing well in the school program. Similar points were made by the other administrator, the principal, who described Geoff's feelings variously as frustrated and rebellious; he felt these attitudes would probably carry over into Geoff's everyday life. It is probable that Geoff would be most happy doing those things at which he could succeed, such as band and athletics.

As the teacher-counselor empathized with the student, he pointed to the possibility that Geoff would very likely want to leave a situation in which he expects to feel "resignation and alienation." He felt that at this stage Geoff could easily give up all efforts in his school work.

The teacher continued to follow the point of view she established in answering the earlier questions by further developing the rationale for retaining Geoff in the eighth grade. She felt that he would probably be reluctant to be retained initially. However, since he is so good in athletics and is relatively young, he might see another year of physical development and practice as desirable at the eighth grade level. At the high school level, it would be necessary for him to pass courses in order to be eligible for team athletics; his present condition would indicate that passing would be questionable at the high school level. She stated again that retention with remediation would indicate a better prognosis.

Problem for Discussion:
10. How would you attempt to explain the fact that some responders feel retention would be devastating to Geoff's personal and school adjustment, while others see it as a favorable alternative?

F.   What would be your suggestions or alternatives for solving or improving the problem situations you identified?

By now the reader should expect to find a wide variety of answers to the question about what to do for Geoff. This is so because some of the responders have already taken a firm positon in this regard, but it is even more important to note that the responders have not identified the problems in the same way. Thus it should be expected that different solutions will be suggested, based on different interpretations of the case information materials.

In the case of the behavioral scientist, as his professional orientation dominated his earlier discussion, it also influences his suggestions for improving Geoff's school situation. He stated that "methods for quantifying academic behavior in the classroom and at home (homework) should be generated. It has been stated that the subject works well for money and poorly without it. The subject should be paid for acceptable daily academic work both at home and at school, and also for long-term behavior changes, (i.e., improvements in report card marks)." The approach being suggested here is that base line information be obtained that will show Geoff's current type of classroom behavior. This would take into account the amount of time he attends to school materials, the number of problems that he completes during a given period of time, the quality of his work on some criteria, and so forth. Once this information is obtained, then conditions (standards) are established for him to receive rewards (money) as he improves on the criterion behavior. Evidently, the behavioral scientist feels that money rewards are sufficient for motivation and that they would have equal application in the school and at home.

Note that an alternative to approaching Geoff's problem this way would be to pay the teacher on a special basis, depending upon her characteristic behavior in the classroom; that is, set up teacher standards and as she was able to provide Geoff an effective program of training, give her special financial awards. In either case, it would be interesting to see how the behavioral scientist would develop these applications in an interdepartmental program at the junior high school level and establish the quantifying procedure in the usual complex school situation.

Problems for Discussion:
11. Is there implied in the behavioral scientist's approach that the same curriculum would be maintained and that as the result of the money-reward system employed here, Geoff would recover his four or five years of educational retardation?
12. Should the responsibiltiy for teaching the educational program be shared on a monetary basis with the parents and should educational training be emphasized in the home?

Wihout being specific, the superintendent suggested that Geoff be put in a position where he could excel without losing face. It would be of interest to explore the meaning of the statement with the administrator, since his answer allows for a number of interpretations.

Problem for Discussion:
13. Is the reader to assume that in order to put Geoff in a position where he would excel, it would be necessary to provide a program for him

that would not result in a loss of self-esteem *if it were public informa-tion?* For example, if Geoff were promoted to the ninth grade, would he have an academic program with materials at the fourth to fifth grade level, the level at which he is functioning in reading? Perhaps the sense of "losing face" has reference to Geoff's own personal considerations of himself. In terms of grade placement, would it be necessary to keep information from him on the exact grade in which he is functioning?

As indicated in his earlier discussion, the principal first proposed to approach the problem directly in discussion with the parents and then referred to the development of alternative procedures within the school program. Initially, he would have the parents and Geoff discuss very frankly with the school authorities and the school psychologist the entire situation as described. Together they would outline possible procedures to improve the school situation. The recommendations for Geoff might be private tutoring or placement in ungraded classrooms. In his approach to school planning, the counseling psychologist tended to agree with the principal at this point. He reiterated the condition of having Geoff continued in the high school program, where vocational courses and on-the-job experiences would be available. However, the psychologist focused on direct counseling services with the student, rather than emphasize so much the need to bring the parents into the picture. Although the teacher advocated retention in eighth grade with remedial training, she also stressed that Geoff's ability in band and athletics has provided him the kinds of experience that will be favorable for his growth. She advocated giving Geoff responsibility in areas where he could experience manual success, such as assignments in drafting and shop.

The teacher-counselor hoped to establish better communication with the school administration and suggested that he would first attempt to interpret the findings and meaning of the case information in all aspects of the case to the school principal. His alternative procedures also included getting Geoff involved in some of his stronger activity areas, such as scouting, music, swimming, and hiking. He continued to emphasize the personal adjustment aspect of the situation by expressing concern about Geoff's social acquaintances and opportunities for making "substitute friends" in his new surroundings.

The reading specialist took a multiple approach to dealing with Geoff's school problems. Her suggestions ranged from educational placement and curriculum materials planning to consulting with teachers on Geoff's problems and the need for personnel services work.

I do not feel that retaining Geoff will really help the situation in any way. Repeating eighth grade may only add to his sense of frustration, and an additional year of junior high school cannot be expected to solve Geoff's academic problems.

Geoff's new teachers should be made aware of his difficulties and they should be encouraged to provide differentiated materials and assignments not only for Geoff, but for other "slower learning" students as well. Unless some type of curricular changes are made, these students will continue to meet frustration in the classroom.

In addition, any special individual or small group help that is available should be provided for Geoff. This might include the services of a remedial reading teacher or some member of the school staff who works with students during their study halls. At this grade level, such work should concentrate on helping the students to satisfy their immediate needs; that is, if easy material on the topic that the students are studying in science or history is available, provide this material for the students. If such material is not available, either write such material or actually read the assignments to the students or discuss the important concepts in the assignment with them, so that their lack of reading skills will be somewhat minimized in the classroom situation.

Guidance should also be provided for Geoff. This would be aimed at helping him to have a realistic view of his strengths and weaknesses (with emphasis on his strengths) and in making future plans.

Geoff's parents also appear to need counseling to help them to have a more realistic view of their son, to fit their aspirations for him to his actual abilities.

Problem for Discussion:

14. Some of the responders favor heavy involvement with the parents in terms of consultation or counseling, while other responders appear to be willing to work almost entirely within the confines of the school program. Discuss the merits of the two approaches and what rationale or assumptions are suggested by these two positions.

G. *How would you go about implementing your suggestions?*

The process of implementing educational suggestions, of course, depends upon the educational evaluation and recommendations that have been made. It is interesting to compare the recommendations of the reading specialist, who has taken a broader view of Geoff's school development and functioning, with those of the behavioral scientist, who has rather narrowly defined the educational problem in terms of his procedures of behavior modification. The reading specialist began by noting that her suggestions would require a cooperative approach, an approach that included all school personnel, the parents, and the school services unit handling this report. The total picture of Geoff's strengths and weaknesses should be provided for both the parents and the school personnel, and their help should be sought in making future plans for Geoff. This, of course, would presuppose a willingness on the part of both the parents and the school to participate realistically in this planning.

By contrast, the suggestions of the behavioral scientist appear to be almost diametric to those of the reading specialist. However, in practice, these differences may be more illusionary than real. Now, for the first time, the behavioral scientist applies his problem-solving techniques to the problems at hand. He has made his evaluation and is now ready to do something about the condition of the subject. The particulars of his approach are a function of the specific conditions in the classroom situation and changes or lack of changes in the dependent measures. ("Dependent measures" referes to behavior deemed significant in terms of educational progress, such as reading scores, social studies scores, teacher grades, participation in class discussion, and so forth.)

The behavioral scientist considers three conditions important in his approach to educational planning.

1. He views daily communication between teachers and parents as essential.
2. He believes that it is important to have reliable and definable standards of classroom performance, and also of homework performance.
3. He believes that reinforcers, money in particular, and anything else that proves to be effective should be provided, contingent upon acceptable reports from school, homework performance, and report card outcomes.

From the point of view of specialist applications, these two responders present a behavioristic approach, on the one hand, and a clinical diagnostic group planning approach on the other. The behavioral scientist appears to ignore much information that has interested other responders. However, a closer examination of his responses would indicate that he has not really ignored this information, he simply does not emphasize it in his communications. For example, his very first suggestion is that there be regular communication between the teachers and the parents. He describes this as an absolutely necessary condition for his behavioral approach. Regrettably, he does not say what they will be communicating about. Perhaps it will be to establish reasonable and meaningful educational goals or to talk about procedures of teaching. Perhaps he hopes to establish a better understanding between the teachers and the parents so that an appropriate reward schedule can be established for effective work. His request for clearer definitions of classroom performance is an attempt on his part to make a concentrated, daily assessment of Geoff's behavior. This approach is facilitated by quantifying observable behaviors over a time period. It cannot be argued, however, that the actions being observed are different from those the teacher has been habitually observing in her day-to-day contact with the student. In essence then, this procedure is an attempt to deal somewhat more systematically with the day-to-day operations of the school as personified by the teacher and the student in the classroom. Similar procedures are being suggested in terms of defining the homework performance.

The behavioral scientist emphasizes the need to motivate the student.

In response to earlier questions, he ignored all aspects of the affective domain; however, it has now become an obvious and significant factor. After all, if money or some other contingency is reinforcing and encourages certain types of behavior, by definition he is talking about change in an affective state.

Perhaps the two most obvious questions that come to mind in assaying the behavioral scientist's comments are his apparent disregard of the reading requirements in the ninth grade and his failure to consider dealing with Geoff's academic problems from the point of view of altering the curriculum or program. As one reviews the suggestions of the reading specialist, it is immediately apparent that she places much emphasis on curriculum materials and on involving other personnel in educational planning for Geoff. She is suggesting that what is going to be motivational for Geoff is to create conditions which will facilitate his learning by providing him with a program in which he can experience considerable success. The behavioral scientist might label this one of *his* reinforcers, although with further inquiry he might be more comfortable staying with some type of token or social reinforcer.

Problem for Discussion:
15. How would the reader go about integrating the approaches of the behavioral scientist and the reading specialist in educational planning and implementation for students like Geoff?

The principal and the counseling psychologist followed similar procedures as they began to implement their educational plans. The principal first suggested having a frank discussion with the parents. Following this, he would suggest private tutoring for Geoff on a regular basis but not until there had been a clearer definition of Geoff's condition in the educational setting, based on test administration and interpretation. He would find it useful to pursue further individual analysis to determine what are the "real causes of Geoff's difficulty in academic subjects" and would anticipate moving Geoff along in the ungraded classrooms at the ninth grade level just as fast as Geoff could demonstrate satisfactory progress. At first, the psychologist suggested the parent conference, followed immediately by what he called "proper educational placement." He is concerned with maintaining close attention to the student's progress. The follow-up procedures are to make sure that the program changes actually meet the student's needs. Of the seven initial responders in this case, only the teacher has consistently taken a position of retention for Geoff in terms of her educational prescription. She suggested retaining Geoff in the eighth grade and getting him immediate help under the school's administration. In fact, Geoff might be eligible for a special program in learning disability for his age group. She continued to focus primarily on obtaining remedial reading help from someone who "knows what he is doing."

The teacher-counselor focused on the pupil adjustment pattern by suggesting that auxiliary activities be implemented, especially those that relate to the earlier successes reported in Geoff's social history. He suggested that Geoff would join a scout troop and be made a leader or assistant leader, since he has Life Scout rank. He also suggested that Geoff would join the school band or possibly form a small combo of his own. He would set up an interview with the principal and see if Geoff could receive some kind of regular guidance services. The superintendent also indicated that the parallel school activities approach might be most productive, that Geoff might "try sports, music, or some extracurricular activity in the first period."

Problems for Discussion:
16. If the educational program remained fairly constant for Geoff as he entered the ninth grade (assuming that he would enter the ninth grade), what limitations would this place upon procedures such as counseling services and supportive social activities?
17. What are the merits of the evaluative approach suggested by the reading specialist and what limitations might be indicated by her procedures? Also, what are the merits of the behavioral scientist's approach to the problem and what limitations might be found in its actual application?

H. What additional information would help you in developing possible solutions to these problems?

This question is one that is a frequent companion to case staffings and case information materials. Almost inevitably, people who are required to make educational planning decisions want more information. They have the responsibilities for predicting which of several procedures might be most useful for the student; additional information may increase the likelihood of successful program development. Obviously prediction is enhanced by the amount of relevant information available and by control over future contingencies. Usually, more thorough and more complete information will provide a better guideline for the prediction of the course of future events. It is also true that most decisions have to be made on the basis of an imperfect view of past history and imperfect knowledge about school personnel and programs in the future. In education this problem is often dealt with by gathering relevant data and pooling professional judgment so that a consensus can be made. This occurs obviously in staffings and somewhat less obviously during informal conferences with teachers, administrators, and parents. A corollary procedure to this is to maintain follow-up on recommendations to make sure they are meeting with predicted success. In educational settings, this is not difficult to do, since the student is immediately available for observation and communication. There are also opportunities for further dialogue with school personnel involved in the revised educational program. The reader will observe in the following discussion that many responders wanted additional information which would help to clarify their particular views of the case and their recommendations.

The principal wanted to know more about the procedures followed in high school with student cases of this kind. In his school system, the ninth grade is part of the junior high unit, and he thinks his suggestions of placement in the ungraded classrooms and tutoring could be handled with success. Since there is still some confusion about why Geoff has fallen so far behind in his academic work, the principal would like to know if this was a result of poor teaching, of Geoff's inability to hear sounds, or of his inattention. Answers to these questions could certainly influence educational planning since this question is related to the development of alternative strategies within the school program.

The other administrator indicated that it would be helpful for him to "be around the boy; by talking to Geoff and trying him out in different tasks, he would eventually find out where Geoff might fit into the school program. He wishes to seek additional information by having Geoff participate in the activities and by getting immediate results on the basis of Geoff's involvement.

In line with his earlier discussion, the behavioral scientist wanted more objective measures of Geoff's academic behavior at home and in school. He requests more information about how Geoff behaves when he is in these two settings and what Geoff is expected to be doing in his schoolwork. He also wants more information about rewards the subject has worked for on past occasions. The behavioral scientist is interested in finding additional reinforcers that might be used to facilitate attention to assigned tasks. His requests open the door to a fairly careful review of the student's educational and family history, should that line of inquiry be necessary to establish the rewards information.

The reading specialist focused her attention on learning more about the student and the alternatives within the school program. Her first line of inquiry was to find out about Geoff's own aspirations for the future and his view of his parents' aspirations for him. She also indicated an interest in knowing what school facilities were available for students with Geoff's problems, how the administration felt about making curricular modifications to meet the needs of these students, and whether Geoff's teachers were interested in helping him make the most of his abilities.

The teacher focused on the family situation as an area of information need. She raised the question as to how this family reacts to pressures in reference to the academic pressures they place on their son. Does the mother feel this child's insecurity which he seems to display with adults? What influence have grandparents and other disgruntled relatives had on Geoff and his parents?

Problem for Discussion:
18. Does the reader feel that the teacher has gone adrift in hunting for related phenomena and explanations to Geoff's educational progress?

Both the counseling psychologist and the teacher-counselor emphasized the need for obtaining more information about the student *from the student.* The psychologist indicated that his first activity would be to have an individual conference with the student. This coincides with the teacher-counselor's interest in learning Geoff's side of the story by finding out what he thinks the problems are and how they should be dealt with. He also would like more information from the academic records of the two schools and the more general background on Geoff. The psychologist requested additional information on the Wechsler subtest pattern, along with school administrative information. He extended his inquiry to the family by wishing to know the extent of the father's role in Geoff's future educational plans.

Problem for Discussion:
19. Why have Geoff's parents been so naïve about his educational progress?

I.   *When reviewing the information available on this student, what assumptions did you have to make?*

As the reader reviews information provided by responders to this question, it will soon become apparent that reference to assumptions made by the responders is most often with reference to the veracity of the case material information. For reasons that are not always obvious, responders tend to view their own interpretations and evaluations as unquestionably accurate. It is often this sense of responder absoluteness the personnel specialist must deal with. The reader will have an opportunity to reconsider his assumptions as further inquiry and clarifications are made. An example of this is presented by the behavioral scientist who made the following as his assumptions: the subject has normal ability; academic behavior at home and in school can be objectively measured; money would continue to be an effective motivator; and other effective motivators could be found and used.

What are the assumptions of the behavioral scientist in his review of the case? Obviously, one is the basic need to find something that will motivate the student. He makes no mention in his discussion as to the appropriateness of goals of the program or the appropriateness of materials for the student. The behavioral scientist focuses on external motivational propensities. Taken at face value, presumably he would be trying to find some means of motivating Geoff, irrespective of other factors that might have value in educational planning. His assumption is that only the motivational state needs to be considered. If the instances of motivated behavior can be counted, then the primary question is how can you change the student's behavior to deal more effectively with assigned tasks? Evidently, the behavioral scientist would not be concerned with the program or the particular nature of the materials, provided that the right reinforcers were found. Where is the teacher an agent of change in his scheme of education? The behavioral scientist does qualify his assumptions to the degree that he feels the subject should have normal ability to learn. It is not too clear why this would be a factor, but perhaps a knowledge of Geoff's real abilities to learn might affect the *kinds* of behavior being reinforced.

The principal also made the point that it is necessary to assume that Geoff has the capacity to do average work if he applied himself to the tasks at hand. He noted the fact that the parents apparently did not have conferences with the teachers in Nazoneth and, therefore, did not really suspect that Geoff was doing poorly in school. The assumption that Geoff has the average capacity to apply himself to the work at hand is an interesting one because it raises the question of whether average ability is a sufficient condition for learning if the task at hand is far beyond the technical capacity of the student. If Geoff is reading at the fifth grade level and his reading assignments are at the eight grade level, the credibility of such an assumption immediately becomes one the personnel specialist will have to deal with. What would have happened to Geoff if the Minowa school had not made an issue of his low educational achievement? Would it also be reasonable to assume that the parents would continue to be ignorant of Geoff's real educational progress or lack thereof? The principal evidently assumes that if the parents had known about Geoff's failure to make expected educational progress, they would have reacted much earlier, if not more vigorously, to the situation.

The superintendent made the following statement: "It may be that the whole picture had things lacking; also, don't depend too much on a test." By "the whole picture" he evidently refers to the school, the family, the student, and whatever else might be brought into consideration. The superintendent's second assumption is that you are not to depend too heavily or too substantially on a test score. Does this indicate that the scores from achievement, intelligence, reading and diagnostic tests are fallacious and that judgment should depend solely upon other factors?

Problem for Discussion:
20. What other criteria would the superintendent employ in dealing with this type of situaton?

The teacher continued to emphasize the home situation and presented a series of assumptions she believes are necessary to make in reviewing the information on the case. She assumed that there were not too many unusual family situations such as the father's being away from home frequently; the harmony between the mother and the father did not exceed normal limits; disagreements did not occur between the parents on child discipline or academic demands; the parents provided honest answers to the questions; and Geoff is as normal socially as he seems to be. It is a little difficult to relate this set of assumptions to the suggestions that the teacher made, namely, retention and tutoring. What difference would it make in terms of educational planning if the father had been away from the home from time to time or that the parents did have some communication problems or disagreements? What if they did not always agree on child discipline? Even if all of the teacher's assumptions were true, the question of why Geoff was having so much trouble in school would still remain to be answered.

The reading specialist also made the assumption that the statements made by the parents are essentially true. She feels that it is necessary to assume the comments they made were really their own views of the problem and not just statements the parents considered to be socially acceptable views. This presents one interesting alternative. By defining the school problems as solely related to Geoff's current educational placement, the parents have placed the responsibility on the school in which he is now a student. They imply that Geoff's failures are the responsibility of the school rather than the parents' or Geoff's personal responsibility.

Problem for Discussion:
21. Why would the reading specialist be concerned about the parents' position being a socially accepted view? Would the reader interpret her comments to indicate that she would look to a better understanding of the family in order to obtain a more realistic view of Geoff's educational adjustment?

The teacher-counselor and the psychologist both reported that they had to make many assumptions in dealing with the case information. The teacher-counselor elaborated his comments by saying that he assumed that the principal of the Minowa school must border on incompetency.

Evidently, the counselor reacted very strongly to the report that the principal contacted the parents over the phone to tell them about their son's educational status. The counselor also assumed that the move from Nazoneth to Minowa affected Geoff's attitude toward school, presumably because of his reported satisfactory progress in the school. The school may have had an easier program, but the fact would seem to indicate that Geoff is quite an emotional child with a fear of failure and that his parents may be pushing him too hard. The counselor developed a case analysis approach, which underlined his earlier suggestions of referral for counseling services. The psychologist noted that there was no anecdotal information from teachers, and he feels that the available information is probably very one-sided. In other words, he is making an assumption that all of the information is not available on Geoff. Additional information about school personnel might add considerably to an understanding of Geoff's status in school.

Problems for Discussion:

22. Based on his earlier discussion, do you think additional information would have altered the psychologist's recommendations for class placement with educationally retarded students, as referred to earlier in the chapter?

23. If recommendations were based on faulty assumptions, why would the personnel specialist be more likely to get school personnel or parents to reconsider their conclusions by discussion of their assumptions?

J. **What assumptions were necessary to make defining the problem(s) as you did?**

The behavioral scientist makes an interesting assumption with regard to his definition of the problems involved in the case: Geoff's developing acceptable academic work rates at home and in the school would have a direct influence on his academic grade point rather than his actual educational achievement, such as skill in reading. Would it be possible for Geoff to have a higher grade point average as a result of an "acceptable academic work rate" but show little or no real change in educational development? The behavioral scientist's basic assumption seems to be that work rates, in conjunction with motivational factors, are the key to solving educational problems. *Question for Discussion:* Would the reader assume that the condition of work rates is *sufficient* for purposes of educational planning? Is academic grade point a *sufficient* criteria for success?

The Nazoneth strategy was to increase the grade point, but this action did not prove to be a suitable educational solution in Minowa. In Nazoneth it worked because Geoff was graded as if he were a slow learner. Work rate, per se, to be educationally viable, must have implicit in it a "quality of response" commensurate with adequate program expectations and adequate expectations of achievement.

Compare the behavioral scientist's teaching technology approach to that of the school principal. The principal made the assumption that in defining the school problems, Geoff was given work to do beyond his educational skill level. Geoff has been lacking in some phase of academic achievement from the early grades; as a result, he continued to fail in the school program. The principal assumed that basic skills are a necessity for satisfactory progress in the school program. Evidently, he believes that Geoff is basically capable of this progress. If past performance is one of the best predictors of future performance, Geoff will continue to progress at about 60 percent of his expected rate in education. This is the pattern he has established during his eight academic years. Even under optimal conditions, it is unlikely that Geoff will progress into grade level functioning in the next year or two in an academic program. Even if he were able to start making a full year's progress each ensuing school year, he would remain four to five years behind his class placement, outdistanced by most of his peers in an undifferentiated high school program. On the other hand, what will happen if even under optimal conditions for learning he continues to make relatively poor progress? He will increasingly fall behind his classmates as do slow and underachieving students who frequently drop out of school.

Problem for Discussion:
24. The behavioral scientist presents a modified learning approach in education. Does the reader judge it as a sufficient program for educational planning?

The superintendent continued to be brief in his comments by noting that he assumed the information given was correct.

The teacher did not suggest any sense of urgency when reviewing assumptions she made in defining Geoff's problems. Her assumptions included reference to the fact that the tests were administered fairly and reported accurately, but this seemed obvious to her, since there was much, much correlation among related test scores. She also made the assumption that Geoff has the ability to learn, as indicated on the WISC. What assumptions was the teacher making in her fairly consistent position that Geoff should be retained in the eighth grade and provided remedial instruction? Surely the assumption here is that this educational procedure will be of sufficient caliber to alter importantly the course of Geoff's educational development. Unfortunately, the assumption of this recommendation is hard to validate in terms of the experience of many in the school setting.

The question might be raised regarding the necessity of very considerable program change at the eighth grade level. Little benefit would probably accrue to Geoff should he simply repeat the program he had failed previously. If program changes are needed, why not initiate them at the ninth grade level? The teacher largely ignores these assumptions of her evaluations and recommendations of the case.

Following her earlier broad clinical approach to the information, the reading specialist assumed that the information given provided a fairly complete picture of the situation and that no major items were deleted. She reported having made assumptions with regard to the actual relationship between Geoff and his parents, the parents' apparent pushing of him toward college and general academic excellence, and Geoff's apparent interest and skill in nonacademic areas (shop courses, band, and physical education). Apparently, she views information as pertinent to educational planning and, as a reading specialist she does not confine herself to the narrow diagnostic information of the reading evaluation. She takes the reading diagnostic information and attempts to use it within the larger context of school, family, and related data. Evidently, the reading specialist did not expect dramatic changes in Geoff's educational progress, even with materials more in line with his actual educational skill level.

The teacher-counselor reported that his basic assumption was that the change in environment had quite a negative effect on Geoff. He evidently was alluding to the change in schools and the process of moving from one community to another. Like most of the other responders, the teacher-counselor believes that Geoff is largely a product of his environmental experiences and his experiences need to be altered to encourage changes in his educational adjustment pattern. The assumption to change the condition and experiences of the student can lead to dramatically different alternatives. For example, the teacher-counselor suggested that counseling services would best facilitate Geoff's educational adjustment, while the behavioral scientist would approach the problem by setting up certain work rates and a prescribed reinforcement schedule.

The psychologist reported the following assumptions: "validity of test scores, test conditions, Geoff's effort or lack of effort, the extent of speech impairment residues, and other handicaps such as financial variables in the home, and so forth." It might be of interest to have a clarification by the responder of his wide range of related assumptions. Upon reviewing his evaluation and approaches to the case, it does not seem likely that there would be any substantive changes in his recommendations (unless some of the information were absolutely invalid).

K. *In order for your recommendations to be implemented what assumptions would be necessary?*

The behavioral scientist did not find it necessary to make any assumptions other than those mentioned in answering the two previous questions, namely, that the subject has normal ability; academic behavior can be objectively measured; money can work as an effective motivator; and acceptable academic work rates would have a direct influence on the subject's academic grade point. The reader may wonder how the monetary approach to classroom behaviors will be implemented in the school program. The question might arise as to how the teacher will define work rates, since she has responsibility for many other students and must plan for all of their activities. The question might also be raised as to how the recommendations of the behavioral scientist would be implemented in a school program that evidently would be far beyond the student's capacity to deal with on an effective level. Furthermore, the behavioral scientist has not dealt with the real possibility that even if the rate of educational achievement were increased, it would be years before Geoff would actually be in sight of the average performance of his class. On the other hand, he may have assumed that the four- or five-year gap in educational attainment would be overcome in a short period of time. There is no way to determine what will happen to the student if the behavioral scientist's program does not succeed. Even with reliable standards of classroom and homework performance, it is conceivable that progress will continue to be at a low, if not improved, rate of educational attainment.

The behavioral scientist has apparently ignored the nature of a curriculum that might be used to assist the student in his educational development. Whatever plans or strategies were recommended, it would be necessary to have them implemented throughout the student's program. Thus teacher activity and staffings would be required to coordinate planning.

Problems for Discussion:
25. Would your school be willing to have the teacher dole out money to this individual student in order to change his studying behaviors?
26. Is the reader convinced that the approach of the educational technologist is a sufficient one for the educational planning of a student like Geoff?

As mentioned earlier, the superintendent would implement his suggestions by having Geoff first try sports, music, and extracurricular activities. In light of these plans, it is surprising to find that the superintendent's first three assumptions concern test scores: (1) the test scores were correct; (2) Geoff did not cheat on the exams; and (3) the persons making reports on this boy had estimated his ability correctly. What have these assumptions to do with the suggestions for implementation recommended by the responder? Rather than use scores, the superintendent apparently relied heavily on case history information to arrive at his conclusions and recommendations. He also suggested setting up a list of objectives and following through with them.

Problem for Discussion:
27. Is this a statement with reference to assumptions or does this statement fit more appropriately under suggestions and methods of implementation?

The principal's first procedure for implementing his suggestions was to have a conference with the parents. He assumed that the parents could work with school personnel and follow through on recommendations made by mutual agreement. His recommendation that alternative procedures be used in the school to assist Geoff in academic subjects was based on the assumption that Geoff would be able to change his attitudes toward failure and attempt earnestly to improve his academic proficiency. Goals would need to be set by him for him to reach. In conjunction with his plan for implementing educational alternatives in ungraded classes at the ninth grade, the principal made the assumption that if necessary Geoff could be guided into the vocational type of work, where an academic college degree is not required.

It is not surprising that the teacher considered the following assumptions necessary for her plans of retention in the eighth grade to be successfully implemented. She assumed that the family could adjust to the retention of Geoff and that Geoff could adjust to retention and be able to progress following it. Two questions might be considered at this point. Are there necessarily better possibilities of developing a suitable program in the eighth grade than in the ninth grade? There is little evidence to indicate that retained students at this age recover in terms of their educational deficits. In other words, based on his school history, the best prediction that can be made here is that Geoff's rate of educational development will remain about the same. By retaining him in the eighth grade, there would be slightly less of a discrepancy between Geoff's educational level and that of his classmates.

Problem for Discussion:
28. Implied in the teachers assumptions is that by repeating the eighth grade Geoff will be able to cope successfully in a program which has in the past been beyond his functional level. Is retention a sufficient program modification for students like Geoff entering the junior high–high school levels?

The reading specialist continued to emphasize the role of the parents in educational planning for the student. She assumed that in the long run Geoff's parents were truly interested in his well-being. In time, they would be able to understand Geoff's strengths and weaknesses, to respect his areas of ability, and to modify their aspirations for him. The reading specialist does not indicate that she expects spectacular changes in Geoff's abilities to acquire educational skills. After all, she has emphasized throughout that both the school and the parents must participate realistically in planning for Geoff in the educational setting. She stated that it was also necessary to assume that the school administrators and teachers would be willing to make adjustments in the curriculum to modify time limits, materials, and the methods of teaching in order to provide for the varying abilities of students in the school. She believes that in order for the school to be effective for the student, *the school must take cognizance of the student's functioning and provide a program of education within the student's ability to benefit meaningfully from the instruction.*

The psychologist's plans for implementing his suggestions were by the use of parent conferences, proper placement, and follow-up procedures. His basic assumptions were that there would be sufficient parental interest in Geoff and his siblings for them to benefit from the conference procedures and that the family is sufficiently mobile to find suitable facilities and resources for Geoff's educational program development. He defined his follow-up procedures as a case study that would be competently initiated in the new setting. Evidently, after reviewing the case materials, the counseling psychologist was not strongly impressed with the school's potential for providing an adequate program for Geoff. He saw as an alternative for the parents to find an educational setting that would be useful for educational planning and program development. The teacher-counselor emphasized the need to reinitiate activities in which Geoff had earlier successes. In this, he assumed that Geoff would be likely to reidentify with some of his old interests, and these experiences would place him in a more favorable position to deal with other demands being made of him. The teacher-counselor also assumed that a more comprehensive understanding of the family and school situations by the new principal would be more beneficial for future school planning. This assumption would coincide with the teacher-counselor's interest in working with the school principal to implement guidance services.

Problems for Discussion:
29. If you were a pupil personnel specialist, what rationale would you use for closely examining the assumptions made by the responders for implementing their educational plans?
30. Contrast the different assumptions made by the behavioral scientist and the principal in their approach to solving educational problems.

EPILOGUE

The reader may be interested in the early educational recommendations for Geoff and the progress made during the intervening year.

The following is a statement from the recommendations section of the school psychology report, which was not included in the case information materials:

The results of the examination were discussed at some length with Geoff's mother. She and her husband were obviously very upset by the telephone call informing them that their son was to be retained in the eighth grade and the principal's report that Geoff would never be successful at the college level. They feel that retention in the current program and grade would not be satisfactory. This approach would not resolve the basic problems of educational retardation and might create another situation of failure for Geoff, as he would be removed from his supportive peer group.

In essence, we spent our time discussing alternative educational planning for Geoff. The need for more information on educational alternatives and immediate follow-up are apparent. Several other suggestions were made:

1. Geoff is viewed as eligible for the special education program for students who have average ability but are low in educational achievement. Clearly, coordinated planning by the Special Education District is warranted.

2. A dialogue and staff conference might be arranged with the Minowa High School personnel to determine if a suitable program of training and tutoring could be worked out in the high school program (the current recommendation of retention notwithstanding).

3. A discussion with a nearby public school is established to determine if they might not have a more suitable and useful educational program for Geoff. Special education consultation might also be sought in this instance.

4. Geoff's mother suggested the possibility of enrolling Geoff in a private school, where a more structured program is maintained and a separation experience from the family unit could be established.

5. Perhaps a fifth consideration would be to work with the parents and their son Geoff on a child guidance basis to pursue avenues of behavioral change within the family structure.

During the summer immediately following the eighth grade, Geoff participated in a remedial reading program with private tutors at a nearby university reading clinic. He received 27 hours of individual instruction with a program of additional work completed at home under his parents' supervision. The following summary was taken from a report completed by his reading teacher after the summer program.

Since Geoff received instructions for just two months it was considered necessary to administer only two post tests to check on his reading progress. It was noted that his instructional level in reading has not changed significantly. Geoff is a friendly boy and rapport was easily established. While attending the summer training program he displayed a reasonable amount of effort . . . Geoff needs much continued instruction in reading comprehension if he is to broaden basic comprehension abilities and to acquire the kind of reading proficiencies necessary for content areas at the high school level . . . The type of material read should be suitable to the type of comprehension ability being stressed, such as locating and retaining information, making references, evaluation, reading, and so forth. The purpose for reading the material should be well defined prior to the assignment, and a check should be made on the accuracy of comprehension at the end of the reading. If Geoff is to show real gains in leisure reading, he must read many books for pleasure in addition to those required for instruction. Progress will be slow if it depends entirely on what he reads during supervised instruction. Geoff should be helped in establishing a regular time for his free reading, beginning with a brief period and gradually increasing it as his interest in reading grows. Frequent opportunities to discuss books he has read should increase his desire to read and will serve to reinforce such skills as he has acquired. All reading as a skill should receive attention only after many of Geoff's difficulties have improved. For reading improvement it is important that he continue with techniques used in the study of word relationships, development of word clusters, and that dictionary skills be reviewed and extended. Instruction in the regular classroom program should be adjusted to meet Geoff's individual needs.

Follow-up contact with the school principal in Minowa indicated that the parents had several conversations with him at the end of the summer. There were alternatives offered for Geoff, either to remain in the eighth grade or enter the ninth grade lower tract in the junior high school program. It was the principal's impression that the parents had been informed of Geoff's lower educational development in the Nazoneth schools. This impression was later verified by correspondence that had been forwarded from the Nazoneth schools to the Minowa school. The principal stated that during the spring of the school year, the parents had been contacted both by phone and written correspondence to report the slow progress of their son. It had not been possible to get both parents to a school conference with the teachers. The principal continues to feel that Geoff is not "college material." The principal was not informed of the parents' final decision and did not realize until he had a request for information that they had enrolled Geoff in a military school about 100 miles from the local community. The principal stated he had no information on the final decision and had not been informed of the current status of Geoff in the private school. He reported that the parents also had contact with the special education district.

A follow-up conference with the special education district revealed that there had been contact with the mother but that she had insisted that Geoff not be entered into any kind of vocational program. Evidently, the parents still felt that Geoff was college material; part of the problem was that they had not held Geoff to adequate educational expectations by setting academic limits for him to operate within. The director of the special education unit also reported the parents had known for some time prior to coming to Minowa that Geoff was having serious educational problems.

A final conference was held with Geoff's mother. She was not satisfied with the programs that had been offered for their son in the local school or through the auspices of special education. The project director of the special education unit had told her that their programs were not suited for her son because most student participants were from poverty-type families. A school social worker had concurred with this opinion. Geoff's mother also stated that they were not satisfied with the recommendation of retention in the eighth grade because Geoff would be required to return to the same school situation in which he had already failed.

Geoff's mother stated that her son is repeating the eighth grade at the military academy this year. He apparently is enjoying his stay there and would like to return to the military school again next year. Her major concern about this plan was that it was necessary for the family to spend approximately $3300 to keep him in private school; the parents also had serious reservations about having him separated from the family. Geoff has been working very hard and producing a great quantity of work, according to reports she has received. Geoff's mother believed that his experience at the military academy had "made him feel real good," and she talked about the fact that he had made rank and had recently been promoted.

As Geoff's mother reviewed her conferences with the public school, she continued to feel that the classroom teacher was very negative about Geoff and was criticizing him for reasons that were not appropriate. She said she probably would have reacted negatively, too, had she been in Geoff's situation. She wished the school could provide a program of training at a level where the students are actually functioning. She continued to feel very negative about the possibility of retention; she was also not enthusiastic about the summer reading program. The teacher had communicated to her that the entire summer program was more or less a diagnostic arrangement. She and her husband may decide to keep Geoff in the military school if he shows progress in reading; this decision would also depend on the type of program available at the local high school next fall. She continued to believe that Geoff is capable of succeeding in college, and she continued to find abhorrent a vocationally orientated program.

During the interview, Geoff's mother stated that the younger brain-injured boy had received no special attention in the school program and had remained in the third grade for the third time this year. She was hesitant to contact the special education district, even though she was urged to do so. She stated that the younger child had a good attitude, so that she was reluctant to have him change his educational program at this time. However, she did complain that some of the materials he was studying at the third grade level, especially the mathematics, was already well within his skill level and were not sufficiently demanding on him.

CASE NO. 2 Jack (Kindergarten, Grade 1, and Special Education)

The case materials about Jack cover three years of his life. During this period, Jack moved from the public schools into a school for special education students.

Information contained in the case materials section for Jack covers a three-year span of time. The letters, demographic background, psychological reports, summary of a case conference, and other materials taken from Jack's file cover the time span from approximately age six to nine, or basically from the fall of 1967 through the spring of 1969. Although the case materials presented here end in 1969, Jack is still very much a part of the lives of the teachers and staff of the Wright Special Education School, who continue to work with him.

A number of approaches have been attempted with Jack over the three-year period involved in the case materials. Some of these have been successful, but none have brought about dramatic changes. Jack did not become a different boy as a result of any of them, although several approaches for improvement have worked. The reader will have an opportunity to compare his evaluations of the case with a group of responders and with a follow-up a year after the case materials were obtained.

The reader should not hesitate in responding because of lack of experience with children just like Jack. One can never have experience with all the possible variations in human behavior. A well-developed set of expectations about human behavior can eventually result from a combination of experience and intuition.

CASE STUDY MATERIALS ON JACK

Remarks by Parents on Family Information Form

Home and Family History:

There are six children in the family. The oldest is a teen-age boy, followed by two girls; then Jack, followed by two younger brothers. The father is a small town lawyer, and the mother is a medical technologist who works at community hospital.

Type of neighborhood. Upper class.
Is house rented or owned? Owned. *Numer of rooms:* 12.

Family social contacts and activities. Local friends—small parties at home —not frequent.
Is the client sociable or does he prefer to be alone? Variable—no special friends.
How does he get along with: Mother. Occasional temper outbursts. *Father.* Submissive.
Brothers and sisters. Fair at best. *Other children.* Variable.
How does child behave in adult company? Acting out.

Describe main behavior difficulties child has in the home. Hyperactive, constant talking, screaming, stamping, negativity, loud talk, constant request for "help" often inappropriate and unrealistic—aloof.

Parents' attitude toward this behavior. Mother tends to be submissive and compliant—frustrated; father—harsh, often punitive.

Interests and Activities:

What are his main interests? Play-acting, "play" writing, "cooking," grocery store, collecting stones.

What recreational activities are enjoyed most? rides tractor, outdoor play —simple games (these he varies from the usual format).

Are there work responsibilities? Limited. *What kind?* Garbage emptying, simple direct requests.

Attitude toward work. Routine work needs constant supervision—more simple tasks are usually well accepted. Quite commonly demands help from older siblings, especially his immediately older sister.

Letter Written by Jack's First Grade Teacher

Jack was placed in morning kindergarten after conferences (on Nov. 1 and 8, 1967) with his parents and conferences with the school psychologist and principal.

He attended first grade in the afternoon. All of his work this year was readiness work. He received no grades. Parent-teacher conferences were held instead. Conferences were held in February and March and on June 1, beside the ones mentioned above.

(Teacher's name)

School Report

Grade.   1.   *Grades skipped.*   None.

Grades repeated.   Kindergarten.   *Age at entrance to school.*   6

Extent of absences.   1966—10 days; 1967—6 days.

Previous Tests:

Name of test	Date given	IQ or grade placement
Lorge-Thorndike Intelligence	11 - 14	86

School Marks:

Subject	Present marks	Past marks	Comments
Reading	D		
Phonics	E		
Arithmetic	D-E		
Writing	D-E		

Special abilities (list them): 1. Play acting. 2. Creating songs about everyday happenings. 3. Talk and tell in detail.

Special disabilities (list them): 1. Manipulation of tools and materials. 2. Not being able to retain work learned in school.

Teacher's evaluation of child's intelligence: Jack has a large vocabulary and a delightful sense of humor which would indicate a higher IQ than indicated above.

School behavior:

Child's attitude toward authority (antagonistic, yielding, cooperative): Jack does not obey very well, after he becomes acquainted.

Behavior in groups (active, shy, aggressive): Outside of our classroom, Jack is very shy with children.

Reaction to success or failure (encouraged, discouraged, indifferent): Success. Enthused. Failure. Indifferent.

ADDITIONAL COMMENTS ATTACHED TO LETTER. Jack does not seem to be able to control himself. His voice is loud and it seems easy for him to become emotionally upset. At times, for no apparent reason, Jack will hurt the other children and will display an outburst of rage.

He lets things unnecessarily upset him and he becomes very quiet and sorrowful or to the other extreme.

Jack is liked by his classmates, but he had not chosen any for a close friend —but neither had he isolated himself from them. On the playground he prefers to stay by me and talk.

Jack and I are very good friends. I am most regretful that I have not been able to teach him as I had hoped to. Jack needs a lot of special help and with a class as large as mine, 36–38, I am not able to give him the individual help that he needs and demands.

I will welcome any suggestions that the Mental Health Center has to offer in order to make me a better teacher for Jack. He will not be ready to go on to the second grade next year, and I wish to keep him in my room; therefore I desire the help of the Center.

Letter from Social Worker to Mental Health Center

November 12, 1968

To: Director, Mental Health Center
From: Social Worker, Wright Special Education School
Subject: Jack

The following is a brief review of our contacts with Jack's family, in the hope you may be able to find a therapist to work with them. I talked with you briefly about this case last week.

Jack has been a student at our school since September 1967. He was referred to us after his discharge from Presbyterian-St. Luke's Hospital in Chicago where he had had a lung operation, and psychotherapy as a result of behavioral problems noted while he was hospitalized. Jack was also examined at your center in May 1968, and a recommendation for treatment of parents and child was made at that time, but it appears not to have been followed through.

When Jack entered school, he was showing aberrant signs of anxiety and insecurity. He talked constantly, was extremely fearful (especially of bodily harm), and related poorly to other children. He had an obsessive need to control every situation, was bodily rigid, and overly concerned about time and order. He had violent screaming fits when demands were placed on him or any arrangements changed.

The recommendation from Presbyterian-St. Luke's was for therapy for Jack. Therefore, when he entered school, I started working with him two times a week and seeing his parents about once a month, the parents also participating in my

Parents' Group meetings. As a result, Jack has improved. He is no longer so insecure; the screaming and talkativeness have greatly diminished.

However, Jack still has many problems. Academically he has progressed slowly. His relationship with peers is fearful or controlling and he is still insecure and has little sense of self-worth. His parents describe him as having fewer tantrums, but not dependable and a difficult child to understand and handle. Jack identifies with the adult world, seems not to know how to be a child, have fun, and so forth. He is unable to talk about himself, or to express any hostility, especially about either his parents or his siblings, his teacher, and so on.

The reports from Presbyterian-St. Luke's did not specifically confirm an organic basis for Jack's problems but thought they were emotional. However, our repeated psychological tests since he has been with us indicate an average intelligence, but problems in visual-motor, spatial, and other areas. In a recent staffing with our consultant, he thought there was sufficient material to indicate some minimal brain damage. He indicated that the potential for individual therapy, therefore, was about exhausted. More important at this point, we see the need for communication and better relationship between parents and child, and help for the parents in understanding Jack's problems and in knowing how to deal with them. Our consultant recommended family therapy with the preference that this not be done at the school. I do hope that you will be able to find a therapist for Jack's family. I have not yet discussed this with them, but they have been cooperative and closely identified with the school, and I feel will accept our recommendation. However, I do not think it would be beneficial to Jack or his family to have assignment in abeyance too long and would prefer to hear from you first to plan from there.

Social worker's signature

Psychological Report

Interview with the Parents

The father appeared for the interview without the mother. He talked about his son in a quiet, unemotional manner. He was ready to admit that Jack's birth was unplanned and that he did not get enough attention in his younger years. Jack became a problem only at the age of five. He became hyperkinetic, restless, very noisy and complaintive. He was very dependent on his mother and would follow her around, talking at the same time at the top of his voice. The mother is usually compliant with him. The father, however, is very authoritative and impatient. He controls Jack by threats of physical punishment and spanking. He expects him to perform in accordance with his chronological age level.

The father admits that Jack has a rich vocabulary and a very good memory for locating various objects in the house but suspects some deficiency in mental endowment.

The impression of the interviewer is that the father regards Jack as a nuisance and is unwilling to accept him the way he is. For him Jack is now "outside" the family. He expects help to come from outside sources and has few expectations about his or the family's being able to help him.

Test Results and Observations

Testing:

Stanford-Binet Intelligence Scale
CA - 7 yrs., 7 mos.
MA - 6 yrs., 5 mos.
IQ - 83

Peabody Picture Vocabulary Test
CA - 7 yrs., 7 mos.
MA - 6 yrs., 10 mos.
IQ - 90

Wide Range Achievement Test
Reading Grade Equivalent - Kg. 4
Arithmetic Grade Equivalent - Kg. 9

Draw-A-Person

Bender Motor-Gestalt Test

Jack was a seven-year, seven-month-old first grade student who was accompanied to the examination by his father. He was somewhat passive during the examination and might be described as shy. He had light blondish hair, and his appearance would be described as average. During the examination, he was moderately distractible but in the structure of the one-to-one relationship presented no management problem. He became increasingly impulsive and began twisting and turning in his chair as his attention began to wander. At times speech would not be described as difficult to understand, and sometimes the volume was rather loud. It occurred to the examiner that there might be some hearing loss.

Results of the SBIS placed Jack in the Dull Normal Range when compared with the norms for his age group. He established a Basal at the Years IV-VI level and continued to pass items through the Year VIII level. He received credit for vocabulary at the Year VIII level, and at the Year VII level received credit for similarities, two things, and repeating five digits. The findings of the Peabody Picture Vocabulary Test (PPVT) were comparable, although slightly higher than the results of the Stanford-Binet test. This may be reflective of the higher vocabulary level that was obtained on the Stanford-Binet test. Educational achievement was lower than expected, based on mental age development. On the Bender Test, Jack had difficulty integrating several of the designs and was not able to plan ahead in his work so that he found it necessary to overlap several designs. Organization was poor and, clearly, perceptual skill level would be considered marginal for school functioning. The drawing of a person was simplified and included a head with poor development of bodily structure.

Recommendations

The results of the examination indicated that Jack had Dull Normal intelligence. He gave the appearance of being slightly brighter than his functional level because he has a relatively good vocabulary. In terms of school planning, it would be recommended that he be placed in a Socially Maladjusted Program —Plan A. A reexamination should be obtained in two years or sooner if deemed advisable by his teacher or school principal. The father feels that he and his wife have developed expectations which are not realistic and he communicated a need for child guidance assistance. It would be recommended that the parents be offered parent counseling services at the Mental Health Center and that during this time exploratory therapy be developed with the client.

Jack was placed in the Wright Special Education School. The following information comes from the Wright School records after he has been enrolled for two years.

Yearly Staffing on Jack (Spring 1969)

ACADEMICS.   Jack has reached the point where he is capable of working at the second grade level in all subjects. He is almost through with the Ginn 2–1 Book, *We Are Neighbors*. When he is settled down, he can read fairly fluently and do the workbook pages with some support. Jack receives much supplementary work in the area of reading —Sullivan Programmed Reading Series Book 3 Level 2.1; Lift-Off to Reading Cycle I Book 8 (Science Research Associates); and supplementary sheets both teacher-made and from the Scott Foresman series. Because it was recommended at the last quarterly staffing that Jack begin to learn to attack words phonetically, the supplementary work is all phonics-orientated. When Jack comes to a word he does not know, he becomes terribly upset and frustrated. He guesses one word after another and becomes more and more upset. When in a reading situation, there seems to be *no* carryover from the phonics instruction. On some days Jack can successfully work independently at these tasks, but the majority of the phonics work is done on an individual basis. Jack continues to read mainly by the sight method and by getting words in context or by using picture clues. He is presently working in the *Two by Two* second grade mathematics book (Harcourt Brace Jovanovich).

No formal spelling program is being used with him at the present time, as the individual phonics work consists of spelling short words and writing sentences from dictation.

Jack's printing has become much more legible lately—no further attempts have been made to teach Jack to learn cursive writing.

BEHAVIOR.   Looking back to September 1967, Jack has come a long way behaviorally. For someone watching him day by day, it is harder to see improvement! His behavior is much more reality-oriented, but as the counselor said last week. "There's room for improvement, isn't there, Jack?" Jack still regresses into being people with various occupations during unstructured times of the day. Jack will still manipulate those who allow themselves to be manipulated.

Jack does attempt more frequently to interact with other children and these attempts are a little more appropriate. Jack still chooses younger children with whom to interact. He tries to manipulate them by grabbing them, ordering them to do things, shouting at them, and so forth. However, there are times when Jack honestly tries to carry on a sensible conversation with older children (for example, field trips and lunch, at times). During the structured morning recess, he participates well with little coaxing.

COUNSELOR. The counselor feels Jack has a great deal of trouble or difficulty with monetary realistic situations. He feels he wants to pay people (his teacher, the nurse, the counselor, and so on) for what they do for him. The question was raised as to whether it might not be a good idea to attempt to get him to "do good deeds and be kind to people" instead of trying to pay them. The counselor has already talked with the father about this and to see if it couldn't be carried over into the home and reported Jack's father is pleased with Jack's behavior at home. An outside relative visited and noticed an improvement in Jack's behavior.

SCHOOL PSYCHOLOGIST. During this year's testing, Jack was relaxed, spontaneous, and didn't get upset by lack of structure.

TEACHER FROM PUBLIC SCHOOL. It was his feeling that the local school could not handle Jack next fall under the present conditions.

Anecdotal Report on School Behavior

The school counselor asked Jack's teacher to try and write down her perceptions of his behavior for a week. She provided the following reports.

5–6, Tuesday: Jack worked very well from 9:00–9:30. He was cooperative and was successful. At 9:30 he went to the hearing center. The girl there said he greeted her with, "I'm Grandpa. I won't work unless you call me Grandpa." She ignored this. Later in the period he was talking about sermons he had to give. At the end of the half-hour she said, "I hope Jack comes tomorrow." He replied, "Jack was sick today; he'll probably be here tomorrow." When he got back to the room, he was perfectly normal —participated at recess.

During the library period, the librarian told a story with flannel cutouts. She said a child could retell the story. Jack volunteered. He had the opportunity to make up part of the story himself. He did not do this; he told the story exactly as she had told it.

I heard no fantasies discussed all day—very little singing.

5–7 (noon): No fantasy so far—Jack has been very loud today. He only mentioned his cub scout meeting once. I noticed that each time he started singing he was not getting individual help or attention.

Jack brought his pipe to school this morning. I told him he could not have it in class, but that he could play with it during recess (which he did).

5–8, Thursday: Played very well at recess—ran when he was supposed to. During the game of kick ball he put his sweater on his head and pretended to be flying when he was running. This seemed like a normal fantasy to me. It was appropriate for the situation.

Jack was trying to manipulate me and the student teacher. He refused to work unless he could check his list. I took him out of the room. On the way out, he said, "You must please me, you must please me."

When I came back to get him in five minutes, he was ready to work.

Jack showed up at this afternoon's recess with a whistle (like mine) and said he was the Traffic Director. He insisted he could not play because he had this job to do. Finally he decided to play. When the upper grade kids came out, he stopped playing and started ordering the other kids around. They got mad and began fighting with him. I had Jack sit down until he could play "right." While he was sitting, he called kids over to tell them what to do.

When we got back in the room, Jack behaved well.

Friday, 5–9: Came in talking about "the Green Man" (this was in the hall)—had his money bag and notes. I told him to put that stuff away. Jack got out his notes during juice and crackers. I told him to put it away—he did.

During recess, he tried to direct traffic. Jack told one girl he would grant her wish —then he took a paper bag out of her hands and dumped the contents on the ground. He then informed her that her wish was granted: she would have gold, silver, and so forth.

Jack's behavior on the field trip was very inappropriate. He tried to walk with me rather than with the rest of the kids. When we told him to run ahead, he ran in a robotlike fashion.

Monday, 5–12: When Jack came in this morning, he said he was "Uncle Fred" and began talking about his fruit stands. I told him that if he said he was anyone else, he would have to leave the room.

This afternoon at recess, he wore a straw hat and bowed to "all the girls," giving a Spanish greeting.

He tried to manipulate the lower grade kids—most of them chased him away— some allowed themselves to be bossed around.

Tuesday, 5–13: Jack did not discuss "unreal" things today. He was, however, rather loud. He came in singing.

He did an exceptional job in swimming today. Very cooperative—said was there to work and learn.

Wednesday, 5–14: This morning Jack came in singing loudly. I told him he could not sing in the room. I threatened to remove him if he did. He went the whole morning without singing—at lunch time he started, so I sent him to his seat.

Jack was very involved with real things today. Morning recess, he did an excellent job on the bars. He worked on writing a book.

No problems today.

Thursday, 5–15: This afternoon, when he could not finish a project he had started, he became very frustrated. On top of that, I insisted he take his whistles home. He refused —so I just walked down to the car with him and gave him the whistles there.

Friday, 5–16: Worried about touching the cows on our field trip; talked about forgetting gloves to milk the cows with. No fantasies.

Monday, 5–19: Was a radio weather man all morning.

Tuesday, 5–20: No trouble.

Wednesday, 5–21: Came in quietly—told me about his cub scout meeting. Seemed pleased. Brought in an airplane that he had made.

Monday, 5–26: Brought a case of plastic bags to school—tried to sell them to others.

Tuesday, 5–27: Tried to pay me for teaching him (play money).

Wednesday, 5–28: No real problem. Jack will not, however, walk with the rest of the class on field trips. He always lags behind and tries to talk with me.

Mondays are always bad—always a new occupation or some type of fantasy. Could this be the result of a permissive week-end, at home, where the storytelling and playacting are either permitted or ignored?

SELECTED REACTIONS TO JACK'S CASE

Reactions to the case materials on Jack probably reflected more differences of opinion among responders than the other cases. One reason for the divergent approaches to the case may be that Jack had already been removed from the public school and placed in a special school. Although Wright School is merely concentrated special education classes, the implication seems to have been that it was a great deal different from special education in the public schools.

The most extreme reaction to the case of Jack was provided by a man who had taught in a school system for three years and then decided to run for the school board. Apparently, it was board policy that teachers in the system could not be board members, so he resigned and obtained another teaching job in a neighboring community. He then ran for the office and was elected. It was during his first year in this dual capacity that he responded to the case materials on Jack. The school board member saw the main problem in the educational setting as "Probably Jack's father, and his desire to have Jack be like others." We could certainly agree that relationships at home, and particularly with the father, would be a related problem, but we question whether this would be the *main* factor influencing the educational setting. Although the school board member might have been 100 percent accurate, we really do not know. Some of his other comments, however, make us question the validity of his interpretation. When asked for suggestions for solving or improving the problem situations, he wrote, "It is difficult to remove a son from his father's influence, especially at Jack's age." Then, when asked how to implement his suggestions, the reply was, "Put Jack in a boarding school." A boarding school would remove Jack from home and his father's direct influence, but would it help Jack?

The father's desire to have his son be like others does not appear to be an unusual parental expectation. Most parents want their sons to get along with other boys, partake in activities of children growing up (that is, riding bikes, playing ball, laughing, and so forth), and develop academic skills like reading and arithmetic. If these are typical expectations of parents, why would the school board member perceive the father's desire to have Jack resemble other children be so atypical that it would require putting him in boarding school? The boy has already been placed in a special school situation. Furthermore, no mentiion was made of how or what provisions should be part of a residential school for Jack.

It would be a sad commentary on American education if this school board member represented the broad spectrum of school board officials. It might be more understandable if this person were ignorant of educational practices. But he has four years of teaching experience and is presently taking course work in order to obtain an administrative certificate.

In contrast to the educational concern of the school board member, we consider the responses to the case materials made by a teacher whose home is on one of the island groups of the South Pacific. He taught high school for six years on his home island before completing his B.A. in English at an American West Coast university. A fellowship to work on an M.S. in education brought him to a large midwestern university. Following completion of his master's degree, he remained near the university to work and to continue his education. He summarized the current work experience on the personal data sheet attached to the case of Jack by saying, "I am teaching at _____. This school provides many challenges, insights, and enlightening aspects of the American system of education. I enjoy working with the students and the school administration. It is an excellent school and experience for me." He teaches fourth grade science and social studies.

When responding to the case materials the M.S. teacher first comment was "Very good diagnosis, interest, and concern for the welfare of the child from all quarters." Whether or not the reader agrees with this evaluation of the case materials, it might be good to emphasize the positive aspects of working with other school staff members, and particularly pupil personnel specialists. With a student like Jack, suggestions for courses of action may not always prove profitable. Yet even in retrospect, one should be positive and emphasize what has been learned from the experience.

Progress through the M. S. teacher's responses seems to illustrate an attempt to analyze and synthesize the materials and draw relevant conclusions. An example of this comes with his answer to question C, "What, if any, do you view as the related problems?" He wrote:

Jack is an "attuned child." A disturbed child will tune in the parent who gives him the most love and tune out the other. This tendency toward selective hearing could be an important source of trouble in the child's later life, reports Dr. Rakoff of McGill University, Montreal. In a study of 32 families, Dr. Rakoff has found that the early trend toward hearing one parent over the other is generalized to outsiders. If the child hears his mother's voice preferentially, he will also have a tendency to listen more to women than men. Such selective listening and exclusion reduces chances of the child's identifying with the parent he hears less, says Rakoff, and, in a larger sense, restricts his perception of the world.

This line of reasoning is continued when discussing suggestions for improving the situation. The responder makes the assumption that Jack's teacher is a female and that his mother is "compliant" to his demands and needs.

Therefore, a female teacher for Jack would fall in a similar situation. He would expect her to meet his demands. A *male* teacher might be in order for Jack. Jack's father sees or used to perceive Jack as an "outsider" and if the male teacher were to act fatherly with firm but gentle demands, Jack's attitude would probably improve toward his father, males in general, and the world at large.

Problem for Discussion:
1. The M. S. teacher's idea about how to initiate change seems very simple. Do you think it would be appropriate or inappropriate to place Jack in a class with a male teacher, and if so, why?

The responder further defined the problem:

The recommendations were good and acceptable, but one may not delve into solving problems such as Jack's in accordance with previously accepted notions as prescribed by research and textbooks. His case is unique and must be dealt with on an individual basis. While a teacher may proceed to assist many such boys through past experiences, still, she must be prepared to find answers to solving problems on an individual basis and be able to apply creative (new) methods of her own. Research goes on in this field!

Then, when discussing the assumptions necessary for successfully implementing his recommendations, he continued:

One must never be deterred from accepting the fact that it is possible to march on with all the scientific researches and know-how to bring a person's behavior into proper balance, in terms of a full command of his faculty. We have all kinds of problems—such as seen in Jack—but we also have scientific tools to eradicate diseased minds. Jack acts, talks, and walks, because that's the way he's made genetically or otherwise. The problem is that we know so very little about the human brain. We must continue to deal with existing problems with the acceptable solutions until such time when better and efficient methods will be procurable.

From the M. S. teacher's last two responses, the reader should have some idea about his future professional goals. In five years he hopes to be teaching and doing cultural research in the South Pacific. The attention he pays to cogent research findings seems to indicate that he is already attuned to the future goal. Although research is not the end-all in working with children or adolescents, professional judgment is still necessary and a knowledge of related research tends to reduce error in our judgments.

The third responder to the case of Jack would also like to be a teacher-researcher in five years. This individual, unlike the M. S. teacher, tends to incorporate his ideas about research into his approach to children. Consequently, his research bent is not nearly as explicit. At the time of responding, this individual had just completed his master's degree in counseling and guidance and was beginning study for his Ph.D degree in counselor education. If completed, he might be a professor instructing readers about pupil personnel services in the schools.

Problem for Discussion:
   2. After reading the counselor's responses, would you like him to be your pupil personnel instructor in graduate school?

The counselor, in some respects, defined the most significant aspects of the case, as did the school board member, although his additional explanation seems to clarify his position. Whereas the school board member's only comment when asked his opinion about the significant aspects was, "Jack's role playing to get attention," the counselor's statement read as follows:

One of the major problems with Jack seems to be a problem of identity. His adoption of different occupational roles at inappropriate times could indicate that he has difficulty in knowing what role he is expected to take. This "not knowing" could also be related to the hostility to authority that appears regularly and to the inability to interact effectively with other children. One of the significant aspects of the case is probably the home situation. I can see the possibility that Jack does a good deal of modeling after his father. The indication is that the father does not show a great deal of love for Jack and that he controls the boy from a very authoritarian position, one which is fairly rigid. It does not seem unlikely that Jack would assume this kind of role in trying to identify with his male role in society.

What, if any, do you perceive as the main problems in the educational setting?

The problems in the educational setting seem to be common to this kind of child. Jack seems to have definite problems in accepting the give and take position that is necessary in the social context of the classroom. Also, in work situations his attention span and his toleration for frustration seem to get in his way a good deal.

The conclusions drawn by the counselor include two themes that reoccur in most responder statements about the significant aspects of the case. It might be profitable for the reader to reread his responses and attempt to identify them.

Holding a Case Conference on Jack: A Hypothetical Example

THE MOST SIGNIFICANT ASPECTS OF THE CASE. Now we present several series of statements made by a diverse group of responders. Each has attempted to identify the most significant aspects of the case in his or her own opinion. The pupil personnel specialist chairing the case conference on Jack will ask involved parties to give their opinion; then the specialist will summarize the major themes presented. The summary will provide direction for the alternatives to solve or improve the situations identified. It is suggested that the reader place himself in the position of the pupil personnel specialist.

The first reaction at the case conference comes from the grade school social studies teacher. He has taught in the same community for eight years and is well respected by the other teachers. In preparation for the case conference, he listed seven significant aspects.

1. Underachievement.
2. High vocabulary.
3. Frequency of role playing.
4. Expectation or determination of the child to be someone else.
5. The bossing of others.
6. Socially maladjustment with classmates.
7. Poor acceptance at home.

After the social studies teacher is the music teacher. This is her first year at this school, since she has just returned to teaching after a 10-year absence. Her two children are both in grade school now, and she seems to function well in the dual role of teacher and housewife. She also drew up a list of seven significant aspects for the case of Jack:

1. The boy probably does have some brain damage.
2. There appears to be some relationship in the home that has some bearing on his actions (as indicated by the last teacher's report).
3. There seems to be an "adult" influence in some way on his actions (possibly related to the above.)
4. He tends to attempt to manipulate other people—particularly those younger than he.
5. He finds it necessary at times to be involved in an "unreal" world.
6. He appears to be able to behave almost normally on some days, and then changes completely.
7. His relationship to his peers seems to indicate some area of great difficulty.

After hearing two responders at this hypothetical case conference on Jack, the reader should be trying to piece the information together. Analysis is the mental process involved. "Analysis emphasizes the breakdown of the material into its constituent parts and detection of the relationships of the parts and of the way they are organized"[1] In looking for the major

---

[1] Benjamin S. Bloom (Ed.), *et al. Taxonomy of Educational Objectives.* New York: McKay, 1956.

relationships between the factors noted by the responders, the reader should ask himself if there are consistent approaches among the responders.

Problems for Discussion:
3. Do the hypotheses of the responders correspond to known evidence?
4. Which responders form the main thesis as contrasted to parts or elements that only serve to support the thesis?

Of the two teachers who reported their ideas thus far, only the first mentioned underachievement. There is evidence to support low achievement, but this is probably not the major thesis. It can be assumed that underachievement is more of an effect than a cause. Although the social studies teacher mentioned achievement level first, his main thesis is probably farther down the list.

The music teacher's first factor was brain damage. There was note of brain damage in the case materials, but the evidence is inconclusive. Even if this were a cause of Jack's behavior, what could we do about it? We could not change the brain damage (except in extreme situations) and would have to work with other factors. Thus, brain damage, if there really is damage, would not be the central theme of the music teacher's analysis.

The reader, as the pupil personnel expert, should look at each list of seven factors offered and analyze the function of the particular communications. Some statements are possibly fact, although there are few absolute facts when working with individuals; others will deal with the responders' values, while still others will imply their intent. In pupil personnel work, we must consider the total communication before piecing the parts together in the synthesis process. As the reader considers the remaining responses in the hypothetical case conference, he should analyze each of them while attempting to synthesize all the communications.

The third person to respond to the case is a young man doing some practicum work in counseling. He has wanted to be a counselor for several years so that after getting his B.A., he began the master's program in guidance and counseling. In general, his approach to school guidance is sensitive and practical. When called upon for his opinion, he prefaces the remarks by saying, "I consider the question 'What are the most significant aspects of the case?' to mean 'What are the causes of Jack's behavior patterns?' " With this introduction, he offers four aspects of the case.

1. His father's attitude.
2. Fantasies.
3. His ordering and demanding-authoritative, inappropriate behavior.
4. His singing is a puzzle (perhaps it follows some one type of event).

In addition to offering the above opinion, the practicum student asks, "This may not be appropriate now, but I was wondering while reading the case materials just how brain damage is identified. Is it done physiologically or behaviorally?"

Everyone seems to turn to the school psychologist for an answer to the question. He says that basically brain damage or brain injury is impairment of the cerebral cortex. It typically shows up in some type of visual-motor coordination. For example, with a boy Jack's age, he might have difficulty reproducing simple drawings. He could be shown a picture of five circles, and then, after removing the picture, probably would not draw five circles. He might draw five dashes, five squares, or something else. The visual picture is distorted or else the motor aspect of the drawing does not function relative to the visual perception. He also suggests a further reference.[2]

The psychologist then offers the ideas about Jack that he had jotted down.

1. Diversity of parental controls—the mother is submissive, the father punitive.
2. Lung surgery—subsequent problems in school—leaves question of surgical insult causing mental condition.
3. Large number of siblings.
4. Parents' expectations.
5. Parents' feelings of being unable to help him—seek outside help.
6. Parents noted problem occurring at age 5.
7. Large vocabulary in relation to SBIQ 83.
8. Problems with other children (fantasies).

The next two individuals to offer their opinions are an industrial arts teacher and a "low track" English teacher. The industrial arts teacher, whose specialty is wood technology, responded as follows:

1. Jack's need for attention from adults would seem to be related to the fact of his being neglected when he was young, because his birth was unplanned.
2. Jack's hearing problem may have much to do with learning within the standard classroom.
3. The way Jack's parents relate to him is also important, for the mother and father are opposites in handling Jack—also the inference that Jack was actually considered outside the family.
4. His father expected Jack to improve but did nothing to help him improve.
5. Jack can be very creative in songs and playwriting is also very interesting and important.
6. Jack's fantasies are being acted out at inappropriate times.

The English teacher indicates that she looked for consistencies in behavior Jack exhibited and in the reactions of other persons to Jack.

[2]Elizabeth M. Koppitz, *The Bender Gestalt Test for Young Children.* New York: Grune & Stratton, Inc., 1964.

Some consistencies are Jack's attention-getting devices, his inability to transfer knowledge to another area (phonics to reading), his loneliness (being a middle child could be a contributing factor). He has a vivid imagination, which he uses both acceptably (in telling stories at school) and unacceptably (attention-getting fantasies). He may be a good mimic, for he has a large vocabulary (the information given does not state how correctly he uses his vocabulary). Jack identifies more with adults. His mother is consistently submissive to Jack's outbursts (it *could* be confusion because she doesn't know what procedures to follow). Jack's father is consistently impatient with the entire situation involving his son.

There doesn't seem to be adequate communication between school and parents, for his mother, who obviously wants Jack to be helped, is submissive to him while his instructors aren't. The first grade environment seems to have unnecessarily been in limbo for Jack. In terms of help he might have received, the instructor, while willing to try, had too many children to give him personal attention.

The yearly staffing indicates that Jack is making progress, yet in his teacher's reports there seems to be so much emphasis on his having to "behave" simply for its own sake, without trying to see why he misbehaves. Perhaps there was not time to include such material in this report; but it seems that in such a school for exceptional children, the instructor would, by the law of averages, write down at least one instance of working directly with him, on his own terms, with his emotional problems.

Problems for Discussion:

As the final responder at this hypothetical case conference, reconsider how you reacted to the case materials.

  5. What personal values came through in your considerations of the most significant aspects of the case?
  6. Do you have a central theme? In other words, just how would you analyze your own responses after an opportunity to look at the responses of several other persons?

AN ATTEMPT AT SYNTHESIS

Cognitive Considerations

Now we are ready to consider the synthesis of the communications involved in the hypothetical case conference. Synthesis is a process and not a single act. Therefore, the reader should have been attempting to establish a pattern or structure from all the communications as each was presented in turn. The final product will be a combining of the elements or parts to form a whole. The counselor, although not part of the conference as written, should be included. After his statement, we asked the reader to look for two themes that he had introduced. These can be attached to the ideas presented by the persons identified as:

  1. M. S. teacher.
  2. Music teacher.
  3. Practicum student.

4. School psychologist.
5. Industrial arts teacher.
6. English teacher.
7. The reader.

One of the ideas that the counselor introduced was that Jack had difficulty in knowing what role was expected of him and the "not knowing" was probably related to his inability to interact effectively with other children. Although not explicitly a part of the statements concerning the most significant aspects of the case by the above six responders (and possibly seven if the reader included it), a related idea was reported by every responder.

1. The social studies teacher included these statements in his remarks:

   a. Frequency of role playing.
   b. Expectations or determination of the child to be someone else.
   c. The bossing of others.
   d. Socially maladjustment with classmates.

2. The music teacher included two remarks that appear to be related to the counselor's theme.

   a. He appears to be able to behave almost normally on some days, and then changes completely.
   b. His relationship to his peers seems to indicate some area of great difficulty.

3. The practicum student also noted two related factors:

   His ordering and demanding-authoritative, inappropriate behavior. In particular, his singing is a puzzle.

4. The school psychologist's only comment indirectly related to the theme was:

   Problems with other children (fantasies).

5. A similar line of reasoning was noted by the industrial arts teacher when he said,

   Jack's fantasies are being acted out at inappropriate times.

6. The English teacher again reiterated this point by saying,

   He has a vivid imagination which he uses both acceptably (in telling stories at school) and unacceptably (attention-getting fantasies). He may be a good mimic for he has a large vocabulary.

The synthesis of all this material would involve a recombination of the perceptions of the school personnel into a more or less unified whole. One example (note that there would probably be several other alternative examples) might be that Jack's inappropriate behavior (role playing and fantasies) seems to revolve around the identification of socially acceptable models of behavior. His occasional failure to function within the limits of acceptable behavior for school situations creates a problem in dealing with both his peers and the school personnel who must deal with him. We will return to this point several times before concluding this case. An approach to handling the problem, or as Question F in Chapter 3 states, "What would be your suggestions or alternatives for solving or improving the problem situations you identified?" requires some type of synthesis on the part of a pupil personnel specialist. But before moving to ways of handling this situation with Jack, it is necessary to bring out the second theme the counselor introduced and attempt to synthesize the points raised by the case conference responders.

The second theme centers on the home situation. The counselor said,

I can see the possibility that Jack does a good deal of modeling after his father. The indication is that the father does not show a great deal of love for Jack and that he controls the boy from a very authoritarian position, one which is fairly rigid. It does not seem unlikely that Jack would assume this kind of role in trying to identify with his male role in society.

Along these same lines, the social studies teacher noted that Jack was not very well accepted at home; the music teacher reported that "there appears to be some relationship in the home that has some bearing on his action." She does not identify any particular person but just notes that some adult probably influences (or shapes) his actions. The practicum student did not make any such comment about adults in general. He put "the father attitude" at the top of his list of responses. Of the case conference responders, the psychologist seemed to concentrate on the home environment more than the other school personnel. Four of his statements were related: diversity of parental controls—mother submissive, father punitive; the large number of siblings; parental expectations; and the parents' feelings of being unable to help. A paraphrase of the industrial arts teacher continues this theme.

Jack's need for attention from adults would seem to be related to his being neglected when young. The way the parents relate to him now is also important. The methods employed by the mother and father in handling Jack seem opposed. Along with this difference in method, there is the inference that Jack was actually considered outside of the family. His father seemed to want Jack to improve but he did little to help him improve.

The final responder, the English teacher, seemed to support the differences in the parental handling of Jack. She said "His mother is consistently submissive to Jack's outbursts (causing confusion because she doesn't know what procedures to follow). Jack's father is consistently impatient with the entire situation involving his son."

All of the above responses concerned the family structure, but putting them together into a workable whole (the synthesis process) is difficult. Again, there is no one way to synthesize. The authors' synthesis of these ideas would read: The parental difference in reacting toward Jack provides for an inconsistent environment in his home. This, in conjunction with his being a middle child in a large family, probably leads to some confusion in identification of appropriate behavior. Jack's father might be the only member of the family who does not react in a consistent fashion toward him. Since fathers are the primary model for sex role identification, Jack might see his father's authoritarian stance as a workable one for him.

Problem for Discussion:
7. Two attempts at synthesis of the material were offered by the authors. In addition to these, what might be acceptable alternative ways to synthesize the most significant aspects of the case of Jack?

Affective Considerations

Up to now, consideration of the case materials has centered on cognitive processes. Cognition includes both the awareness of the materials and judgment about them, but probably does not include affect to any great degree. It is our opinion that the affective domain is a very important aspect of pupil personnel work. Feelings, emotions, and degrees of acceptance or rejection will often influence or shape suggestions or alternatives for improving problem situations. Therefore, before we attempt to continue our hypothetical case conference to consider what should be done for Jack, we need to consider how the participants felt about the situation.

Again, we begin with the counselor's response. This time, responding to the question "How would Jack be likely to feel about this situation?" he replied, "I think that Jack would feel fairly comfortable." The implication of this statement might be that Jack has adjusted to his special class and his home situation quite well. It could be taken even further and suggested that Jack likes his fantasies and outbursts. Although anything beyond the counselor's statement is pure speculation, it seemed out of context to mention Jack's "fairly comfortable" response after he had suggested that Jack had identity problems and problems in knowing what roles to assume (see p. 84 for the counselor's earlier statement). His identification of problem situations might suggest a statement about Jack's feelings more similar to that of the science teacher, who wrote:

He becomes frustrated when unable to do certain tasks. He must be aware of his difficulties to perform well at times. He is probably confused most of the time.

Although it might be expected that the counselor would give a response along the same lines, the music teacher's comments lend some support to his idea that Jack would feel fairly comfortable:

I have a hunch that Jack really enjoys the attention he is getting. He seems to want to relate more to adults, but his unnatural relationships with his peers are probably by this time, or at his age, a situation of which he must be at least partially cognizant and must cause him some self-doubts.

In one respect, this is almost a compromise between the ideas expressed by the counselor and the science teacher. In another respect, the music teacher's statement could be considered a synthesis of the two reports on how Jack felt about the situation. If the music teacher had responded in the same manner as the third responder in a real live case conference, we would consider her a "good" pupil personnel person. She would have worked in her own ideas while making the apparently opposing views of the first two responders more palatable to each other.

The next responder, when following the original order for the hypothetical case conference, is the practicum student. His response might be considered an excuse for not answering, rather than an answer:

I think Jack would be the only real source; without knowing his conscious or subconsicous motive, I couldn't say.

Responses like this one suggest a point that needs reiteration. In the introduction and in Chapter 2, we noted that pupil personnel service is an art and not a science. One of the basic factors upon which pupil personnel service rests is professional judgment. At times, restraint in making judgments is very appropriate, yet one should not confuse the decision to wait for further data or more time for interpretation with a complete departure from the situation. The former is, at times, a part of judicious decision making, while the latter would not be a revered quality of pupil personnel specialists. We have no real knowledge whether the practicum student's response is one or the other, but our intuition leads us to suspect avoidance. Our experience in training pupil personnel specialists suggests that too infrequently preservice trainees are afraid to act whenever the pressure of making professional judgments arises. The mark of a professional pupil personnel specialist is one who can stand up for his ideas, yet is willing to change positions when logical discussion suggests more appropriate judgments.

The psychologist, in his reactions to the affect question about Jack, does seem to make professional judgments. These judgments seem to be logical extentions of his comments on the cognitive aspects of the case.

1. Jack apparently likes the special attention he gets.
2. Quite obviously, it is frustrating for Jack to cope with his academic and peer environments.
3. Jack is probably feeling uncertain how he should behave—Mother is permissive and submissive when he rants, carries on, and role plays his occupations. Father, on the other hand, is punitive and rejecting.

Points 2 and 3 were also brought out by the industrial arts teacher.

His (Jack's) feelings toward his teacher are those of a friend but one who sometimes puts restrictions on him. He feels his peers are to get kind of close to sometimes, but most of the time they don't need or want him.

He probably feels his father's resentment and feels his father doesn't love him. His feelings toward his mother would involve insecurity concerning her love for him.

It is interesting to note the similarities and differences (an obvious difference is the practicum student) in interpretations of the affective domain. As with the cognitive responses, the feelings about the persons involved (particularly Jack, his teacher, and his parents) have to be analyzed and synthesized before devising a course of action. If some persons in the environment have particularly strong feelings about Jack that might deter his progress, it is valuable from a pupil personnel viewpoint to get these feelings into the open. Sometimes, this method can clarify and improve a situation, while at other times it might indicate that certain staff changes would be in order. An example of this has already been brought into the case: the M. S. teacher's suggestion that Jack be placed in a class with a male teacher. Hopefully, the female teacher involved would not feel hurt by such a suggestion. Sometimes, hurt feelings among professional staff can create bigger problems than those of the student being considered. Personnel specialists *must* perceive attitudes and suggestions for improvements as possible aids in helping the students. Taking these same communications as personal affronts will not facilitate the process. Yet, at times it is difficult not to take something personally. There is no known panacea for interpreting comments as professional communications rather than questions of professional competency, except emotional maturity.

A hypothetical example might involve the teacher who spent two weeks writing the notes on Jack included in his case materials (pp. 79–81) and the English teacher involved in the case conference. These two women do not have much in common and thus do not always see "eye to eye" when discussing how to handle staff and student problems. With this background, consider how Jack's teacher might perceive the English teacher's response to the question "How would Jack be likely to feel about the situation?" Her statement was:

I believe I can see one factor leading to his outbursts. No one in his environment seems to be trying *hard* to understand him. Either their attention is, at best, divided among many youngsters (his instructor), or else they are thinking more in terms of themselves (his parents).

Problems for Discussion:
8. What do you think is the intent of the English teacher's comments?
9. How can you bring up touchy issues in case conferences without alienating other staff members?

Additional Responder Reactions: A Broader Point of View

In addition to the comments by the hypothetical case conference participants, many other school personnel responded to the case of Jack. Some of their ideas on how Jack would feel about his situation follow. These are included to provide a still broader cross section of types of school personnel who might be involved.

1. A special education teacher concentrating in training deaf children responded:

He would feel frustrated, which was just what he felt at the time he was brought to school. Evidently, the fear reactions Jack showed are the results of the actions of an ignorant father trying to suppress what he does not understand or want to understand.

2. A 26-year-old female teacher of German who was working on her master's degree in guidance and counseling (taking a practicum at the time she responded to the case of Jack) wrote:

I'm not quite sure—I haven't been able to make up my mind about the level of awareness the boy might have about his situation. I have the feeling that he doesn't really understand—doesn't actually perceive himself and his situation as it is. However, his reactions to feelings he doesn't understand are nevertheless *very* real.

3. This responder was a first-year school psychologist. He comments:

Apparently Jack is able to block out certain facts about reality. Perhaps this may occur with his emotions.

4. This individual had been teaching a junior-level, general educational psychology course required for persons in teacher-training for several years. His comment on the affective domain started with the idea:

Possibly Jack was too immature to realize that his behavior was not conforming. Although this may or may not be true, it should be noted that he did have a consistent need to manipulate people. When trying to solve these problems, I do not feel that Jack will notice pressure being put on him.

5. The responder is the M. S. teacher who was introduced earlier in this chapter.

Jack can be rational in terms of the teacher's goals only to the extent that he is *able* to pursue a particular course of action; he has a correct conception of the *goal* of the action; and he is *correctly informed* about the conditions surrounding his action.

6. This responder was a graduate student from the Far East, who was training to become a school psychologist.

I suppose that what Jack has been doing is right to his conscience. The problem is that people around him don't understand him or sympathize with him. The indications of his feeling of insecurity in some situations would support this assumption. In addition, he does not understand himself or the circumstance around him very well; otherwise, he wouldn't bring up so many fantasies.

7 and 8. The final two responders included in this section have similar backgrounds. Both had majored in psychology as undergraduates and were unable to find suitable employment upon completion of the B.A. degree. Jobs teaching psychology in secondary schools are hard to find. Partially because of this and also because of their interest in working with children, they entered a training program for pupil personnel specialists.

Jack would be likely to feel unwanted and ignored. Much of his inappropriate behavior at school—loud singing, fantasies in which he usually plays the role of an adult, and so forth—are attempts to get attention in the school setting, particularly from the teacher. He apparently fails to receive this attention at home. He would be frustrated and anxious.

Jack would probably view almost any situation as a possible source of attention. The actual reason for attention that he does receive, however, would probably be somewhat of a mystery to him because of the inconsistent reactions of various people to the same behavior. His constant desire for "help" may indicate not only a desire for attention but also a complete lack of self-confidence, the feeling that he cannot possibly succeed without help.

Problem for Discussion:
10. Attempt to integrate your response to the case of Jack with those of Responders 1 through 8. In this process, consider how differences of opinion might be reconciled. For example, Responders 4 and 5 stated almost opposite views. How might you work with these responders?

Suggestions for Improving the Situation

Now that we have considered the varied perception responders had of Jack, let us turn to possible means of working with the situations identified. Two questions were listed that involved means. The first was "What would be your suggestions or alternatives for solving or improving the problem situations you identified?" Many responders did not realize that the question immediately following (it was on the next page of the mimeographed form they wrote on) was one which read "How would you go about implementing your suggestions?" Consequently, the what and how responses were often worked in together. Therefore, when reporting responder information, we will include both statements labeling the first, *suggestions,* and the second, *implementations.*

Since this case seems to lend itself to the order first introduced in the hypothetical case conference, it will be continued here. The initial responses, which seem to set the tone for subsequent case conference responses, are those of the counselor.

Suggestions:

I would probably try to work with Jack on some of the specific problems indicated. For example, the intolerance for frustration and the attention span problem might lend themselves to some type of behavioral therapy. I also might try to involve Jack in some group work, possibly where he could benefit from some peer social models.

Implementation:

In working with the specific problems, I would set up a structured interview situation and would also enlist the aid of Jack's teacher and parents. For the group work I probably would not involve myself directly. I would, however, work with the group leader in setting up the models and the general situation.

It is interesting to note that the counselor would employ a counseling technique and would involve himself in the process. This is probably the mark of a fairly confident individual, since the case of Jack might be considered more difficult than many others encountered in school situations. Getting involved might also be characteristic of his professional identification. For example, we might expect a social worker to offer a suggestion for improving the situation that involved home visitations and work with the parents, while the counselor might be expected to get involved in direct services with the child.

Problems for Discussion:
11. Even though the counselor would involve himself in the one-to-one counseling with Jack and consultation with his teacher and parents, he probably would not involve himself in the group work. Why do you think he might get involved in one way and not in another?
12. The reader should already have some feeling for the case responders. Before reading their suggestions and means of implementation, speculate on how each might involve himself; that is, what personal involvements, if any, will the science teacher, music teacher, or practicum student note?

The social studies teacher is the first responder.
Suggestions:
1. Offer more rewards, rather than punishment.
2. Try and help the family and others to accept the probability of the child's potential in school work.
3. Try to provide some manual training, very basic, to develop an interest and pride of accomplishment in the boy.
4. Work with a counselor or others to help this boy perceive and accept his role.

Implementation:
1. Check with experts in child behavior.
2. Counsel with teachers, family, and close friends.
3. Search for areas of interest the boy has.
4. Try different approaches to try to solve some of his learning problems.

The points raised are really quite broad and somewhat indecisive. The social studies teacher suggests using positive rewards for behavior. This could be a universal suggestion for children because it has been found that punishment does not change behavior as rapidly as once thought. Yet, the social studies teacher is not specific when it comes to attempting implementation with Jack. Here a pupil personnel worker might come to his aid. The pupil personnel specialist should be knowledgeable enough about operant techniques to make *specific* recommendations about what type of reinforcers could work; yet one difficulty we have found in training school counselors and psychologists is that they are often too passive. In conferences with teachers, they sometimes nod their heads rather than try to extend the person's knowledge or offer specific proposals that might be implemented. Thus, in addition to agreeing that more rewards should be employed, the pupil personnel specialist could initiate a discussion of the types of reinforcers that seem to affect Jack. Within the context of the resulting interaction, some appropriate means should be identified. Closure can then be handled by deciding which of these will be attempted and what the consequential behavior change might be. The issue will still be open-ended, in that the rewards might change or continued consultation be necessary if the behavior does not change, but at least some definite plan of action has been decided upon.

The second suggestion of the social studies teacher is also broad and might be considered somewhat of a universal. In paraphrased form, it might read "have realistic expectations and accept children for what they are." To bring this about, the teacher's suggested means of implementation was counseling with appropriate persons. Unfortunately, some persons might not have realistic expectations for counseling outcomes. It would be appropriate to attempt helping the parents to better accept Jack through counseling. It would be unrealistic to anticipate counseling the parents *into accepting* Jack. The long-range outcomes of a pupil personnel specialist's program sometimes rest upon such differences in approach. If the school staff looks upon counseling as a process that might be helpful, the prospects are positive. If the school staff expects the pupil personnel specialist to counsel persons into *accepting* specific points of view, the long-range view is not optimistic and the counseling aspects of the program will probably fail. Such distinctions must be made early and reiterated whenever appropriate.

The third suggestion of the social studies teacher brings out two aspects that need comment. The most obvious is that there is usually something that every child does well. At times it is difficult to identify a child's strong points, but when noticed they should be reinforced. The social studies teacher thinks of this as some type of "manual training." Manual training might imply an overworked assumption that is too often found among teachers: if a student does not do well in an academic setting, he can work with his hands. Manual training, or now more frequently called vocational and technical education, has become an unfortunate stereotype. Most teachers, who have themselves been successful in school, tend to reinforce education-seeking behavior. One way they see to get rid of students who do not exhibit such behavior is to put them into industrial arts or vocational classes.

We stress this because of knowledge about Jack that might not have been apparent in the case materials. Jack's strengths seem to lie in his verbal behavior and his management of other children. At times, these skills work to his detriment but they are still strengths for him. Psychomotor skills, needed in manual training, are one of Jack's biggest weaknesses. The other children reject him because he has difficulty catching a ball, for example. Therefore, when the social studies teacher suggests an activity that probably would involve high psychomotor performance, the suggestion becomes debatable.

The remaining point this teacher brought up was for the staff to help Jack to perceive his role. This suggestion seems to defy comment because of the word role. Does Jack only exhibit one role? If so, we do not have any idea what it is. There is a sociological approach (beginning with Mead[3]) that uses roles to define personality and show how children are socialized (boys playing the role of father, and so forth), but this does not provide any leads on the social studies teacher's suggestion. His comments in response to the implementation do not seem to provide any clarification. Thus if the written communications on p. 96 are the only ones available when holding a case conference, we might do one of two things. We could seek clarification or move on to points (possibly raised by other persons) that seemed to have more credence. Following up the latter might be the more pragmatic approach because case conferences frequently generate more courses of action than can reasonably be initiated. But faced with these alternatives, one will have to rely upon professional judgment.

The music teacher answered the questions on solutions and implementations more fully than either the counselor or the social studies teacher:

Suggestions:

1. In the educational setting he seems to operate best on a one-to-one relationship. If this could be provided, he might progress better academically but it would probably negate an improvement in his social development, which he also needs.
2. As was suggested, the mother and father, as well as Jack, would probably benefit from counseling. Since there appears to be an inconsistency between how Jack is treated in the home and how he is treated at school, this should be removed. And even if the inconsistency of the treatment by the two parents were removed, it would probably help.

[3]J. Herbert Mead, *Mind, Self and Society*. Chicago: University of Chicago Press, 1934.

3. Since Jack is going to a hearing center, I assumed there was an indication of some loss. This might be explored more fully as a partial cause of some of his actions.
4. As the father indicated, there was lack of attention to him in earlier years; perhaps Jack needs *extra* attention, of a positive nature, at this time.
5. We have little indication of how the siblings react to Jack. If they could be included in a positive reinforcement of his need for manipulation somehow, perhaps he might develop better peer relationships.

Implementation:

1. If at all possible, I would try to teach Jack by himself so that all his needs could be provided for. If not possible, I would try to put him in the smallest possible class.
2. I would try to arrange at least a weekly counseling session with the parents to attempt to reconcile the differences in their approach to Jack. I would also attempt to get across to them the necessity of consistency between school and home. (The teacher who removes him from the room when there is a problem seems to have an effective tool, and this could be attempted at home.)
3. I would want to consult with the hearing specialist to see if any impairment there could conceivably be causing some of the problems, and how they could be eliminated if such were the case.
4. For the fourth suggestion, I would also attempt, in the counseling situation with the parents, to see if some arrangement could be made for each of them to spend some special times with Jack alone.
5. If the siblings, at least the older ones, could be taught to be consistent also in reacting to Jack, he might be helped to better peer relationships.

You have now read the suggestions and means of implementation for two teachers. Those from the social studies teacher were so broad that some discussion was necessary. On the other hand, the music teacher's responses appeared quite specific and almost self-explanatory. Hopefully, these two sets of reactions will illustrate the need for specifics in pupil personnel work. As a further illustration, we consider the responses of two graduate students who are enrolled in a master's degree program. The first one has already been introduced as the practicum student in the case conference. His responses involving suggestions and implementations were consistent with the points raised earlier when defining the problems in the educational setting.

Suggestions:

Find out the *cause* for his behavior. Is something organically wrong with his brain? If not, is he being led consciously by some motive, or is it unconscious? What *is* that motive?

Implementation:

Not knowing enough about the field of psychotherapy, I cannot be specific. However, this area is where I would recommend concentration.

Now, we compare his responses with those of another student at the same stage in a degree program, practicum student 2.

Suggestions:

1. Further parent counseling to help the parents understand Jack's problems and how to deal with them more effectively. As the parents seem relatively willing to cooperate in this way (that is, participation in Parents' Group meetings), this would be advantageous.

2. The retention of Jack in his present educational setting. The student still has too many inappropriate behaviors to be well accommodated by the public school. He continues to need more individual help and attention than could be given him in a normal public school setting. Since special reinforcers appear to be important to Jack, a program of action based on considerable social reinforcement for desirable behavior—by teachers and parents—might be fairly successful. It would seem particularly beneficial during parent conferences to urge the parents to try their best not to reinforce—with their attention—fantasy behavior in their son and to attend to and praise those reality-oriented responses exhibited by Jack. These principles should be explained and demonstrated for the parents, with periodic visits to the home and the schoolroom, to determine if the procedures are being properly and consistently employed. This program of action seems warranted, particularly as the teacher's daily behavior observations of Jack would seem to indicate.

    Also, would a program of perceptual training be possible and/or feasible?

    In the academic area, the use of programmed material might be tried out with Jack. The teacher would, initially, heavily reinforce (with her attention) any correct responses made by the student on such material. The teacher would slowly switch to an intermittent schedule of reinforcement, with increasing intervals of time between reinforcements. Indepedent working behavior would also be reinforced.

Implementation:

1. Establish regular parent conferences.
2. Instruct and demonstrate reinforcement procedures to teacher and parents.
3. Plan periodic checks to see that the procedures are being properly employed. (If these procedures are successful, the reinforcers will be reinforced by more appropriate behaviors in the student.) Record and graph Jack's behavioral progress.
4. Review and revise procedures as needed.
5. See that programmed materials are developed or obtained as needed.

It is almost painfully obvious how the specific step-by-step implementation procedure provided by practicum student 2 would be more appropriate for pupil personnel practice. We cannot stress enough that for work to get done, procedures must be outlined in case conferences. If this preliminary work is omitted, the participants will leave the meeting and probably continue reacting toward, and demanding of, students in the same manner they used before the conference. In some cases such behavior might be appropriate, but the rationale for holding a conference would most likely preclude this. Conferences are held to gain perspective and decide upon plausible changes that are deemed appropriate.

Since deciding upon plausible changes is one of the primary functions of a conference, the reader should again use the processes of analysis and synthesis of communications. Earlier in this chapter, it was noted that two ideas seemed to reoccur when defining the problems involved. They were synthesized as:

1. Jack's inappropriate behavior (role playing and fantasies) appear to revolve around identification of socially acceptable models of behavior. His occasional failure to function within the limits of acceptable behavior for school situations creates a problem for him in dealing with his peers and for school personnel who must deal with him.
2. The parental differences in reacting toward Jack provide for an inconsistent environment in his home. This, in conjunction with his being a middle child in a large family, probably leads to some confusion in identification of appropriate behavior. Jack's father might be the only member of the family who does react in a consistent fashion toward him. Since fathers are the primary model for sex role identification, Jack might see his father's authoritarian stance as a workable one for him.

A major question that must be considered is the degree to which the suggestions for improvement and means of implementation would appear to provide workable solutions as reflected in the recombination of the school personnel's perceptions of the problems. Then, from the possible workable solutions a procedure or series of steps must be formulated (the synthesis process).

Note to Reader. The reader should review the suggestions for improving the problem situation and means of implementation before going on to responses of the participants remaining in this hypothetical case conferences. He should also keep in mind the synthesis process in reading the following responses.

School psychologist's suggestions:

1. Arrange for more extensive counseling for parents with continuing feedback to them of what to do with Jack and how to handle him.
2. Whenever possible, advise Jack's siblings and peer group to ignore his fantasizing occupational roles.

His means of implementation:

1. Continue relationships in counseling already established with parents.
2. Reinforce Jack's needs to them and possibly extend group counseling technique to entire family.

Synthesis is the pooling of various ideas into a more or less unified whole. For the school psychologist this unit appears to be a therapeutic approach. The industrial arts teacher adds some new dimensions.

Industrial arts teacher's suggestions:

1. Try to explain further how the parents' attitude toward Jack concerns his improvement.
2. Try to change parents' attitude to a more concerned position toward Jack.
3. Possibly ask some of the more well-adjusted students to include him in their activities.
4. Encourage Jack to write plays and songs; possibly the class could act out one of his plays with Jack directing. He might like to perform one of his songs also.
5. Continue individual attention to Jack with much encouragement and reassuring comments to help build his confidence and security.

Implementation:

1. Explain to the father that his lack of concern for his son is obvious to Jack and he should try to correct this.
2. Encourage Jack's mother to help him or tutor him at night and on the weekends. I would suggest that the mother have a conference with the teacher as to what to teach and how to go about it so there will be a uniform approach.
3. Ask the entire class to write plays or songs and have them perform the best entries of all of them written.
4. Continue special schooling in the described manner already presented, with the idea expressed to Jack that eventually he will be back at the standard public school.

Problem for Discussion:

13. How would you synthesize the ideas of the industrial arts teacher with the school psychologist's therapeutic orientation?

Our final responder, the English teacher, adds still another dimension in addition to counseling.

English teacher's suggestions:

1. If his instructor really isn't trying to help in terms of the child's special problem, I'd point this out to her most forcefully or see that he was placed with another instructor.
2. Since mention is made of a counselor, I assume Jack is being seen periodically. Perhaps a more rigorous schedule of counseling would aid. I certainly would investigate counseling for the parents.

Implementation:

1. One would have to talk diplomatically with his instructor and, at the same time, ascertain whether or not there were other qualified special educational instructors available. Getting Jack's parents to agree to in-depth help for Jack, as well as for themselves, would not be a problem. We

already know they have voluntarily put Jack in the hands of specialists. I get the feeling that Jack is almost a social stigma to his father. If the father feels that becoming a client himself will hurry up the process of removing this stigma, he'll agree to seeing a counselor. The mother seems like a reed bending in the wind, so there would be no problem convincing her she should become a client for her son's sake.

We will attempt to synthesize the communications or suggestions and means of implementation for the case conference responders, but before we do it might be profitable to look at a few of the comments of responders not included in the case conference group. There are four other responders who include some additional points or have interpreted the case materials in a slightly different manner.

A. Suggestions from an Asian graduate student with two years teaching experience in his home country:

1. I would suggest, first, to withdraw Jack temporarily from school if no improvement on his part occurs under the current circumstance, and give some more special treatment for emotional disturbance until some progress has been noticed.
2. I would also suggest, next, to retain him in the school under the condition that some special treatment for his problems be made available and cooperation on the parts of parents is secured.

Implementation:

1. The first suggestion could be carried out only with the agreement of the parents; otherwise, Jack will be segregated into a special class prepared to deal with similar troubles.
2. As for the second one, a special teacher would be needed and the contact between the parents and the school should be frequent. If both can't be fulfilled, some help other than that available from the school setting will be recommended.

B. Suggestions from a German teacher:

1. Get some extensive medical tests of brain damage—recommendations accordingly from a specialist.
2. Get as much information as possible as to the state of his hearing—audio health.
3. Possibly try a few more tests of visual-motor and spatial reactions to attempt to identify more clearly if there are real problems in these areas, too.
4. Work with parents more closely for understanding and empathy; possibly work with family as a group, including siblings, to achieve a home atmosphere that does not contribute any more to Jack's feelings of insignificance.

Implementation:

1. Encourage the parents to make an appointment for Jack to see a neurological (brain) specialist for tests and diagnosis; request a report from the specialist contacted for my own use with recommendations according to findings and, if treatment is needed, encourage or see to it that it is done.
2. Conduct appropriate hearing evaluations.

3. Investigate ways (for instance, tests) to help identify visual-motor and spatial difficulties; administer them—depending on results, make recommendations for treatment.
4. Try to set up weekly family group meetings of Jack's family, perhaps also a part of a larger group of families of other children like Jack; and hopefully at least monthly counseling sessions for parents with me and teacher(s).

C. A teacher-trainer's suggestions:

1. Work further with the parents; stress the facts that their attitudes toward Jack must be the same and that they consistently treat his behavior in the same manner.
2. I feel there should be more communication between the school staff and the parents. As noted by Jack's teacher, "Mondays are always bad. . . . Could this be the result of a permissive week-end at home?"

Implementation:

1. Counseling with the parents on a once-a-week basis, then later once a month. Also, there should be meetings between the parents and teaching staff to make sure that Jack's behavior will be dealt with consistently.

D. Suggestions from a trainee in a program for pupil personnel specialists with an undergraduate major in psychology and no school work experience:

1. The major area for improving Jack's over-all adjustment seems to be in any improvement that might take place in his parents' attitudes and resultant behavior toward Jack. The steps that are taken to improve this relationship would depend, to a great extent, on whether or not parent-family counseling has been taking place during the time that Jack has been in the special class, and on the parents' willingness to actually change their perceptions of, and aspirations for, Jack. If a good relationship exists between parent and counselor (or if family counseling has not been undertaken), the parents should be encouraged to provide a more consistent pattern of responses to Jack's behavior. They should also be encouraged to provide him with some individual attention at those times when his behavior is "normal."
2. If a hearing loss has been discovered, therapy to minimize the hearing difficulty, along with classroom procedures that will take this problem into account, should be provided. In addition, training to improve Jack's perceptual skills may be necessary.
3. Within the classroom, Jack should be led to more independence. Since Jack needs or asks for so much attention, and since he has developed such a close relationship with his teacher, this must be done in very small steps. When he is asked to work independently, it should be for a very short time at first and should involve a task in which Jack will be successful. The tasks should be very well structured.
4. Jack's problem with reading and independent word attack may be somewhat helped by auditory training, within the limits of any hearing loss that may be present. Any instruction in phonics should be geared to such auditory training. In addition, attack word skills need to be integrated with actual reading situations rather than treated merely as supplementary work. Jack cannot be expected to utilize skills until he is shown how to do so.

Implementation:

1. The implementation of these suggestions would require the cooperation of all those who have contact with Jack. Parents, teachers, and counselors must jointly decide on a course of action and then all follow through on a consistent pattern of behavior. If any one of those intimately involved varies his reaction to Jack's behavior, Jack's pattern of responses will not be changed permanently.

Which Suggestions Should Be Followed?

When looking at the many and varied list of suggestions and means of implementation identified by responders, it would appear that selecting a few to follow would be difficult. Yet, most of the suggestions follow along a few main themes. In terms of frequency of occurrence (a) counseling with the parents or (b) working with the family were the major themes. Suggestions involving either points a or b were as follows:

Social studies teacher:

b. Try to help the family and others to accept the probability of the child's potential in school work.

Music teacher:

a. Plan weekly counseling sessions with the parents to attempt to reconcile the differences in their approach to Jack.
b. Help the siblings to be consistent in reacting to Jack.

Practicum student 2:

a. Further parent counseling to help the parents understand Jack's problem and how to deal with them more effectively.

School psychologist:

a. Have more extensive counseling with parents.
b. Extend counseling technique to the entire family (advise siblings to ignore his fantasizing).

Industrial arts teacher:

a. Explore further the parents' attitudes toward Jack concerning his improvements. Try to change the parents' attitude to a more concerned position toward Jack. Also explain to the father that his lack of concern for his son is obvious to Jack and he should try to correct it.

English teacher:

a. Get Jack's parents to agree to in-depth help for themselves.

The synthesis of communications offered earlier was that the parental differences in reacting toward Jack provided for an inconsistent environment in the home. This went on to include Jack's probable difficulty in identification of appropriate behavior; also, Jack may identify with the rigid attitude taken by his father (see p. 101). The synthesis of suggestions and the means of implementation are an easy step after reconsidering the earlier consolidation of the major problems. Almost without exception, counseling, working toward parental approval, and accepting Jack as the person he is would be our suggested combination of the separate elements.

In some respects the synthesis of ideas concerning parental counseling is not really synthesis at all. It would be more like taking the same total concept (the whole), which reoccurred again and again, and merely rewording it. This point might seem to be too much of a simplification, yet we made no claim in Chapter 2 that analysis and synthesis in pupil personnel services had to be difficult. This is just a process of drawing ideas together, and when there is agreement it will be a relatively simple task.

Another suggestion for improving the situation involved individual counseling for Jack. Four of the six hypothetical case responders, five of seven if we include the counselor, included related statements:

Counselor:

I would work with Jack on some of the specific problems indicated.

Social studies teacher:

Work with a counselor to help Jack perceive and accept his role.

Practicum student:

Some type of psychotherapy.

Industrial arts teacher:

Continued individual attention to Jack, with much encouragement and reassuring comments to help build his confidence and security.

English teacher:

More rigorous schedule of counseling and getting Jack's parents to agree to in-depth help for Jack.

Such statements seem to imply that individual counseling would be one of the major ways to attempt to change Jack's inappropriate behavior (role playing and fantasies).

The synthesis of the major problems involving inappropriate behavior revolved around the identification of socially acceptable models of behavior. Additional suggestions offered by responders follow.

Counselor:

Involve Jack in some group work to help him benefit from some peer-social models.

Practicum student 2:

Implement a program of action based on considerable social reinforcement for desirable behavior.

Industrial arts teacher:

Possibly asking some of the more well-adjusted students to include him in their activities. In addition, it might be valuable to encourage Jack to write plays and songs. Possibly, the class could act out one of his plays with Jack directing. He might like to perform one of his songs, also.

One procedure that might include both the counseling and the modeling aspect would be to hold group counseling sessions. If this were done, much as the counselor suggested, we would have taken into account almost all of the responder suggestions.

Only five suggestions for improvement were provided by case conference responders that have not already been included when considering which suggestions should be followed. Three of these, offered by the social studies teacher, were in such a general nature that they provided no substantive direction. One, by practicum student 2, called for retention in the present school to provide the necessary attention. This could be carried out without any real plan of attack, since it is of a continuing nature. The only remaining suggestion that deserves further attention came from the music teacher: to consult with a hearing specialist to check if there might be an impairment that could be causing problems. The pupil personnel specialist should make a note of this and make sure that Jack gets tested. Some teachers are in a better position to note physical impairments than others. Checking out such questions can usually be done rapidly and can frequently be handled by the school nurse.

A RETROSPECTIVE HISTORY—FAMILY BACKGROUND PRIOR TO THE CASE MATERIALS

Shortly before the end of the time period covered in the case materials, a counselor at the mental health center began working with Jack's parents. From these conferences and from talking with other knowledgeable parties, a general family history prior to the time Jack began school was obtained. The counselor attempted to piece together some of the information composed mostly of retrospective reports, into the following general narrative.

The History

Two quite typical children were born to the parents in rapid succession, soon after Jack's father was graduated from law school. Four years following the birth of the second child, after initiating an independent law practice in a metropolitan area, another daughter came along. One year after this, Jack was born. Based on observation of the elder boy, the first-born child; and the girl, the second-born child, it would be expected that this younger set would be considered typical middle class children. There is little retrospective evidence that Jack's first three years deviated from this expectation, although his immediately older sister (she shall be called Sara) seemed somewhat atypical. She was slow at developmental skills and appeared to have some type of retardation. Both parents recall sensing this but were unable to identify a reason for Sara's slowness.

Soon Sara was being transferred from one specialist to another for examination. The final diagnosis was an irregularity of the inner ear which caused some difficulty in coordination, as well as a hearing loss. Treatment to correct this physical problem required a trip from suburbia to an inner city hospital every other day.

Jack, being one year younger than Sara, found himself in the same rigorous schedule. Every other day he went along on Sara's hospital trip. He came home to a family concerned about her progress. Sara, Sara, Sara, for almost a year. Finally, Jack was old enough, four, to be placed in a preschool and no longer had to accompany his mother and Sara; although by this time her treatments were becoming less frequent because of an improved condition.

All of this time, the father became more and more involved in his practice and was also asked to lecture on law at the state university. He found himself being forced to leave home by 6:30 a.m. each morning to beat the freeway traffic and unable to complete the requirements of the day by 9:00 p.m. This pace finally made him and his wife decide to change locations. An offer came along to act as attorney for a new state hospital located in a town of 10,000. This opportunity would provide a substantial stable income with the opportunity to supplement his income with a small private practice. Probably as important in making him decide to take the position were other factors—a chance to hunt and fish, which had been impossible with the demands of a big city lawyer; the regular hours that were possible when living five or ten minutes from the job.

The house in suburbia went up for sale and plans were made for the move. The shift was not made as quickly as expected because construction of the hospital facilities was delayed and the house did not sell. The mother recalled this period as the worst one of her life.

Sara still needed to be taken into the city frequently. The house always had to be clean because you didn't know when someone would come to look at it, and we so wanted to sell it. I was in the early months of my fifth pregnancy. Mr. ——— was trying to reduce the time spent away from home but couldn't. And all in all it was miserable. I'd never want to go through it again.

Little was recalled concerning Jack during this stage, except that his nursery school teacher reported that he was having some difficulty relating to the other children. The move still had not materialized when Jack started kindergarten and similar reports were heard, but with three other children and then four other children (another boy) no apparent overt concern seemed to occur on the parents' part.

Finally, after moving and becoming somewhat settled in their new community, although their home had not yet been finished, Jack started first grade. One week after school started, the teacher requested a parent conference. She had found Jack almost uncontrollable. He would not sit still, talked extremely loudly, and always was in some kind of conflict with the other children. The parents and teacher decided to try it a little longer, but soon it became apparent that Jack was too immature to handle the first grade. He was placed half a day in kindergarten and half a day in first grade. Although not satisfactory, this arrangement continued until late fall when Jack began getting ill. At first, it was little complaints about pains, which rapidly grew into big complaints. After several unsuccessful examinations, it was discovered that he had a cyst on the inside of a lung which would have to be removed. Arrangements with the best lung surgeon in the middle west were completed in early winter for the operation. After the holidays the mother, father, and son packed up for the trip to the hospital 300 miles away. Both parents recalled the reactions of the boy during this period quite vividly. He was afraid and would behave in quite unusual and loud ways. The Jack you read about in the case materials had arrived.

EPILOGUE

Case materials presented on Jack came to a close near the end of an academic year. The epilogue on this case adds one calendar year of experience, the reports falling almost into quarters of the year in a progression of experiences.

SUMMER. Counseling with the parents, begun in the spring, was continued. The mother, who worked rotating shifts at the city hospital, found it difficult to make many of the regularly scheduled counseling appointments, but Jack's father attended regularly. On at least three occasions, he called the counselor between sessions to respond to considerations raised at their meetings and to report on incidents in the home. One of the major problems discussed with the father was his set of expectations for Jack. It was hard for him to think of Jack without projecting to the future. At first, these projections took the form of "How will Jack ever get along as an adult?" With continued contacts, the father appeared to accept the reality of Jack as a boy who could be worked with; he began to see that the here and now had to be handled before getting upset about the future.

During the summer, Jack was seen five times by the same counselor. The school held a summer camp for its students, and each Monday they had a one-hour session. It was during these sessions that many of Jack's inappropriate ways of reacting came out. An example was the other boys' teasing of Jack at the dinner table. They liked to kid him because he would scream at them. His predictable way of behaving just reinforced the action of other boys and made their teasing more frequent. When discussing this in counseling sessions, an attempt was made to get Jack to consider ways of reacting to their verbal comments and gentle pokes. His suggested modes for coping with his peers were:

1. Tell them that if they didn't stop he would call his mother and she would take him home from camp.
2. Bring candy from home and only give it to the boys if they were nice to him. (Jack had a history of bringing things from home that the other boys took away from him.)
3. Bring his little five-year-old brother, who was a "little tough guy," to camp to beat up the boys who weren't nice to him.

Question for Discussion:
14. What would have been the reaction of the other boys to Jack if he had suggested these alternatives to them?

At the end of the summer the counselor found it disappointing that Jack did not seem to be introspective enough to realize the folly of some of his means of dealing with other children. On the other hand, the parents' apparent change in attitude was encouraging. The father was more accepting and the mother, although not seen too frequently, appeared less accommodating to Jack. The mother's change may have been attributable to the father's greater degree of participation in affairs concerning Jack in the home.

FALL. After school began, a marked change in the case seemed to occur. Both parents agreed that the home situation had improved a great deal. Jack seldom had outbursts and those that did occur seemed to have provocation. The situation finally appeared to be in hand, as far as they were concerned, and in their opinion Jack was behaving almost like a "normal" child. Counseling sessions with Jack also seemed to be going along well. He no longer carried on in the relatively free atmosphere provided. Confrontations between the counselor and Jack during the summer seemed to have smoothed out the situation. His self-reports were that things were going along well. As a consequence, the contacts were reduced to every other week half way through the fall.

Evidently things were improved but not to the degree that the counselor sensed. He was initiating a research project in the fall and did not retain the close teacher contacts that had been in effect prior to this time. This was unfortunate because Jack was still having peer problems that were ignored because they were not reported in the sessions. Once contact with the teacher was again initiated on a regular basis and the quarterly staffing was held, a different plan of attack was decided upon.

WINTER. Beginning the first week after Christmas vacation, two counselors began working with Jack's class. It was a sort of semigroup counseling. The main topic was behavior in the classroom, but the group often changed to other topics. One of the big problems with the group procedure was that the children reinforced each other in deviant behavior. Almost without exception, the other seven children in the class had some type of behavior problem. In the semiunstructured atmosphere provided, the children acted out and began to get recognition for inappropriate behavior.

The main advantage of the group procedure was that the counselor could observe how Jack reacted to the other children and see how they reacted to him. Then, immediately following the group session, an individual counseling session was held with Jack. Prior to this, Jack had reported that things were going along well, but after seeing the class together, inappropriate behavior could easily be identified by the counselor. Many of Jack's reactions to the other children were so much a part of him that they were not seen as different or inappropriate. It became much easier for the counselor to make progress with Jack under these circumstances.

Following the individual sessions Jack, the counselor, and the teacher talked for a few moments about the types of behavior Jack exhibited in class. Jack told the teacher the type of appropriate behavior he and the counselor had agreed would be better for him. Jack agreed to try and maintain his behavior during the week. She kept a record of the number of times Jack had to be reminded to act in the prescribed manner. The teacher reported that this procedure did bring about a change in Jack's class behavior. He was much easier for her to work with when dealing with academics. But there was still the problem that Jack did not behave in an appropriate manner outside of the class on the playground.

CASE NO. 3 Del
(Grades 3 and 4)

The parochial school seemed more effective as Del's parents attempt to help him find a place for himself in the public school program. Del's development in reading has been slow and laborious. By the fourth grade, school problems and appropriate educational planning have become inextricably interwoven with teacher and parent resentment, and a later diagnosis of "organic brain disturbance . . . dyslexia with a visual perceptive disturbance."

In this chapter, the authors will approach the case study-responder comments with a different focus from that employed in the previous chapters. The focus will shift from the broader between-responder differences, as in the case analysis of Geoff, to an in-depth inspection of the *interaction* between individual responders and the extensive pupil data. The clinical review of Del will emphasize the significant dyad, with both the responder and the student serving as models of significant information. This method will result in a shift in emphasis from the question-by-question approach to include an intensive assessment of the responder's personal professional history and evaluation strategies. Thus a comparatively different reporting format is utilized. For Case No. 3, each of seven responders will be presented primarily as separate cases in their unique analysis and synthesis of the referred pupil. The authors' comments will emphasize on the "within" characteristics of the dyad, the unique interactive processes, and the responder's perceptions of the student data. In contrast with the case of Geoff, comparative statements "between" responders will be minimized. Therefore, each case dyad will be an integration of the responder's background information, his or her evaluative statements, and the various areas of student assessment.

After reading the case information on Del, the reader should complete the questions in Chapter 3. He should be increasingly sensitive to his own biases and the different points of view and personal motivations of his colleagues, having already reviewed the two previous student cases. In class discussions, the reader-responder has had to examine closely his own motivations and critically review the assumptions of his professional conclusions. There should be a heightened awareness and sensitivity in this process.

CASE STUDY MATERIALS ABOUT DEL

Remarks by Parents on Family Information Form (Third Grade, Winter 1968)

Describe what problems are present at home, at school, in the community. Child has difficulty reading. He went to Kindergarten at Old Larson and apparently did well. He went to first grade at St. Andrew's. He was slow but was doing all right. They taught sight reading and phonics. St. Andrew's closed, so he went back to Old Larson in second grade. They taught phonics. At the close of second grade, the teacher said he was making progress. Del makes fairly good grades in other subjects but does not appear to be progressing in reading. He is now in third grade, and he has gone from a "D" in first quarter to an "E" this past quarter.

Home and family background. The parents were married in the mid 1950s. The father has five years of college training and is an employed insurance manager. The mother is a high school graduate who has occasional employment as a salesclerk. Both are in their early forties. There are four children in the family, three boys and a girl; Del is the next to the youngest child. The older boys are in high school. They live in a rural community of about 10,000 population. Family activities include golfing, fishing, swimming, and so forth. The religious affiliation is Catholic. The parents describe Del as sociable; he gets along "well" and "normally" with all members of the family. Relations with friends his age are described as "very well," and he prefers to be with boys, or children his own age.

Developmental history. Birth was full-term. Del sat alone at 4–6 months, walked at one year, spoke his first words at 9–10 months, spoke in sentences at 1½ years, and had bladder and bowel control at 1–1½ years. No speech problems were noted.

Interests and activities. Swimming, baseball, and building models. Work responsibilities included burning trash, mowing the lawn, setting tables, and washing dishes.

Medical information. Del has no medical abnormalities. Vision is corrected for myopic. (Reference: school medical report.)

School situation. The parents described his grades as average, although they reported, "He does have trouble in reading and has been tutored intensively for reading."

(Parent signature)

School Report

Public School Report, Winter 1968

SRA Achievement Series (Third grade, October 1967):

Language Arts

	Capital punctuation	Language usage	Spelling	L. A. total
Grade	3–6	2–7	2–8	3–1

Arithmetic

	Arithmetic reasoning	Usage and concepts	Computation	Arithmetic total
Grade	1–	1–6	2–7	1–5

Reading

	Reference material	Interpretive graphs	Comprehension	Vocabulary	Reading total
Grade	—	—	1–8	1–9	1–8

Composite
2.4

Third Grade Marks

Subject	First 9 weeks	Second 9 weeks
English	B	C
Reading	D	E
Social Studies	C	B
Science	B	A
Arithmetic	B+	C−

Attendance record. Good. Del has only missed 6½ days of school this year, most of which were due to a strep throat.

Special academic interests (please list). Del seems interested in science. He does his best reading on scientific material, but it is impossible to let him read this type alone. On a recent science test he read the material with enough comprehension to make an A.

Special academic difficulties. Del can write legibly at times. More often, he scribbles and turns in sloppy papers. His reading is the major difficulty. He reads at the first to second grade level. He knows sounds and can comprehend phonic rules.

Classroom participation. He participates well in classroom work, although he tends to wander away from the subject being discussed.

Testing Program. (Achievement, Intelligence, Reading, and so forth):

Name of test	Date given	Grade level when given	Scores
Botel Reading	Sept. 1966	2nd	Pre-Primmer
Botel Reading	May 1967	2nd	1.5
Botel Reading	Dec. 1967	3rd	2.0
Weekly Reader Oral	Dec. 1967	Free reading 1.5	Instructional Level 2.5
			Frustration Level 3.5

Social adjustment:

Describe this child's relationship with peers. Although it would be unfair to classify Dell as a bully, the children prefer not to include him in their play. He is very immature and desires attention.

How does this child participate in groups? Del demands attention and will try to take over conversations. In groups, he's ignored more or less.

What roles does he usually assume (leader, follower, passive, aggressive, and so forth)? He is aggressive but does not have leadership qualities, nor does he follow other leaders.

What is the child's response to authority? Del ignores authority. He acts chagrined when reprimanded but five seconds later is back doing the very thing he was scolded for.

What is this child's general physical appearance? Del is large for his age, clean about his person, well mannered, and well dressed.

Are any particular health problems apparent? (Describe.) None, although we at school have asked for an eye checkup, as he frowns, rubs his eyes, and acts sleepy or tired. He holds his head in his hands as if he hadn't the strength to hold his head up.

What is the relationship between the school and this child's parents? The relationship has been good. However, the parents became very upset when Del was given an E in reading the second quarter of this school year (January 1968). Because of the strained relationship at the present time between the parents and myself, I would appreciate your keeping my information confidential. The mother accused me of disliking Del because I told her he was not very attentive in class. Quite to the contrary, I am very fond of Del. He is a likeable child, and I am anxious to determine why he has the reading problem. Del seems to be playing a game with us. His mother tells me he is very concerned about his school work. His attitude at school is quite the reverse. He couldn't care less. If I keep him in at recess to complete an assignment, he must be constantly supervised or he will get up and look out the windows, draw pictures, and so forth. At our conference, his father said that Del was like that at home also.

Del came to our school from St. Andrew's Catholic School the last year it was in operation (it closed because of lack of teaching staff). Most of the children coming from St. Andrew's to our school tested out below the average of the students in our school. The parents have said repeatedly that they felt the boys were getting a better education with us. Yet the mother said at our conference she felt the trouble began with Del's admission to our school. Another teacher and I have both worked with the child to the best of our abilities. We frankly don't know what to do next. I suggested Del come to the Special Education Division. They can determine what should be done. We shall cooperate in every way.

(Teacher signature)

Reading Examination Report (Spring 1968)

Capacity for achievement. It is estimated that Del's capacity to learn to read is at least at grade level. For the purpose of this report, Del's present grade level (3.8) will be used as the guideline for estimating possible strengths and weaknesses in reading.

Analysis of Reading:

1. *Word discrimination.* The *Huelsman Word Discrimination Test* is designed to show how well students use length, internal design, and external configuration in perceiving printed words. None of his choices on the test items were correct. In this instance, it is possible that Del did not understand the directions or that he was feeling the pressure of the testing situation.

2. *Sight vocabulary.* On the *Dolch Basic Sight Vocabulary Words,* Del could recognize words in the high second grade reading range.
3. *Silent reading.* The *Gates Primary Reading Test* was administered to ascertain Del's silent reading abilities.

Area	Grade level score
Word Recognition	3.3
Sentence Reading	3.7
Paragraph Reading	4.4
Average	3.8

When interpreting the above scores, one must note that his survey test is designed for administration to a *group* of children and that the norming procedures are based on group administration. Therefore, when this test is given in a clinical situation, it is generally assumed that the scores will be inflated. More realistically, then, this test average should be interpreted as indicating Del's current silent reading achievement at approximately a 2.5 grade level. To further evaluate Del's abilities, the silent reading portion of the *Durrell Analysis of Reading Difficulties* was administered. This test consists of paragraphs of varying difficulties and provides for observing aided and unaided oral recall of the content of the paragraphs read, checking for mechanics of silent reading, and characteristics of recall. Del scored at a level between medium and high third grade. There was no excessive head movement or finger pointing. However, there was continuous vocalization, both silent and oral; such vocalization decreases reading rate. Visual imagery was good.

Since a test of this type depicts the frustration level of a child's silent reading ability, *2.5* shall again be used as Del's silent reading level in this report.

4. *Oral reading.* On the oral reading section of the *Durrel-Analysis,* Del scored slightly above middle third grade level. On the next most difficult paragraph, there were gross mispronunciations, hesitations, omissions, and substitutions.
5. *Word attack skills.* The *Boyd Test of Phonetic Skills* was administered to discover the areas of phonetic skills that have not been mastered.

Del did seem to have mastered the use of beginning consonants, except *n* and *v* and the consonant blends *gr, sw,* and *cr.* He substituted the *kl* sound for *ch* and *sl* for *sc* and did not seem to know *ar, aw,* and short sounds of beginning vowels *e, u,* and *o.* Final *e* did not signify a long vowel sound within the word for Del.
6. *Auditory discrimination.* On the *Wepman Auditory Test,* Del seemed to have no auditory discrimination problem that would interfere with his learning necessary phonic skills.

(One year later, Del continued to make less than satisfactory progress during the fourth grade, so that the parents sought further medical consultation and educational information.)

Medical Report

(Correspondence from a medical neurologist to the family physician—spring 1969.)

Thank you very much for referring this very interesting patient to me, the son of an insurance executive who seems to be quite intelligent. There is a reading problem for some years although the patient is not retarded and is doing very well in other subjects. He has been nervous since the third grade. Psychological evaluation has revealed a high IQ. He has had difficulty getting along in public schools and does better in a parochial school. Apparently his reading test shows good comprehension but poor visual perception.

The EEG is striking inasmuch as there was a marked paroxysmal slow dysrhythmia, nonfocal, consistent with a convulsive disorder or organic brain disturbance.

The complete neurological examination is negative. He is nine years old and weighs 105 pounds. He is 4'1" in height.

This is a common problem in my practice and is classified as organic brain disturbance with superior intelligence. The phenomenon which bothers the patient now is most likely dyslexia with a visual perceptive disturbance.

I have worked quite closely with the Special Education Program on such problems. I have a patient that has the same primary problem who has been helped considerably with a program set up by the school and supervised by the Director of Pupil Personnel Services.

I would recommend Dilantin Infatabs twice a day.

(Physician's signature)

School Report

(Fourth grade teacher, St. Andrew's, Spring 1969)

Please state in some detail why this child is being referred for an evaluation. Describe what problems are present at home, at school, in the community: Del started to have a reading problem when he was in the second grade. Earlier, he had transferred to the public school because St. Andrew's closed. He has improved, but we had special help with his reading this year. Also St. Andrew's has reopened and two teachers have been helping him in school.

Is this child sociable or does he prefer to be alone? Sociable.

How does this child get along with: Mother. *Normal.* Father. *Normal.*

Special academic difficulties. Reading.

Classroom participation. Average.

Testing program:

Name of test	Date given	Grade level when given	Scores
Stanford Achievement	Jan. 1969	4	Av., 3.4
Stanford Mental Ability	Nov. 1968		IQ 88

Social adjustment:

Describe this child's relationship with peers. Good.

How does this child participate in groups? Average.

What roles does he usually assume (leader, follower, passive, aggressive)? follower.

What is the child's response to authority? Normal.

What is this child's general physical appearance? Larger than average for age group.

Please discuss briefly any problems (social or academic) that have been observed in this child's siblings. Older brothers progress in school better.

What is the relationship between the school and this child's parents? Good. In previous school, relationship not so good.

(Teacher's signature)

School Psychological Report (Special Education District, Spring 1969)

Background Information:

At approximately the second grade, it was brought to the parents' attention by his second grade teacher that Del was having trouble in reading development. The reading difficulty became acute in the third grade; Del had transferred to the public school from St. Andrews. He received a failing grade in reading while receiving acceptable grades in his other subjects. He was not allowed to go out for recess and was often punished for his poor reading by the third grade teacher, according to the parents' report. His parents noticed a change in his attitude from a happy child to a more nervous and unstable child during this time. Del had some visual-perceptual training by the local optometrist during the third grade.

Del was brought to the reading supervisor for a diagnostic reading evaluation in Spring 1968. Deficiencies were identified and recommendations were made. In the fall of 1968, Del was given a tutor in reading. The tutor gave Del reading help after school for an hour each night. After the parents, the school, and the tutor noticed little reading improvement, he was taken to Kansas City to see a medical specialist for a neurological examination. In turn, he was referred back to the school for education planning.

Parent Interview:

Both parents seemed quite anxious to find methods to help Del with his reading difficulties and were willing to do whatever would help him. The mother appeared quite dominant and admitted that because of Del's problems he was probably spoiled.

Much of Del's nervousness and "poor" attitudes toward school were the fault of the third grade teacher, according to the parents' report. They felt that with individual help and good teaching, Del might not have had some of the reading problems that now exist. They felt the third grade teacher had given up on him, and consequently Del had given up, too.

After the third grade, the parents felt that Del lost his motivation and his easy-going happy attitude. He also declined in his ambition to compete athletically as well as in other areas. He seemed to develop a greater appetite during this time.

Both the parents are happier with St. Andrew's School and feel that Del is happier there, too. The father is impressed with the school's uniform reading program.

The parents are obviously most concerned over Del's condition and are willing to place the blame in many directions. Because of this extreme concern, Del probably does not get the normal chance to develop independence and self-confidence. Perhaps, this concern has also caused the parents to push Del (with tutors) quite hard to develop adequate reading skills.

Testing:

Weschler Intelligence Scale for Children
Verbal IQ   94
Performance IQ   111
Full scale IQ   102

Wide Range Achievement Test
Reading Grade Equivalent   Test I—3.5, Test II—3.8
Arithmetic Grade Equivalent   4.5

Peabody Picture Vocabulary Test — Form B
Chronological Age   9 years, 8 months
Mental Age   11 years, 11 months
Intelligence Quotient   116

Bender Motor — Gestalt Test

Draw-A-Person

Test Results and Observations:

Del was a nine-year-old fourth grade student (Fall 1969, St. Andrew's School), who would be described as clean in appearance and well dressed in casual summer clothing. He was accompanied by his parents for the examination. He stated that he was taking medication. A review of the correspondence from the physician would indicate Del is taking Dilantin Infatabs twice daily. The doctor offers a diagnosis of "organic brain disturbance . . . dyslexia with a visual perceptive disturbance." During the current examination, Del was cooperative, but as the testing progressed, he became tired and mildly distractible. Del wears horned rimmed glasses and removes them from time to time when consistent visual application is needed on motor tasks such as the Bender Test. No speech problems were noted and he complained of no health or social problems.

The results of the WISC indicated that Del has normal intelligence when compared to the norms for his age group. There was a notable discrepancy between verbal and performance areas of functioning, with a wide scatter among the various subtests. Verbal tests were in the normal range, except for his ability to deal conceptually with problems in a social context. On the performance tests, Picture Arrangement and Block Design were beyond one standard deviation above the mean, while the Coding test, which requires visual-motor responses, was below the mean by the same amount. This latter observation would coincide with the physician's report of visual-perceptual problems. The higher findings of concept development on the Peabody Test suggest by comparison with the Weschler Test results that Del is having difficulty in verbal problem solving and application. The visual-perceptual problems were markedly in evidence on the perceptual motor tests, Bender Test, and Draw-A-Person. Del's efforts here were grossly labored and slow. Eventually he is able to deal with the concepts involved but the process of completing the required tasks is impaired.

(Psychologist's signature)

CASE EVALUATIONS: ANALYSES AND SYNTHESES

The reader has now carefully reviewed the case materials of Del and completed the eleven questions in Chapter 3. As a responder-participant, the next step will be to learn about other responders and their approaches to the case. The reader's own perceptions, evaluations, and recommendations to the case should be very much in his thoughts during this review. The reader-responder should compare his strategies with those of other responders to assay their strengths and understand their professional perceptions. It is equally important to follow up this review with class discussion. The experience of publicly conceptualizing and discussing educational alternatives for a student closely simulates the real world of professional education and is significant for the reader's professional development. In education, professional services operate in the public domain and must constantly be evaluated in light of the social context and shifting values.

Information about Responders and Responders' Perceptions, with Authors' Comments

THE READING SPECIALIST. The reading specialist is a 28-year-old, advanced doctoral assistant in a college reading clinic to whom the reader was first introduced in the case of Geoff. The reader will recall that she has administrative and clinical responsibilities in the reading clinic and supervises practicum students in reading education. She also provides direct clinical services in diagnosis and evaluation of referred reading cases. Previously, she taught first grade in public school for two years, and worked as a remedial instructor and teacher consultant for another year. Her undergraduate training was in elementary education, and her doctoral emphasis is on curriculum and instruction. The reading specialist sees her main job role as "helping teachers learn to vary their teaching methods and materials to better meet the varying abilities and needs of students—to get the emphasis on reading to learn rather than learning to read." She is married and her husband is pursuing graduate work in English. In the future, she sees herself in an occupation that would combine university teaching (being a trainer of reading teachers) and active work in the public schools as a reading consultant.

The reading specialist began her evaluation of the Del case information by noting at the outset that the parents had a great deal of concern about their son's academic progress. The situation was seemingly compounded by a poor relationship that developed between the public school and the parents. She feels this occurred because of an apparent result of the parents' tendency to project blame for Del's reading failure on the third grade teacher. Evidently, the parents chose to place the responsibility for Del's reading difficulty on instructional processes, rather than on a possible intrapsychic or organic problem in their son. They defined the problem as external to the child, primarily existing in the teacher's methods of instruction and her perceived attitudes about the boy. The reading specialist began scrutinizing the information provided by professional personnel regarding Del's functioning from the broad perception of the parents' way of viewing the school condition. She pointed out that there is a diagnosis of a convulsive disorder or organic brain disturbance and medication had been prescribed to ameliorate the behavioral symptoms of the disorder. Associated with the neurological impairment is Del's visual-perceptual difficulties and apparent reading problems.

The reading specialist reports that three basic assumptions underlie her initial comments on the most significant aspects of the case. She feels the parents must be genuinely concerned about Del's reading problem. Her second assumption is that the report by the teacher of the parent-school relationship is accurate. The final comment is that the case information presented is both accurate and represents a thorough report of the significant aspects of the situation.

Within the educational setting, the reading specialist reports that the major problem has been defined as Del's reading difficulty. As she peruses the case information, she thinks that the "reading problem" may have been exacerbated *because* of the manner in which the third grade teacher dealt with the student. For example, she points out that the teacher required Del to stay in at recess to complete his reading assignments. Evidently, as a reading consultant, she does not view this as an appropriate procedure. This appears to be a case in which the reading specialist views the third grade teacher as planning strategies that did not adequately take into account the student's unique problems of acquiring reading skills in light of available information. The point is further clarified as she discusses other assumptions underlying her evaluation approaches.

In defining the educational problems as she did, the reading specialist notes at the outset that Del has made no clear-cut progress in reading as a result of the individual tutoring opportunities. She predicts that his lack of progress in reading will continue under these conditions. As a reading specialist, it is interesting to note that she expresses concern that Del will tend to resent individual instruction and extra tutorial help when it distracts him from involvement in other activities which may interest him and bring him more success. Judging by the numerous opportunities he has had for failure and frustration in learning reading skills, this might conceivably include almost any other age-related activity. The reading specialist also operates on the assumption that there is, in fact, a visual-perceptual learning problem and, as she previously stated, the parents are genuinely concerned about Del's academic difficulties. She maintains a high level of importance on family and affective considerations, as well as the learning disability itself.

The reading specialist defined the main problem in the educational setting as one of reading difficulty and makes a direct transition to the related problems question as an association with the organic brain disturbance. She believes that such a medical diagnosis could have a direct bearing on Del's reading problems as well as the visual perceptual problems. She notes that Del's vision difficulties could be influencing his reading achievement. Apparently, prescription glasses were not obtained until late in the third grade, and their corrective effect for the perceptual problems is not known. Her second, related problem point is that while the parents maintain much concern about their son's academic difficulties, they have a strong tendency to place the blame for his reading failure squarely on the school. This becomes a second major factor in the educational problem. The reading specialist raises a third point by noting the possibility that invidious comparisons may have been made by the parents among Del and his older brothers, thus creating an unsupportive and anxiety-producing condition in the family constellation.

Although there is little direct mention of Del's feelings in the report, the reading specialist suggests that it is quite probable that Del has learned to dislike reading because of the parents' anxiety about his low reading skills, the related school frustrations associated with reading such as being kept in at recess to finish his work, and the additional hours of special tutoring he has had to participate in. She thinks that Del has probably experienced a great deal of frustration in this process, since he cannot readily achieve in an activity deemed so important to everyone around him.

The reading consultant believes that Del's reading difficulty could and should be handled within the regular classroom. (At the time of the initial reading examination he was "interpreted" as reading approximately one year below his actual grade placement.) Since Del is reading this close to his actual grade placement, it would seem safe to assume that (1) he is making some progress in reading and (2) there are other children in the classroom who are reading at approximately the same level.

Recognizing Del's need for continued regular class placement is only the first of the procedures the reading specialist would recommend in educational planning to help Del in the area of reading and in the instructional process. Both the parents and teachers must stop designing punitive reading situations for Del. He must be recognized as a student with *specific* learning problems with an organic etiology. He should not be forced to give up recesses and other activities that are a normal part of the school program in order to finish his assigned work in reading. The individual reading tutoring program should also be discontinued, since there has been little or no progress as a result of these procedures. If Del is made to give up his free time in the afternoons with no favorable results, he is almost sure to look upon such instruction as punishment.

The main focus of the reading consultant's advice is that of creating a favorable learning atmosphere in the regular classroom for helping Del. If he is reading approximately one year below his actual grade placement, it is very probable that other students in the class are reading at the same level and could profit from many of the same instructional provisions which should be made for Del. In a general way, she makes a point of this by noting that materials at varying reading levels need to be provided for all children in class, since classes are ordinarily heterogeneous and students cannot be expected to be reading at the same level. Other materials than just fourth grade level basal readers need to be included among the classroom materials if basal readers are used for the major portion of reading instruction.

The reading specialist feels that Del's keen interest in science should be used as a springboard for teaching reading. The teacher should select science materials to show Del how he already is able to capitalize on the reading skills he does possess, rather than start from the position that he is unable to read such materials in isolation. This will provide him the important, added motivation necessary for acquiring additional reading skills. It might also be profitable to provide Del with specific training in visual perception in view of his reported visual, perceptual difficulties.

How would the reading specialist go about implementing her suggestions? She suggested that a conference be set up with the parents, the classroom teacher, the reading diagnostician, the psychologist, the reading coordinator, and/or the curriculum coordinator for the school. At the meeting, each person would present relevant information about Del's activities and the related reading problems. The function of the group would be to establish a mutually agreeable approach to educational planning and program implementation. Suggestions from the participants cannot be *imposed* on the teachers involved, especially those recommendations concerning classroom management. In the reading specialist's experience, it is unlikely that the suggestions will be implemented unless the teachers and the parents are active participants in the planning session.

The plans of the reading specialist for staffing and educational management are necessarily based on four assumptions. The first is that Del's parents would be willing to discontinue the individual tutoring. Parenthetically, she stated that it is possible the parents may feel that by providing such instruction they are absolving themselves from blame for Del's educational problems. As parents, they must provide a different type of family relationship experience for the son. Her second assumption is that the school must have facilities and programs for visual-perceptual training or be able to develop such alternatives. The learning disability problem must be defined as a school problem in the context of the educational program. The last two assumptions refer specifically to the educational program *in the classroom.* Here, she states that the teacher must be willing to make necessary adjustments in classroom procedures to encourage Del's active participation. The teacher must have available, or be able to obtain, reading materials at varying levels of difficulty for use in fourth grade classroom instruction. This is simply a basic requirement for adequate instruction to meet the needs of all the students in the teacher's room.

THE RESOURCE TEACHER FOR THE VISUALLY HANDICAPPED. The resource teacher is a forty-year-old graduate student in a counseling and guidance program, who has had 13 years of public school teaching experience at the high school level. She taught mathematics and vocal music, and worked one year as a part-time counselor. Her most recent position in education was that of resource person for the visually handicapped. She began graduate work in the area of the visually handicapped before transferring into the master's program in counselor education. She received her bachelor's degree from a western university with a study emphasis in music education for the first two years. During the latter part of her program, she shifted to a distributive major in education with an emphasis in mathematics and history. She expects to complete her master's degree at the end of the current academic year and obtain a position in secondary guidance. Her occupational goals are to continue her role as a housewife and to be employed as a school counselor. Her husband is a university professor and they have twin children, eight years of age. She has taken graduate work at four universities.

The resource teacher began her evaluation of the case materials by first making a clear statement regarding her opinion of the most significant aspect of the case:

Del obviously does have a reading problem and most everyone is aware of it. As yet, neither the parents nor the school have been able to help him with the reading difficulties.

The concern of the parents is also a significant aspect of the case. Although they are well intended, apparently the parents are pushing Del too hard, thus aggravating the situation. She indicates that there were conflicting data in the case report, but she assumed in defining the problems this way that the test information was valid. In order to proceed with her analysis, then, the resource teacher operates on the premises that Del really does have dyslexia, is of normal intelligence, and has no other perceptual problems. She assumes that one or the other of the teacher's evaluations of Del's peer problem relationships is incorrect, since they are discrepant in their interpretation of his social functioning.

Two points in relating the main problems to the school setting are emphasized by the resource teacher. Her first observation is that the parents' *feelings* toward the public school appear to have had a definite bearing on the educational planning and Del's situation in the classroom. There is a conflict of opinion on how well the third grade teacher handled the situation (Del's reading failure), but the resource teacher points out that at least the teacher referred the boy for special education planning. In retrospect, it appears that both the student and his parents were happier when he was attending the parochial school: no crises, no problem.

For her second point, the resource teacher is unable to understand what was done with the results of the various evaluations, since the teachers appeared to interpret the test findings to fit their own preconceived notions of the case. There was little evidence of any recommendations being made as the result of these procedures. She assumes that no follow-up procedures were initiated by the consulting personnel because in only one instance was there a reference to new specific plans. Evidently, communication between the two schools was poor.

The resource teacher is "rather curious as to the reason the two different teachers perceived Del's relationships with his peers so differently. Although the first teacher indicated she liked the boy, there apparently was some very bad feeling on his side."

Problem for Discussion:

1. How would the reader explain or reconcile the different ways the teachers either perceived Del's social behavior with his peers or the ways they reported Del's classroom behavior to the parents and educational consultants?

It may be surprising to find that the resource teacher "does not know anything about dyslexia." She assumes that some suggestions could be made to help Del overcome or at least ameliorate the effects of the reading handicap, in addition to the use of medication. She questions if the medical approach has anything to offer.

The reader may find it alarming that a resource person for the visually handicapped would be so unknowledgeable about reading problems and remediation. But such is the case, for the resource teacher states that she would "feel very frustrated," since she knows nothing about reading disorders and so much testing had been done without concrete recommendations being offered. A lot of valuable student and staff time has been wasted in the administration of tests because the results were not used for any purpose. Also, Del would probably experience a great deal of frustration in his predicament because of being pushed by his parents and not helped in the school program. "It rather sounds as if he is acquiring bad eating habits and perhaps not getting the proper diet or enough exercise."

The resource teacher offers three suggestions for improving the school program for Del. She thinks it might have been helpful if a school counselor had been available to observe the first teacher, in an effort to determine the validity of the teacher's negative comments about Del.

Problem for Discussion:

2. Is the resource teacher suggesting that early intervention in the teacher-student dyad might have had a facilitating effect on Del's reading and overall educational development?

The resource teacher would have wanted specific recommendations made after the first series of reading tests were administered. She believes that the whole area of specific remedial procedures was left too vague. Once the diagnosis of dyslexia was made, the special education program should have had a staff consultant trained in reading disabilities who would have assisted the student in his reading development and the teacher in developing remedial procedures. If no resource person were available an effort should have been made to find out the best possible methods for helping Del. These recommendations should have been placed in the cumulative folder so that continuity in training could have been established.

The next assumption made is that resource information could be used to help the student. The resource teacher does not indicate what procedures should be utilized to insure that the student receive the necessary help, of course, since there is still uncertainty about what might be the best procedures to initiate at this point. In addition, all aspects of the student's school program must be considered, so that planning can be on an integrated basis. The parents must be involved in the planning and make an effort to relieve some of the pressure they are placing on their son.

One of the surprising aspects of the resource teacher's evaluation is that as a resource teacher for the visually handicapped she offers virtually nothing in terms of procedures which might assist the student and teacher in the areas of visual-perception and reading training. It may be that as a resource person for the visually impaired, she does not view the student as having visual problems per se. She may make a clear discrimination between problems on a visual level (sensory level) and problems on a perceptual level (cortex problems). As a visual resource teacher, she would seem to have little to offer in this case in the way of remedial assistance, consultation, or training. As a consulting student personnel specialist, she raises many important questions about the kind of planning that needed to be established. It might be of interest to know how the resource teacher would define her job responsibilities in the school program as she analyzed the case of Del. Is it at least remotely possible that the occurrence of dyslexic students has been infrequent in her experiences at the secondary level? What usually becomes of dyslexic elementary students as they struggle through the educational process?

THE ENGLISH TEACHER.   The English teacher is a 46-year-old doctoral candidate with a major in English education and a minor in philosophy. Her program emphasizes training nonnative speakers of English. She eventually hopes to have a position in which she will train teachers, who in turn will have responsibilities similar to those she has undertaken. She has a published text in this field emphasizing comprehension, critical analysis, literature, and creative writing. Previously, she was employed for 13 years as an administrative assistant to a university president; prior to that, during World War II, she was in the armed forces.

In reviewing her own personal history, the English teacher reported that she had "minor brain damage," diagnosed as dyspraxia, and she takes Dilantin medication on a regular basis as a control for a seizure pattern and disruptive psychological correlates. When she tires, she sometimes has minor articulatory problems. After reviewing the case of Del, she felt she was able to understand his frustrations and identify with his problems. In her own home, reading was neither discouraged nor encouraged. Reading materials were not readily available, and this was not a family pastime. She was 15 years old before she saw her first professional play, and family activities were confined to entertaining guests at formal and informal dinners. Although the English teacher was an honor student throughout her academic career, the available money was spent educating the male members of the family. This was felt to be expedient. At the present time, her husband is a university professor of English and drama, and their children are grown and married.

The English teacher began her evaluation of the case by reporting that the most significant aspect is Del's obvious awareness that he is some-how "different." Thus she thinks any urging and unusual challenges that increase the social pressures might very well prove frustrating and threatening to him. The sibling rivalry may also be another such perceived competitive factor. Dyslexia is an obvious source of frustration to him. Dilantin, which is an anticonvulsant, is a sedative that often results in innervation and interferes with coordination. This is more often the case when pressures and fatigue are contributing factors. The inconsistency of the parents' and teachers' reports reflects some lack of communication and/or ability to define and relate pertinent data honestly. In addition to organic problems, Del is obviously failing to cope with social requirements; intellectually he is capable of doing much better in this regard.

Another factor the English teacher comments on is the traumatic experience of a neurological examination. The fact that Del volunteered to the psychologist that he was taking medication suggests to her that he is aware of his "health peculiarities" and probably defines them as personal inadequacies. The English teacher sees all of these influences as threats. Del's mother, described as a dominant person, may also have inhibited his development of a sense of independence in activities and decision making—this may be the major factor involved in his difficulty in "problem solving."

Problem for Discussion:
3. Does the reader sense any relationship between the English teacher's personal background and the intensity and type of interpretation she has made of the case materials?

The assumptions made by the English teacher in her evaluation were:

1. The goals were valid in terms of Del's needs.
2. There might be unreported or undetected variables in Del's case.
3. He could develop skills and interests that others might develop.
4. He could be helped.
5. Those involved in the case study could use their energies and knowledge to assist Del.
6. His parents' observations would not necessarily be reliable.
7. The test data might not be "absolutely reliable."
8. The English teacher might fail in an attempt to assist him.

The English teacher indicated that all of the previous comments may contribute substantially to explaining Del's behavioral pattern in the educational setting. She notes specifically that he may have residual problems in sustaining a "normal" attention span and in dealing with small reading units with comparative adequacy. (Note his test scores on paragraph units, which suggest Del's lack of attention to, or awareness of, details in socially oriented subject matter.) She considers significant that Del's mathematical skills are his highest ones. She describes this type of work as nonsocial, independent, highly structured, and often unimaginative. Again, she relates the *specific kinds of educational problems* back to the broader range of associated information as interpreted by her in the preceding discussion. She thinks that *all* these influences affect his final pattern of behavior.

Problem for Discussion:
4. In terms of an educational evaluation, what advantages or disadvantages might there be in the strategies of analyzing and defining specific educational problems in terms of a broader range of related problems, as the English teacher has done?

On an affective level, the English teacher's reaction to the situation is to feel "extremely sympathetic." She sees that resultant social problems have become manifested as a symptom of Del's sense of frustration. He has lost rapport with those who represent authority, and his inclination is to be aggressive with peers who "often ignore him." The English teacher would not only refer him to a qualified counselor for help but would make every effort to help him feel accepted and to appreciate his own individuality. She would give him as many opportunities as possible for creative and imaginative expression. She would have Del do more work with story telling, improvision in preparation for reading, dramatic activities, and the reading of stories. It might help for his teacher to find ways of making him aware of the frustrations other students experience academically and/or socially. She hopes that after considerable reassurance, Del would respond to a nonthreatening environment and could develop a comfortable rapport with his teachers. He would probably respond sporadically with enthusiasm and manifest indifference or rebellion at times. Then the English teacher adds parenthetically that "I am not a professional psychologist and don't feel qualified to anticipate his responses." She hopes that if Del has opportunities for success he will respond positively.

Problem for Discussion:
 5. Noting for the moment that the English teacher is not a "professional psychologist," what are some of the characteristics indicated in her communications that might make her an outstanding teacher?

In implementing her suggestions, the English teacher would have open classroom discussions, emphasizing verbal activities and free individualized reading opportunities. She might use token rewards in some form as a means of implementing some of these activites. She feels that opportunities to tell stories read by one student but not necessarily by other students might afford some encouragement to Del inasmuch as he obviously seeks attention. This might be a way of giving him recognition on the basis of a constructive activity and might also stimulate his reading interests. Her assumptions here would be that Del's involvement with his class would be validly founded and that their work together could provide opportunities for mutual success and growth. This would minimize the probability of unfavorable outcomes. Planning time would be required so that the enhancement program could be established for the entire class. The new procedures would require the approval and cooperation of the involved people. The English teacher hopes that she would be capable of implementing new methods with or without any necessary assistance, as the case might be. She hopes that the Hawthorne effect would result.

It is apparent from her comments that the English teacher is placing a great deal of emphasis on individualized planning and working with the student to promote motivation for reading. It is interesting that this "nonpsychologist" teacher wishes to learn as much as she can about the student so that she can utilize this information in her teaching preparation. In addition, she would like to find out more about how Del feels about himself, his classmates, and adults. What kind of books does he enjoy? What latent interests can be cultivated? Games often reveal this information. For example, the English teacher would provide the following open-ended statements:

I went to the store and I wanted a book about_____.
He liked me because I_____.
I did not like him because he_____.
Better than anything else I like to_____.
Adults are always_____.

She would have the sentences completed as either an oral or written activity. Among the statements less specific questions could be interspersed: "My favorite fruit is_____," "It is fun to_____," and the like.

Problem for Discussion:
6. If the reader is not already aware of what the "Hawthorne effect" is, based on the English teacher's suggestions for educational planning, what might you surmise she is talking about in this reference?
7. Why does the English teacher assume that the learning process will be facilitated by more effectively socializing the learning experiences and by providing materials related to the student's interest?

THE ACADEMIC ADVISOR.   The academic advisor is a 31-year-old divorcee, whose ambition is to combine work as a guidance counselor with that of taking care of her two children. She hopes some day to remarry. She describes her background experience: a mother for eight years, three years work experience as a secretary to a men's physical education department, two years experience teaching general music on the elementary and high school levels, and substitute teaching at the junior high school for six months. She is now pursuing a master's degree in counselor education. As an academic advisor, she helps students complete their plans for graduation and directs them toward counseling, testing, and other areas of need. She received her bachelor's degree in 1960 and hopes to complete a master's degree and specialist's certificate before terminating her training program. As her main occupational role, the academic advisor feels she must help students academically and vocationally or must know where to refer them if they need further assistance. In many ways, this defines the job of guidance counselor in the public schools. She is also considering specializing in the area of school psychology.

In reviewing her personal background, the academic advisor reported that her father was a minister; when she was a child and a teenager, the family traveled with him a great deal. As a result, her attention was "always focused on people, their motivations, behavior, and relationships." She did not recognize this interest of hers as having vocational potentiality until she reached adulthood and was teaching. As a music teacher, she found that students readily came to her with their difficulties and that she was not well prepared to advise or counsel them. She feels that she would prefer doing this type of work compared to teaching music, so she is now pursuing her graduate program to "learn as much as possible."

The academic advisor's family has a history of suicidal tendencies; at least three have committed suicide in the last 10 years. This has motivated her to learn what can be done for people and/or children with emotional difficulties. Her failure to achieve satisfying parent-child relationships and a good marriage has further stimulated her reading in psychology. She has discovered through reading and working with her children that bad, unhappy relationships can be considerably improved through a knowledge of psychology and efforts to apply it in human relationships. She has also learned that it is considerably easier to learn about human behavior than it is to apply it. She herself has undergone psychiatric treatment.

The academic advisor began her evaluation of the case by pointing out that Del is losing ground academically, and this has been going on for a long time. He may have physical problems that account for the lack of academic development; also, the intense pressure by the second grade teacher for him to improve probably aggravated the situation. Del has maintained a prominent position in the family and, to a degree at school, by not progressing in reading. This situation would be reversed if he were suddenly to start showing adequate progress. *The academic advisor analyzes the case information by developing a theory that would account for Del's behavior as an attention-maintaining or attention-getting process.* To do this, she assumes the parents were reasonably accurate when they stated that the home relationships were good. The second grade teacher probably was frustrated at her own inability to cope with the situation, especially since she liked Del. Del was capable of continuing in the regular school activity even with the brain disorder; intellectually he is capable of learning more than he has actually accomplished. She also assumes that the tutors were competent teachers.

The academic advisor assumes Del is being "rewarded" with attention for school failure (failing to pay attention in reading) and for not taking the responsibility for his lack of work. Del felt more secure in a Catholic school, although parent dissatisfaction has been an aspect of the case throughout his school career. The school day may be too long for him, particularly with tutoring for his reading disability. His concentration span may be shorter than necessary for his class sessions because of his brain condition. In so defining the problem, the academic advisor again assumes that Del needs to be the center of attention and is using his failures as a means of obtaining it. Thus she feels that he is capable of progressing at a generally normal rate.

Del's lethargy in physical activity and his increased food consumption are interpreted as his way of "letting others live his life for him . . . letting go of his own active participation by saying: 'I give up—you do it for me.'" Her final assumption is that Del's failure in the public school setting was largely affected by his parents' unhappiness at the closing of the parochial school and his placement in the public school.

Problems for Discussion:
   8. Even if the academic advisor's interpretation of the data is not one you would agree with, what general advantage might accrue from conceptualizing the problem at a theoretical level? How would the reader explain her interpretation of the data, which accounts for Del's academic failure both on an organic and a psychosocial basis?
   9. If the latter is true, why did the parents refer Del for another evalua-

tion after he returned to parochial school in the fourth grade?

10. To what degree do the other stated assumptions reveal the focus of attention of the academic advisor, as a responder?

In her further evaluation, the academic advisor feels that Del's social aggressiveness is also a part of his need for attention. The poor child-parent relationships have evolved from his disappointing academic progress. The reader may wonder about the logic of these comments, since the academic advisor has strongly argued that the failures are reinforcing his attention-seeking habits. She further declares that Del has established an attitude of "not caring," which has made inroads into all areas of his life. Now, he will do virtually nothing to remedy this situation himself and he insists on letting others do it for him.

The academic advisor feels there definitely could be an improvement for Del in the school program if the physical condition is not the only cause of his problem. As a parent, she would feel frustrated with all this "professional help" with nothing more shown for accomplishment. She feels Del is on his way to continued failure; now, there is nothing *he* can do about it.

What alternatives or suggestions would the academic advisor make to improve Del's condition in the school setting? First of all, she would take pressure off of Del to read better. She would not remove all the attention he is getting, however, as he would then feel everyone had given up on him. She would have a discussion with Del to tell him that he must want to do his school work and that the primary responsibility for success lies with him. Other people can help, but he must be the main person responsible for his learning. Let him know frankly, not subtly, that he will be left alone until he wants help. The parents and teachers will stand by and be ready when he wants them. This would require patience on everyone's part because Del would not be at the center of attention.

The academic advisor must assume she is reasonably close to being right in order to implement her suggestions, and the parents and teachers in turn must accept her assumptions. The parents must be emotionally capable of accepting Del as he is and not as they want him to be. She also assumes that Del will wish to improve academically and socially because he is unhappy with his present situation.

Problem for Discussion:

11. Is not this assumption contrary to her interpretation that failure in reading has led to a rewarding state of affairs, since he has received so much attention for this nonadjustment pattern? Why would this condition also be interpreted as an unhappy situation for him?

If Del is to read better, eventually *he* must make the necessary efforts to accomplish this goal. He must accept his own responsibility for learning. The parents must take the pressure off Del and still give him an appropriate amount of attention. The academic advisor would discuss with the teacher how she can let Del "go his merry way" without pushing him. For instance, if he has not finished with his work, he may stay after class to finish it or take it home if he wishes. In either case, let him do as he wishes. When he does not choose to do it, it will be up to him to accomplish the task without supervision. Help him only if he asks for help. She would appreciate knowing more about the brain disorder. It is possible that he can learn to work around the difficulties if he knows what they are.

THE BEHAVIOR MODIFICATION SPECIALIST. The behavior specialist is a 24-year-old doctoral student majoring in educational psychology: human learning with an emphasis on the experimental analysis of behavior. His undergraduate study was in experimental psychology. He has had one year of half-time experience as a psychologist applying behavior modification procedures to retarded children and doing research in the area of behavior modification. Previously, he completed an internship, in which he supervised experience in various kinds of behavior modification programs. He perceives his current occupational role as that of producing changes in human behavior for more efficient learning, together with research closely related to practical problems. Professionally, he sees himself as a psychologist making contributions by virtue of his research, teaching, and writing. In reviewing his own background, the responder stated that he is from a family of two teachers and he is "generally dissatisfied with education, thinking that it should specify its goals and try to create enjoyable educational programs for all concerned."

The behavior specialist approaches the case information by initially noting that Del's reading is below normal and his parents are concerned about it. *He does not feel that Del's interest in reading has been sufficiently encouraged.* The approach that has been utilized has been primarily negative; for example, Del was kept in from recess to finish reading assignments and his interest in reading science material was discouraged, rather than encouraged and broadened. The many hours of tutoring in reading were probably quite a drudgery for both Del and the specialist. Since Del is somewhat behind in reading, the behavior specialist interprets this as possibly holding down Del's IQ and restricting his success in school. It seems that the school problem is not diminishing. The behavior specialist would tend to minimize the medical reports and would rather consider the problem in terms of poor learning conditions, aggravated by transfer from one school to another.

In approaching the case information as he did, the behavior modification specialist makes the assumption that Del could read better if provided an efficient learning environment, where mild punishments and frustrations in reading did not occur. He also assumes that Del is okay physically ("no wires missing"). He assumes that "Del's behavior can be modified by the environment."

Problems for Discussion:
12. In what ways might you defend the responder's comment that since Del is somewhat behind in reading, this may well be holding down his IQ?
13. How would the reader account for the behavior modification specialist's assumption that Del must be okay physically and at the same time wishing to minimize the medical reports?
14. What contributions, if any, does the reader feel the medical information might make to the educational evaluation and planning for the student?

In further developing his concept of the case, the behavior specialist indicates that Del has probably built up at least a strong dislike for reading and is undoubtedly very distraught but does not know what to do about it. He considers the school situation unfortunate but hardly hopeless. He explores several alternatives for educational planning. To begin with, the problem situations are mostly in the past—they cannot be "undone" at this point in time. Perhaps, at best, *we* might learn from our experience with Del to be more effective with other children. The second grade teacher probably expected too much of Del, while the reading specialist apparently never found a sufficient way to motivate him for remedial purposes. Maybe the parents should have been brought into the training program.

The behavior specialist would now suggest that all concerned persons (parents, teachers, and possibly Del's siblings) be asked to encourage any reading that Del does. He should be provided games, magazines, books, and other intrinsically interesting materials that he can enjoy and be successful in reading. Complaints to Del about his reading failure should be minimized. Whenever he succeeds in reading, whatever the level or content, he should receive praise and recognition. These activities are based on an assumption that parents and teachers are sufficiently able and motivated to implement them. The behavior specialist states he "would be motivated enough to prepare a meeting and follow-up for two planning sessions of three or four months." He would get the parents and teachers together and ask them for suggestions on how to motivate Del at school and at home. He would have the parents work directly and briefly with Del before supper with simple reading materials and reward him for completing his activities. Gradually, *carefully*, they would increase the difficulty level of the reading material, insuring Del all along that he can be successful in reading and begin to enjoy reading. As a consultant on the case, the responder would be responsible for maintaining follow-up procedures with the parents and teachers.

The behavior modification specialist has presented a model of behavioral change for the referred student that emphasizes positive motivational factors and the prescription of teacher and parents behavior toward the student. There are many similarities between these proposed plans for the student and those given by the previous responders in this chapter. *Note*: Before proceeding to the next case, quickly go back and review the previous three responders' comments to determine if their recommendations include those of the behavior modification specialist.

Problems for Discussion:
15. What additional procedures did the earlier responders include among their recommendations?
16. How are their approaches similar to those of the behavior specialist and for what reasons do they differ, especially when considering specific procedures of remediation?

THE ASPIRING SCHOOL PSYCHOLOGIST. The school psychologist is a second-year graduate student working in the specialist program to prepare for a school psychology internship in the state of Illinois. As an undergraduate, he studied a broad range of psychology courses, including experimental psychology, learning theory, motivation, personality, social psychology, physiology, industrial psychology and statistics. He is preparing for a professional career in education as a school psychologist and later hopes to continue his training in a doctoral program. At the university, he has had work experience as a laboratory assistant, maintaining rats with water and food, and completing some data analysis. During the summer, he worked as a waiter on a train; prior to that he had been a produce clerk for a year and one-half in a local supermarket. As a professional psychologist, he believes his future role will be multiple: participation in curriculum planning, diagnosis of learning problems, remediation of classroom behavior (reducing undesirable behavior as well as promoting or instigating desirable behavior), consultation with other staff members, the making of referrals, and so forth. He sees his main occupational goal as that of helping teachers use their talents more effectively in the teaching of students.

Reviewing his own personal background, the psychologist indicates that he comes from a family of five children, with four younger sisters and brothers. He has had many opportunities to observe their behavior in the family setting and to some degree in the school setting. He thinks this has provided him with information and experience that will enable him to look "objectively" at other children's behavior and to understand some of their motivations. His background in psychology has helped him to learn to raise important questions following the observance of behavior: why did it occur, what is maintaining the activity, and how might it be changed or strengthened? He is familiar with various psychological principles that supposedly endow him with the ability to make objective observations and to develop conclusions regarding behavior. He is not certain, however, just how valuable this background is at the present time.

As the aspiring school psychologist begins to evaluate the case information, he thinks that Del's reading difficulties in school and his visual-perceptual problems are the most significant aspects to the case. Different teachers have evaluated Del in different ways, which is confusing the issue, and the parents (especially the mother) are biased in their assessment of the school programs. The parents are seen as spoiling Del, which has hindered his development of self-confidence and independence. He sees Del's behavior and disrespect for authority as attempts to obtain more status.

The psychologist found the reading examination report to be very subjective and the self-assumed proficiency of the reading interpretation to be biased. He considers the neurologist's report unclear and thinks it could contain more information. It is necessary to assume the evaluators were competent and were honest in what they said, but he feels that both of these reports may be seriously questioned. Furthermore, he thinks that there must be additional and relevant information about the student which is not available or has not been reported.

Problems for Discussion:
17. What characteristics of the reading report is the school psychologist responding to as "very subjective"?
18. Differentiate between a subjective and an objective professional reporting.
19. Is there a slight overcriticalness in the aspiring school psychologist's evaluation?

The psychologist believes that there are several main problems in the educational settings. At the same grade level, the Catholic school appeared to be teaching at a lower instructional level than the public school. Therefore, a unique condition developed so that the parents were more satisfied with Del's performance in the parochial school and the problems did not become a major source of irritation until Del transferred to the public school. Also, the third grade teacher's use of punishment in the public school may have been more detrimental than helpful to Del. There are conflicting reports in the evaluations of Del's academic skills. Sometimes he performs well on tests and at other times his performance is below par. There are conflicting views regarding his capacity to interact with his peers. In making the evaluations specific to the educational setting, the aspiring school psychologist operated on the assumption that he did indeed know something about student behavior and mannerisms, and that he is somewhat qualified to define the problems in the manner indicated. He hoped there was sufficient information available for him to define the problems accurately, but he again qualified the statement by indicating uncertainty about this.

The psychologist points out that the parents are not actually able to help improve Del's performance in the school setting, although they are trying to help him as best they can. Unfortunately, they are viewed as hindering his development, along with other factors operating on Del that could be causually related to his low reading performance. The parents spoil him, which not only discourages his development of independence but fosters aggressive behavior and disrespect for authority. In addition, Del does not get along well with his peers, and the schools themselves have been inconsistent in their expectations. Apparently, Del does "well" at the Catholic school but then has been required to work harder at the public school. This is an educational activity he is not used to doing so that his grades suffer, his parents become worried, and even the pupil-personnel specialists evaluate him differently.

How is Del likely to feel about this situation? The psychologist would expect to find the student's feelings ranging from frustration, anxiety, and anger to outright despondency. Del seems to be "lacking proper motivation," except in science, as one of the teachers pointed out. It is now necessary for all those concerned to make an honest, sincere effort to present as clear and true a picture of Del's problems as possible. Not only does Del need help in his school work, per se, but also in his relations with pupils in the usual school routine. *Comment:* The psychologist views the conflicting teacher reports from the different schools as both failing to place Del in an appropriate educational perspective. He also interprets these reports as reflecting different curriculum standards between schools, particularly with regard to expectations for student achievement.

Problems for Discussion:

20. Is it possible that the referring teachers did, in fact, genuinely view Del differently from each other in their respective school settings?
21. Does the reader have the impression teacher information may have been biased in some manner due to the nature of the school-parent relationship?
22. What would Del's condition have been in the third grade if the public

school teacher had decided to give him passing grades rather than create an educational confrontation with the parents?

What did the psychologist recommend for Del's educational planning, given the available alternatives? To begin with, all concerned individuals should get together and pool their information in an effort to reassess what has transpired and to arrive at a worthwhile synthesis of the cumulative student information. The parents need to understand that they have been spoiling Del and should attempt to make some changes in their approach in order to facilitate changes in Del. Furthermore, he recommends the possible need for more extensive testing, and perhaps retesting. Evidently, the responder is not comfortable with the conflicts among the current reports. The psychologists may give Del additional tests; there also needs to be a more thorough evaluation of the home setting. It is important to talk over Del's situation with the parents and try to get them to provide an atmosphere at home that will encourage Del to become more self-sufficient. To implement his recommendations, the psychologist reiterates that his recommendations are as expert as those of other concerned parties.

Problem for Discussion:
23. Does the parental spoiling interpretation of the case offer a substantial theoretical leap from that proposed in the academic advisor's attention-getting explanation or the behavior modification specialist's unrewarding-environment position?

THE GUIDANCE COUNSELOR.   The guidance counselor is a doctoral student in counselor education with seven years of professional experience in education. Previously, he taught English at the junior high school level and was a counselor at a youth project. He served three years as a high school guidance counselor with job responsibilities of personal counseling, vocational and educational guidance, and group testing. At the present time, he is a teaching graduate assistant at the university and has delegated responsibilities on a funded research project. His academic background includes a bachelor's degree with a double major in English and speech, and a master's degree earned three years later with the support of an NDEA fellowship. He views his main occupational role as that of teaching and research, with the emphasis on teaching school counselors and participating in research related to counselor education. In five years, he sees himself mainly doing reading, writing, and fishing. Teaching and counseling will be continued on a need basis. The counselor comments, "One piece of information about myself may be of help to you in interpreting my responses. When I feel short of time, and especially when the task is a bit laborious, I will not give as complete thought as I should before writing my response."

Problem for Discussion:
24. Is it possible such a communication offers a rationalization not only for vagueness in a case evaluation, but also provides an excuse for errors in judgment and prejudicial interpretations?

In his review of the case, the counselor points out six areas that are significant in his evaluation of the information on Del. The medical diagnosis of "organic brain disturbance" was apparently substantiated by psychological testing. In combination, the strong parental concern and the punishing efforts of the third grade teacher were accompanied by a decline in Del's reading at grade placement. Apparently, Del's ability to read science material is superior to that of other content areas. The counselor educator feels the parents have a biased attitude about parochial versus public school education, much favoring the former system. He interprets Del's declining interest in nonacademic areas as indicating a withdrawal-from-challenge pattern with implications of further potential for failure. Additionally, he notes inconsistencies among the teachers' reports, and between the parent and teacher reports with reference to Del's relationships with his peers.

Problems for Discussion:
25. Would the reader interpret the parents' concern for Del's reading problems as a cause of the reading problems or as a consequence of their awareness of the reading problems?
26. Did the third grade teacher "punish" Del for not reading at grade level by giving him individual help and attention?
27. Were her efforts to help Del at recess a cause of the reading failure or indicative of the reading failure?

The counselor's assumptions closely parallel his analysis of the significant aspects of the case. Thus he concludes that the following test results and reports must be considered accurate and valid: medical findings, reading tests, and psychological findings. Reports of the parents and teachers must be considered "somewhat" valid. Classroom grades probably reflect with some degree of accuracy Del's actual reading ability and performance level in the classroom.

In the process of defining the main problems within the educational setting, the counselor again emphasizes the improper action of the third grade teacher in keeping Del in for recess to work on reading. She may not have handled him appropriately, although he thinks that not enough information is given to say for sure. He notes that the reading teacher was unable to help Del improve his reading performance and the school may not be exploiting Del's interest in science to the fullest extent. While reiterating earlier assumptions, the counselor hopes that he possesses some ability in making student personnel judgments. The final assumption is that Del shares the counselor's perception of what the problems are and he notes that is "*some* assumption!" One cannot say how Del feels about this situation without talking with him, and even then the counselor might not know how he feels. Del might feel like a failure because of the assigned label of "poor reader" or, on the contrary, he may be quite pleased at all of the attention he is receiving as a result of the reading handicap. His relationship with his peers may disappoint him or he may be quite pleased, depending on the referenced situation.

It is not surprising to find that one of the counselor's recommendations is to have either a psychologist or counselor establish a personal relationship with Del to assess the nature and intensity of his feelings and to help him cope with them more effectively. Furthermore, he would inform Del's teachers of the unique aspects of the case and encourage them to be patient, supportive, and reinforcing of reading performance "and other areas as well, of course." The reading teacher may again try to help Del with some new techniques, in light of the medical report. Both the classroom and the reading teachers may wish to capitalize on Del's interest in science when selecting reading materials. The counselor educator would try to implement his suggestions by asking for a case conference of interested teachers, administrators, counselors, psychologists, and nurses. He would help clarify the available student information and help the professional faculty to establish feasible objectives. Program methodology would be formulated and further suggestions requested. He would ask the school administration to supervise the program.

What assumptions must the counselor make to have his recommendations successfully implemented? First, the teachers must be sensitive and professional enough to understand the child and his problems. Second, they must be capable of feeling and manifesting those kinds of behavior necessary to communicate patience, support, and reinforcement. Third, the reading teacher must possess the skills, techniques, and flexibility necessary to implement a new reading program that will help Del. Finally, he feels that the psychologist-counselor must be capable of establishing a proper relationship with Del to assess the student's feelings and provide personal help. The only additional information requested would be to know more about the organic brain damage and how to help such handicapped students.

Problems for Discussion:

28. Describe the model of counselor-educator suggested by the guidance counselor's approach to the case and his recommendations for educational planning.
29. What do you see as the contributions of the counselor to this case and what are his expectations of other school personnel?

EPILOGUE

After the reading and psychological evaluations were completed, a conference was held with the parents, and later with school personnel to discuss recommendations. These recommendations were summarized in a report, a portion of which is included verbatim as follows:

The findings of the psychological examination were discussed with the parents. As was noted earlier, they are quite upset with the educational problems their son is having and tend to project the blame for his reading failure on the third grade teacher. Several considerations should be made in planning for Del's educational program during the next several years.

First, he is making some progress in reading but he will be handicapped in the usual classroom situation because of visual motor impairment.

Second, the potential effects of medication have not as yet had the opportunity to establish their worth in terms of the educational setting. The medication may help Del in this regard.

Third, Del is eligible for educational planning and consultation with the special education district. He is suitable for placement or educational planning in the program for children with neurological impairment. A joint conference should be established between the parochial school and the special education district to develop suitable plans for Del within the two district programs.

Fourth, Del may well benefit from specific visual perceptual training. The earlier program was attended to only abortively, according to the parents' report.

Fifth, the examiner agrees with the parents about their concern for having Del being involved in a tutoring program an hour each evening after school. The problem needs to be defined as an educational problem in the school setting. After school Del should have and needs to have the same opportunity for play and social activities as other children his age.

An extensive program of remedial reading instruction was provided the classroom teacher by the reading diagnostician, and copies of the psychological and reading reports were made available to the special education district, the parochial school, and the consulting neurologist. The reader will recall the resource teacher's grave concern over the lack of specific recommendations as presented in the case materials. A verbatim report of the recommendations by the reading consultant completes the case information on Del.

Results of the reading tests given indicate a difference of approximately one year between Del's average achievement in reading and his estimated capacity to read, which is his present grade placement (3.8). His chief difficulty seems to be in the area of word identification and word attack skills. He should begin with instructional materials on a middle second grade level and progress to more advanced materials as he learns the necessary skills.

Del should have instruction in the following areas:

1. *Sight Vocabulary:* The Dolch words that Del does not know should be presented frequently in a variety of situations. He might be given each word on a separate card and permitted to write the word on the back of the card after he has called it correctly. The words should be used in experience stories and in meaningful sentences. It is important to note that the 17 words he does not know are *sight* words and should not be attacked with phonetic analysis skills. He might also be placed in a situation with another child who does not know some of the other sight words. They might work with the same stack of sight word cards and compete in calling the most words correctly, each building a stack of cards with the words he knows.

Scott Foresman *Linguistic Blocks* would furnish further guided practice in word recognition in a challenging setting that would provide repetition of words in context of a meaningful sentence.

A picture dictionary, such as is suggested in the last section of this report, might help Del to learn other words by sight. In fact, several might be put at his disposal so that he might read and write more independently.

He might also use supplementary basal readers such as *All Through the Year,* level 2 (Harper & Row). It contains self-help sections such as "Let the Sound Help You," "Let the Sentences Help You," and "Words You Can Get Yourself."

2. *Word Attack Skills:* Consonants *v* and *w* and the consonant blends *gr, sw,* and *cr* should be presented in familiar words. Other words should be written and the consonant or blend to be learned should be underlined. Substituting a blend for a single consonant sound may help the child learn it, e.g., *l*ow, *gr*ow, and *cr*ow; *d*ay, *sw*ay. As these skills are mastered, Del should receive instruction in the other phonic areas such as the final *e* rule. Emphasis should be placed on the application of these skills in actual reading situations.

If *Word Games* of SRA's Reading Laboratory Series is available, it should be used independently with Del. The first four games would provide a review and would reinforce his knowledge of the letters. At the same time, he would be learning how to play the games so that he could work more independently while learning the subsequent phonetic and structural elements.

Linguistic Blocks are geared to be helpful here, too, and several workbooks are good for learning in this area.

3. *Silent Reading:* Independent silent reading should be fostered by supplying easy-to-read books on a variety of topics. Worksheets containing detailed directions should be supplied, but a limited time for carrying out the directions should be allowed. The teacher might hold up flash cards which give simple directions for brief tasks requiring physical activity, such as "Sit down," "Stand up," "Draw a ball," or "Look out the window."

From time to time, other literary areas, such as easy to read children's magazines, should be introduced by his teacher or by the librarian. Since much vocalization was observed, Del should be taught to "think the words." One of the techniques often successful is to have the child read silently while placing his fingers on his lips.

4. *Oral Reading:* Some help should be given by the reading teacher in oral reading to strengthen and reinforce Del's word recognition techniques as well as

his sight vocabulary. Oral reading, however, should always be preceded by an opportunity to read the material silently. Del should always be given a purpose for reading, such as to answer questions, express feeling, or "be another person."

5. *Leisure Reading:* Del must be allowed to read books of his own choosing that are written on his independent reading level (between 1.0 and 2.0). It would be well to allow him to purchase a book he has read and likes so that he might start a personal library. From time to time, other literary areas, such as easy-to-read magazines, should be introduced by his teacher or the librarian. Suggestions of some of these are listed in the next section of this report.

Suggested Books for Del

All Through the Year. (To be used as a supplementary reader.) New York: Harper & Row, Publishers, 1966.
Childrens Activities (periodical), Child Training Association Chicago.
Dolch First Reading Books: *Once There Was a Monkey; Once There Was a Dog; Big, Bigger, Biggest; Dog Pals;* and *Tommy's Pets;* Champaign, Ill.: Garrard Publishing Co.
ELKIN, BENJAMIN. *The Big Jump and Other Stories.* Chicago: Follett Publishing Company, 1958.
FLACK, MAJORIE. *Angus and the Ducks, Angus Lost,* and *Angus and the Cat.* New York: Doubleday & Company, Inc., 1962.
Jack and Jill (periodical), The Curtis Publishing Company. Philadelphia.
PALMER, HELEN. *Do You Know What I'm Going to Do Next Saturday?* Indianapolis: Bobbs-Merrill Co., Inc., 1964.
Playmates (periodical), A. R. Mueller, Cleveland, Ohio.
REED, HALE C., and CRANE, HELEN W. *My Picture Dictionary.* Boston: Ginn and Co., 1963.
ROSSNER, JUDITH. *What Kind of Feet Does a Bear Have?* Indianapolis: The Bobbs-Merrill Company, Inc., 1963.
Story Parade (periodical), Story Parade, Inc., New York, N.Y.
TRESSELY, ALVIN. *Rain Drops Splash.* New York: Lathrop, Lee and Shepherd Co., 1946.
Very First Words, A Picture Dictionary (A dictionary of words and sentences to help the child read and write independently). New York: Holt, Rinehart and Winston, Inc., 1966.

Suggested Teacher Materials

BOND, GUY, and WAGNER, EVA. *Teaching the Child to Read.* New York: Macmillan Company, 1960, pp. 185–200. (Developing word recognition.)
BOTEL, MORTON. *How to Teach Reading.* Chicago: Follett Publishing Company, 1962, pp. 49, 51. ("Order of Teaching Consonant Sounds and Blending".)
Consonant Lotto, Garrard Press, Champaign, Ill.
Eye and Ear Fun, Book 1, Webster Division, McGraw-Hill Book Company, New York, N.Y., 1946.
WILLIAM S. GRAY. *On Their Own in Reading.* Glenview, Ill.: Scott, Foresman and Company, 1960, pp. 14–23. ("What Is Involved in Word Perception?" Also Chap. 4. "Word Analysis at the First Stage of Progress.")
HEILMAN, ARTHUR. *Teaching Reading.* Columbus, Ohio: Charles E. Merrill, Inc., 1961, Chap. 6.
Linguistic Block Series, First Reader Level, Scott, Foresman and Company, Glenview, Ill.

Sounds We Use, Benton Publishing Co., Fowler, Ind.
TINKER, MILES, and MCCOLLOUGH, CONSTANCE, *Teaching Elementary Reading*. Appleton Century Crofts, Inc., 1962, (Chap. 21, "Recommended Practices in Second Grade," (contains suggestions for developing silent reading skills.)
Word Games, Reading Laboratory I, Chicago, Ill.: Science Research Associates, 1962.

CASE NO. 4 Sally
(Grades K through 1)

CASE STUDY MATERIALS ABOUT SALLY

Sally's mother had few complaints about her daughter's adjustment pattern at home before entering school. However, the separation was difficult for Sally, and as she is now scheduled to enroll in an integrated enrichment class, the mother seeks consultation with school personnel.

Sally is a first grade Negro child who came to the attention of the school counselor when her mother expressed serious concern about the child's general development. The following information was obtained in the process of the school's involvement in the case.

School Report (Completed by the Classroom Teacher, February 1969)

Sally entered kindergarten, September 1967, and has progressed to the first grade without incident.

Academic adjustment:

Does above average work in all subjects.

Attendance record. Good.

Special academic interests. Does excellent written work.

Classroom participation. Does not volunteer.

Testing program:

Kuhlmann Anderson Test: Jan. 20, 1969. First grade IQ-115

What is the relationship between the school and this child's parents? Good.

Teacher signature
February 1969

Parent Information Report (Completed during February 1969)

Why is this child being referred for an evaluation? Describe what problems are present at home, at school, in the community. Personality problem? Described as shy by people not knowing her well. After being around her for a period of time, it is agreed she is not shy. What is the word to describe her? One expression I hear often is "she lives in a world of her own." Always reticent at school or around groups of people. Alternately quiet or friendly and with adults she has always known. At home *sometimes* aggressive or demanding. On the whole—well behaved. I sometimes wonder about her hearing.

When did the problems described above first begin? She has always been this way.

Has the child ever been examined or received treatment for this problem before? No.

Home and family history:

Sally lives with her natural parents and two older siblings, a nine-year-old brother and a thirteen-year-old sister. Her parents are in their late forties. The father has an eighth grade education and is employed as a lathe operator. The mother completed high school and is employed as a salesclerk. Family and social contacts are described as "few—Sunday school and friends in occasionally."

Family's religious affiliation: Methodist.

Is this child sociable or does he prefer to be alone? Likes to be alone at times; sociable with one person at a time.

How does this child get along with: Mother: Good. *Father:* Good. *Brothers and sisters:* Good.

How does this child behave in adult company? Sometimes friendly and at times she has to whisper everything to me.

How does this child get along with friends his own age? With one or two fairly well—if well acquainted. In a group—not at all.

With whom does this child prefer to be? Black children in the neighborhood or her sister.

Developmental history:

No special problems were reported except "controlling bladder—has been going to the doctor and taking medicine for about four years."

Interests and activities:

What are this child's main interests? Likes books extremely well, reading and writing.

What recreational activities are enjoyed most? Rides bike a lot and enjoys swimming.

Are there work responsibilities? Very little. *What kind?* Picking her own things up.

Attitude toward work: Very slow.

Parent signature
February 1969

Medical Report (by Family Physician)

The medical report revealed no problems except a "history of enuresis and problems emotional in nature."

Physician signature
January 1969

Counselor Interview of Mother (April 1969)

Sally's mother came alone to the parental interview. She was an older, mature appearing Negro woman who was attractively and conservatively dressed. During the interview, she appeared to be frustrated and perplexed, since she could not describe her daughter's difficulty and could not understand why her daughter would have problems. Her husband was not mentioned until this interviewer inquired as to his feelings about Sally. Her reply was that her husband was too permissive with their children, but that he did not agree with this accusation.

After much discussion, one point seemed to reoccur over and over and that was: "Sally doesn't associate with kids at school. What will happen if this situation gets worse?" The mother had received feedback from other parents that the school was concerned about Sally. When she inquired at school she found that the physical education teacher was concerned about Sally because she would often refuse to participate in class activities. However, she was doing quite well in all other classes and was considered one of the best Negro first graders, so the school personnel were not overly alarmed about her lack of participation. The mother indicated to this interviewer that this was not unusual for Sally because she is stubborn and will not do what she does not want to do. The mother said that even during her dancing lessons she occasionally would refuse to participate.

Sally is described by her mother as a child who will not mix in groups; a child who is shy with her peers, but not with adults; a child who wants to do what she can well; a child who is quiet, but capable of temper tantrums; and a very bright child.

Even though Sally wants to do things like washing dishes or crossing the alley to see the only kids her age in the neighborhood, the mother had felt that she is not old enough and has restricted her on these matters. Recently, the mother has allowed Sally to cross the alley to visit these girls. She feels that Sally lets these girls take advantage of her, but the mother admits that Sally has been happier since playing with them.

Sally will be going to a different school this fall for the second grade as she was chosen to be in a special enrichment class. She will be taking a school bus and there will be integration at this school. The mother was concerned about both of these matters but was hoping that Sally would develop some effective peer relationships in this new environment.

Psychologist's Report (Testing, April 1969)

Wechsler Intelligence Scale for Children
    Verbal IQ 81 (see discussion)

Peabody Picture Vocabulary Test
    Chronological Age   7 years 6 months
    Mental Age   6 years 2 months
    Intelligence Quotient   91

Wide Range Achievement Test
    Reading Grade Equivalent   2.6

Thematic Apperception Test (selected cards)

Vineland Social Maturity Scale
    Age equivalent   5 years 6 months

Test Results and Observations:

Sally was a 7 year, 6 month old Negro child who would be described as rather pleasant and cooperative during the examination. She was responsive to inquiries and alert, and commented freely to the examiner about playmates and activities. Speech was spontaneous and sentence structure sufficiently complex for her age. No affective disturbances were noted.

The results of the testing indicated an apparent deficiency in problem analysis, problem solving, and coping with novel problems. Thus her intellectual function was borderline, which would appear to be representative of her functional level in comparable situations. Applications were poor. Sally would get tense, and look rather helplessly to the examiner to solve the problem. She looked to friends and her mother to deal with problems she was faced with on projective testing. Many responses were personalized, suggesting considerable immaturity.

She was seen as an overly dependent child who could not cope with novel situations. She would not attempt activities that could possibly make her look wrong or bad.

CASE EVALUATIONS: CASE ANALYSIS AND SYNTHESIS

The case of Sally differs from the previous studies in that earlier responders had the opportunity to review the student information under two conditions. The case information was presented to 24 responders clearly indicating that Sally was a black child, as shown in the preceding case information. About a half dozen statements were included in the report to communicate Sally's race: "Sally is a first grade Negro child . . ." "With whom does this child prefer to be? Black children in the neighborhood or her sister . . ." "The mother is an older Negro woman . . ." "Sally was a seven year, six month-old Negro child . . ." "However, she was doing well in all other classes and was considered one of the best Negro first graders . . ." Thus half the subject responders evaluated a protocol of a referred Negro child. The remaining 24 responders were given the case information with all references to racial characteristics and skin color deleted. The question being posed at this point is: What significance, if any, does information about racial background have to do with a responder's evaluation of the case?

The starting point for the reader is to go back and assay his own evaluation of the student information. Were racial references included in the review and planning of the case? If so, on what basis were these interpretations made? How significant or nonsignificant is this information on an individual student basis? Rather than presume the answers to these inquiries, the questions were posed by having a variety of professional people in education and educational training programs complete their analysis of Sally's case materials without comparative knowledge. Some responders were simply informed that she was a black child and others that she was a child with no color reference, presumably nonblack.

There are clearly instances in educational settings in which skin color is an important although superficial factor, since variation in skin color is just one of the differentiated characteristics of the people of the world. For example, in one school building there are no black students, in another no white students; the black students eat their lunch at a separate table in the lunchroom; proportionately more black students leave school prior to graduation, and so forth. These observations imply segregation and discrimination, and present a social-cultural problem in the school setting.

On the other hand, are there instances in which color is considered a significant factor because it represents a stereotyping or a biased opinion of the responder? Does a beautiful black Sally differ from a beautiful white Sally in terms of individual educational evaluation and planning? Did the responder incorporate race reference and skin color as significant educational variables in his evaluation of the case materials and his recommendations for educational and/or family planning? What assumptions were made, either including or excluding this information?

Responder evaluations to the case information on Sally are presented in the following sections to amplify these questions. The reader should decide after each numbered statement whether the comment was taken from the protocol of a responder who thought Sally was black or white. The third estimate of these criteria is "not discernable." A protocol chart may be set up as follows:

Case information protocols	Black	No color reference	Not discernible

Other subject responder data will be included when the additional information will add meaningfully to the reported comments. Consideration was made of the skin color of the responder when the authors initially perused the 48 protocols utilized as source material for this chapter. This proved to be of little value, since evaluative comments were unrelated to the color variable among the responders themselves. Therefore, no attempt has been made to apprise the reader of this contingency.

Responders' Perceptions and Recommendations

A. *From the available information, what in your opinion are the most significant aspects of the case?*

1. The overprotective nature of the mother to Sally's problems with other children.
2. The existence of enuresis points to an emotional problem, yet the teachers found little classroom difficulty except in physical education.

3. Sally's dependency on her parents and on her teachers for approval of certain of her behaviors. Her lack of ability to cope with novel situations is probably a function of this dependency.

4. She is the youngest of three children and of older parents. Sally does not interact well with peers (adult-oriented). She prefers other black children or her sister. The father is permissive.

5. The haphazard way this particular case is being handled by all those concerned with the welfare of Sally. The medical report indicated no problems; however, there is no indication of a metabolic or hearing examination having taken place.

6. Dependency and lack of problem-solving abilities are very much related to her difficulties in dealing with groups. Intelligence quotient discrepancy indicates something.

7. The distinct possibility of a worsening situation. Overanxiety on the part of the mother has apparently been transferred to the child. The proposed change to another school, with the additional factor of integration, would indicate a possible increase in anxiety on the part of the child.

8. The mother seems to be more concerned about what other people think of her child; this attitude seems to be developing in Sally, since she seems to need the support of others in order to do anything. The teacher seemed to express the attitude "as long as she doesn't interfere with the way I want the classroom run, she is a good kid." There seems to be little communication between the mother and father.

9. Her mother is strict with her and her father is permissive. The difference in child rearing could cause stress to the child. Her social development is apparently below her chronological age by two full years and her mental age is also behind her chronological age.

10. Why did the mother learn of the teacher's concern through the neighbors? Why didn't the teacher contact the mother and/or a guidance counselor? Why did the parents not resolve the problem on discipline at an earlier date? Also, why did Sally do above average work in school, yet show so poorly on tests given by the psychologist?

Child-rearing practices and Sally's dependency problems are the most frequently cited aspects of the case materials that are deemed significant by the responders.

Problems for Discussion:
  1. Is there any likelihood that these phenomena have a relationship to our concepts of black-white cultural patterns?

B. What, if any, do you perceive as the main problems in the educational setting?

1. Sally's teachers have not socially rewarded approximations, on Sally's part, to adequate social skills when she is interacting with other children on a personal and a group basis. A twenty-four year old Laotian doctoral student who was trained in the French system of education notes that one minor problem in the school is that a Negro neighborhood may not be a very healthy environment for learning

experiences . . . The school does not do all that it can to help pupils before any problem develops.

2. Sally has been placed in an enrichment class in a different school at this time.

3. There seems to be a concern about the child as a Negro, which seems odd. I think a more complete file would help, particularly if it contained anecdotal records. There might be a possible lack of concern for individual differences on the physical education teacher's part with no concerted effort to bring Sally out.

4. There is a lack of communication in the classroom. Sally knows the answers, since she does above average work, but she does not give verbal answers voluntarily.

5. Though Sally's reading ability is good, basic and mature social skills must be developed also.

6. The educational setting provides reinforcement for Sally's academic behaviors *and* for her dependency on clearly defined situations. The educational setting (in general) doesn't reinforce responding to novel situations.

7. Since Sally does not engage in disruptive behavior, her teachers are prone to "leave well enough alone." Her lack of participation in group events is accepted, since this doesn't create a discipline problem. Unfortunately, far too often, "rote" behavior is encouraged by teachers as opposed to creative behavior . . . Sally has learned to follow instructions in a well-defined classroom and home environment.

8. The competitive basis of our school system would seem to be the problem. Sally does well on an individual basis but seems to fall short of the mark when she is required to integrate into the social environment of the school's atmosphere.

9. The child appears to lack confidence in her own ability. Other than in physical education Sally appears to be doing quite well in school. The problem may be primarily related to the home situation.

10. The probable lack of individualization within the curriculum which will allow for any kind of compensatory education. The recording of information in the student's folder—she will be marked, stereotyped—the rest of her school career. I am not sure the extent to which, or whether, the "problem" is being forced on her.

In Question B, many responders confined their comments to problems in the school program and the teachers' failure to deal adequately with Sally's nonadaptive behaviors. The home-school behavior pattern remains prominent.

C. What, if any, do you view as related problems?

1. Could the permissiveness of Sally's father have caused part of her problem? Was she aware that her parents disagreed on how she should be reared?

2. It would be helpful to know whether the home environment is intellectually stimulating or has provided few opportunities for developing problem-solving skills.

3. Basically, the child lacks an opportunity to fulfill herself socially and intellectually. Her social opportunities include older people and her environment does not offer her enough opportunity to learn responsibility.

4. A lack of communication between the child's teacher, parents, doctor, counselor, and psychologist. Incomplete data which would not allow a proper diagnosis of this child. A paucity of information from a medical aspect. The mother is better educated than the father, possibly the dominant parent. Sally never has the challenge of fending for herself in a new situation or the opportunity of experiencing the give-and-take of social intercourse with her peers.

5. Obviously, Sally's difficulty in controlling her bladder could have serious consequences for her interaction with other children. One or two incidences of "wetting her pants" in school could evoke ridicule and teasing from her classmates, thus making Sally even more timid or hesitant to become involved in group activities.

6. Older, restrictive parents could have caused Sally to be dependent on adults and the reason for the poor WISC scores. The refusal to participate in physical education could be an attempt to strike out at her parents to refuse to obey an adult.

7. Related problems could be mainly environmental, which seemed to be the basis of Sally's problems. In particular, her mother's apparent greater rigidity than the father and authoritarian decisions seemed implied in her comments. Also, Sally may have a lack of advantageous learning experiences from her environment.

The focus of related problems again stems back into the home, with particular emphasis on maternal overprotectiveness and socialization problems. Judging by the distribution of responses we have obtained in this section of the chapter, problems of too much "momism" and too few friends are not those with racial boundaries.

The reader is probably beginning to sense that among responder perceptions, there is little apparent use of the concept of race and color as viable data for purposes of educational analysis.

Problem for Discussion:

2. Does this observation fit your preconceived notion of such a finding? Are you surprised to learn how quickly the color phenomena is dispensed with in professional dialogue?

D. How do you feel about this situation?

1. I feel that Sally's problem is remedial. The mother seems ready to listen and to accept help regarding her behavior in this problem. The child has a record of many good assets for school success. Understanding, time, and patience can help her overcome her "apparent" inadequacies but not her real inadequacies.

2. I feel the child is intelligent but does not know how to handle herself when in front of people. She may be self-conscious and very shy. She may be a one-track-minded person because she cannot face a situation in which a complex problem may exist. She does not do well in abstract thinking, which results in poor application. I feel the teachers who have Sally as their student are not helping Sally enough to solve her personal problems.

3. I would not be overly alarmed because the problems may be partially healed just by chronological maturation. As she grows older, she will have greater latitude and with this she will have greater experience in problem solving and decision making. While she may remain behind her peers, she may eventually catch up provided no other peripheral problems occur.

4. Sally is having emotional problems adjusting to group and peer situations. She is functioning on the borderline; her problems will probably become more acute if not dealt with now.

5. Sally should not be permitted to continue in this one-sided development of

her academic skills. Ability to interact successfully with peers is at least as important.

6. Some effort must be made to introduce Sally to a more realistic give-and-
take type of social life with her peers. Her mother has taken a step in the right
direction by allowing Sally at least to cross the alley and play with girls her own
age who live there.

7. As far as Sally is concerned, I would not be overly anxious and concerned
but would let the time factor help her, along with other suggestions which may
be forthcoming by her teachers, parents, counselor, and psychologist.

8. This writer would consider whether the basic problem might primarily
reside with the mother. The school personnel was not overly concerned and the
behavior of the child did not seem too atypical. It is possible that the mother has
difficulties of conflicts which if resolved might operate to change the child's behavior.

Because of its subjective basis, this question on responder feeling will
be answered in a variety of ways by different readers. Some responders
tend to view the child's condition with alarm; others with considerable
acceptance and an expectation that she will recover from the current
situation with the passage of time. The last responder was even inclined
to view the mother as the principal person needing help.

E.   *How would the student probably feel about this situation?*

1. Sally probably would have preferred that she be left alone. The special
treatments (tests, and so forth) are novel treatments and therefore threatening.

The following statement was provided by the supervising school
counselor with 11 years of school experience.

2. Sally's way of acting is a way of life, her life style, or the way she has always
behaved towards "the game." What would a six or seven year old think? Is she
miserable? She may feel "uneasy" if an adult or peer doesn't react or if she feels
they may react to her behavior . . . Be *shy*—they do the nice thing and leave her
alone . . . Nice people wouldn't embarrass her further.

3. The student shouldn't feel anything in particular, unless the enrichment
program is for slow children and then she might wonder why she is put into it, as
she does good work. She probably isn't aware of the reasons she doesn't participate.
Since the only information obtained in this case study came from the teacher,
parents, physician, counselor, and psychologist, it is beyond practical comprehension how you can be asking someone else how the student felt about the situation
when *no one asked her!* You know there are social scales that at least attempt
to deal with this very question by asking the child (subject). Since you deem
this question pertinent enough to ask it, why haven't you dealt with it in your
study??

4. I would expect that the student would feel more social pressures and a
greater degree of frustration than most children. She may also be disturbed by her
bed wetting. However, while she may internally be concerned with the fear of not
wanting to look bad, she should become much more social upon a modification of
her home environment, a resultant of counseling. She would probably resent and
reject the changes if they were handled poorly.

A doctoral student in behavioral modification provides the following
information:

5. I have no idea.

6. Sally does not realize how much she depends upon others. If all her help were suddenly stopped, it would frighten Sally. The usual thing for Sally to do when she really has to try to cope with her problem is to seek help. Sally does not realize that what she has learned is to be applied.

7. A first-grader could hardly be expected to have a mature and objective viewpoint concerning such problems as seem to be indicated in Sally. Sally would probably resent any attempt to force her into more social activity—we have seen that she is very strong willed. She is also very intelligent and would see through any too simplistic kind of logic that might be employed to urge her in that direction. Yet somehow she probably misses the kind of activity she sees the other children enjoy. (This statement was provided by a supervisor of student teachers.)

8. Undoubtedly Sally is aware that something is definitely "going on." She may become even more upset. During the testing period this fact was clearly illustrated. She appears to be a very sensitive girl and this immediate concern may cause her to withdraw inwardly even more toward her peers.

9. Since she is a normally "sensitive" child, the feelings of anxiety of this student would be increased by her mother's concern for her behavior.

10. Frustrated. She would be likely to feel defeated without enough opportunity to succeed among her peers. She probably feels that her "other world" is much better than the one she is estranged from.

Somewhat in the pattern of the previous question, the concept of "feelings" led to a wide variety of responder interpretation. Variously, Sally is thought to feel threatened, miserable, shy, embarrassed, social-pressured, frustrated, frightened, upset, sensitive, anxious, defeated, and estranged.

F. What would be your suggestions or alternatives for solving or improving the problem situations you identified?

1. Sally's parents should allow her to play with her peer group and allow her more self-expression in the home. She should be given responsibility commensurate with her age and abilities but should be excused from vigorous physical education activities until she has overcome her enuresis.

2. Have the teacher encourage Sally to participate in class. Work in small groups could be arranged by the teacher for these purposes: (a) encouragement of social interaction with peers, (b) alleviation of fear of failure and of being wrong, and (c) development of problem-solving skills.

3. A family counseling situation where the parents and child are involved. The purpose of this would be to clarify the problem to the parents and suggest how they can help improve her behavior. The parents may be given training and reinforcement in shaping behavior. The child should be interviewed to find out how she feels with her relationship with her peer group. Sociograms should be given in the school to change seating arrangements and structure play time to maximize Sally's relationships and adjustment to others.

4. Keep Sally in the same school she is in. The teacher should give her assignments she is able to do and gradually increase the degree of difficulty. A thorough medical checkup and the problems of enuresis should be solved first. Since Sally has a pretty good relationship with adults, a counselor should be assigned to her.

5. The mother should be encouraged to be less protective and more willing for Sally to fend for herself and to try to accomplish certain tasks or overcome

certain difficulties even though there is not a 100 percent guarantee that she will be successful. The mother should also be encouraged to provide opportunities for Sally to meet more girls her own age first, perhaps, in her own home where she is more secure and then in other circumstances and surroundings.

6. Place Sally in a small group in the classroom where she would be involved with classmates in completing projects. Place her in a leadership position to see if she communicates with fellow committee members. Place the two neighborhood children whom Sally plays with in the same class so Sally might begin socializing in the school setting.

7. Leave the situation alone but continue to monitor Sally's interaction with children at school and at home. Instruct the mother to allow Sally to go across the alley and to provide loving approval for any movements on Sally's part which approximate efforts to interact with children and groups of children. Ask the teacher to cooperate and keep an eye open for any social behaviors which occur on Sally's part. When these behaviors occur, they should be immediately reinforced with praise and approval.

8. Both Sally's parents and her teachers should begin to reinforce her for independent behaviors. This might at first involve praising her for social relationships she now maintains, gradually requiring that she approach other children before she is praised ... Creativity is more difficult to shape. Teachers and parents might refuse to answer Sally's questions, suggesting instead means by which she, herself, can find the answers. Sally might be encouraged to ask questions about the materials assigned and to explore alternative ways of dealing with a specific task or assignments, rather than rely on previously acquired responses.

9. My suggestions would be to allow Sally to attend the environmental enrichment program which would stimulate already manifested academic interests. Counseling for the mother should coincide with this change, trying to promote greater latitude for Sally in her environment and to lessen Sally's dependence on the immediate family. Parental encouragement to bring home friends, subtly handled, could be of assistance. The low score on the Picture Vocabulary Test might be raised by the new school experience, as the test is probably geared to white, middle class students. Sally's teacher should attempt to bring Sally into the larger group.

The comments provided by responders for solving Sally's problems were almost all geared toward certain procedures designed to alter the child's learning experiences. Virtually all responders assumed that Sally's self-concept, social skills, and problem-solving behavior could be enhanced if she were encouraged to change her activity pattern. Except for the last statement, where the PVT was alleged to be racially biased, the concept of helping the child to become a more effective individual appeared to have no racial connotations. Evidently, both blacks and whites are thought to have extraordinary capacity to respond to changes in their social and learning environment.

G. *How would you go about implementing your suggestions?*

1. I believe that a child who is good at bike riding and swimming at this age would certainly make friends. These are activities that can be done alone but also in groups. Sally's mother should enroll her in a swimming class, and her aptitude for this would probably help her confidence. I would take her out of the enrichment class, find out why she does not participate in dancing, and find another

activity such as Junior Girl Scouts. The mother should ask the daughter if she wants to be in this new activity.

2. I would go over Sally's case with the teachers and find out from them what would be an appropriate reward to use as a reinforcer. If they weren't already familiar with the techniques involved, I would explain them and then meet with the teachers daily to work out problems. If it would be possible to observe the classes without being seen, I would do that also. The counseling sessions with the parents would be used to let them try to see themselves as each one views the other. The counseling sessions could also be used to explore the dependent-independent relationship between Sally and her parents.

3. Provide the teacher with problem-solving material. Have Sally's parents seek additional professional help. Gradually insist that Sally try to do the things she does not want to do. Have learning activities in the form of games and simple problem-solving puzzles. Have Sally be delegated more responsibility at school and at home.

4. I would consult with someone who knows much more about the problems of children than I do. I would consult not only with the child's teachers but others as well. I would review her case with them and ask for advice. I would work as closely with the parents as possible.

5. Provide social reinforcement for the teacher's adherence to the program I suggest. Be very authoritative with the parents.

6. In discussions with the mother I would stress that the problem is not extremely serious as yet and it may be rather easily solved by allowing and encouraging Sally to participate in and to solve her own problems. Sally should decide what she would like to do as cogently as possible on her own with minimum assistance from her mother. However, stress that simple permissiveness is not the answer because Sally will still not be learning to solve things. I would also stress that chronological maturation may solve some of the problems.

7. Once the problem was defined through the process of elimination, a family education program would have to be undertaken so as to implement the environmental changes necessary to Sally's adjustment. Each member of the family would have to be made aware of his part in helping the child and this would have to be done in a simple and unobtrusive manner.

Increasingly, the reader may be sharing the observation of the authors that the concepts involved in psychoeducational evaluation and planning are surprisingly uncontaminated by racial characterization and innuendo, as developed by the above responders. This is a somewhat unexpected finding in that the responders themselves represent a cross section of students and professional people in education in a geographical area where racial tensions are present. Perhaps one of the best ways to circumvent racial compromise is to think of each person one meets as a unique individual.

Why have the responders so often avoided the pitfalls of prejudicial interpretation? Did the reader find this true in his own case analysis? One possible explanation may be that *professional applications* in education tend to circumvent the tendency toward racial biasing. Was there a sense of social review of responder interpretation by the authors that tended to filter out racial overtones? If this is true, then openness of dialogue should be expected to create the professional atmosphere *least* likely to be influenced by unconscious or calculated racial bias.

H. What additional information would help you in developing possible solutions to these problems?

1. More information is needed about the child's behavior at school and the teacher's opinion of the child's status. More information is needed about the husband-wife relationship. Why was the father not interveiwed? Is the home intellectually stimulating? How are the other children doing in school? Are they having similar problems?

2. Whom does the child emulate in the family? When did bed wetting begin and what is the consistency of the problem? What in the child's experience has made her a nonexperimenter? If her behavior is indeed neurotic, to what degree does a professional trained in psychoanalysis and child psychology feel Sally deviates from the norm? I would be extremely interested in the socioeconomic status of the family and the child's physical environment, that is, ghetto or not.

3. How do the family members get along with their neighbors? Is the home a place to "live and grow" in or a place "not to get dirty" in, since the mother worked? The emotional history of the mother? Has the mother always worked outside the home or did she begin working after Sally was born? More specific information from the family physician—"problems emotional in nature." The nature of these problems? The father's viewpoint would be helpful in determining the assessments made by the mother.

4. There were no real data with numbers related to the problems of low rate social interaction and class participation. Without objective measures of this I cannot really tell "how bad" the problem is, or, if what I can do to help the problem is in fact producing changes.

5. Personal knowledge of Sally's interactions with her peers, her parents, and her teachers. When does she participate? What are the conditions in effect? What does she enjoy?

6. Anecdotal information on how Sally functions in the regular classroom situation. The kinds of problem-solving situations that tend to frustrate Sally. More information about the sibling relationships. Test on abstract reasoning ability—mathematical ability.

7. A reexamination of intelligence. More information might influence any decision about transferring Sally to an enrichment class. (I wonder if she was referred because of her high ability in reading and writing or her lack of socialization.) Typical teacher reactions (if any) when they find an IQ score which is Low Normal (91) instead of Above Average (115).

8. More information on the child's family background, race, socioeconomic status, parental attitudes on rearing the child, marital relationship between the parents, and so forth. More information on the child's health, especially on her bladder control problem.

The requests for additional information are varied, with interest extending to the child, the teachers and school programs, and the parents. Social-economic concerns are more clearly noted. The last response in this section came from a no-color reference protocol, with the racial question raised. Sally's differentiated intellectual, emotional, and social functioning are the main issues of inquiry. The earlier questions about the unexpected, unbiased interpretations continue to demand explanation. Are higher education and professional training in education antidotes to responder prejudice?

I.   When reviewing the information available on this student, what assumptions did you have to make?

1. That Sally's behavior was just normal for her age. Nothing was really very, very important to be frantic about. Children have their own peculiarities just like adults. As long as she does not trample upon the rights of others and as long as her behavior does not annoy so many people, I would assume her behavior was normal.

2. That the child was in a class with other students with whom she could identify intellectually. The child had not had any extreme traumatic experience with her peer group. That the father is actually permissive.

3. Sally is an intelligent girl. She is mentally lazy (in a way). Sally has been able to have others perform the tasks that were difficult for her. Sally has been sheltered by older parents and older children in the family. She does have the ability to solve problems.

4. I have the feeling that the child's mother discusses in her presence the anxiety she has in regard to Sally. The mother is fearful of Sally's riding the bus and attending the new school that is integrated.

5. Sally was having problems developing stable peer relationships. Probably her classroom work was affected. She has not developed mature attitudes toward herself and the group. Overdependence upon parents and friends. Skills in problem solving inadequate.

6. One must assume that a problem of some kind exists. The problem may primarily be concerned with the child; it may be a problem resulting from the mother's perception; or it may be a problem which is reciprocally related.

7. The information was not biased. The problem was Sally's and not her mother's. It was significant information.

8. The child may have problems. The problems may be a result of many factors, namely, physiological, psychological, educational, and environmental. Detailed information is necessary to understand the child's problem.

The question of assumptions elicits the broadest and least consistent responses among the responders themselves. Even a cursory reading of the assumptions-of-information review lends support to this observation. While previewing the same case information statements, sometimes with resulting similar interpretations, when asked to clarify the nature of their assumptions the responder was as likely to assume the child is "normal for her age" (first statement) as to assume "the child may have problems . . . a result of many factors, namely, physiological, psychological, educational, and environmental" (last statement). The assumption spectrum ranges from the significance of intrachild characteristics, such as intellectuality and emotionality to interactive social contingencies such as aging parents, parental permissiveness, and unstable peer relationships. Some of the complexity of applied pupil personnel services is illuminated by these findings. Different sets of assumptions are likely to influence responder treatment of case materials. Perhaps this same phenomenon exists among the readers as they have tried to decipher the protocol questions.

J.   What assumptions were necessary to make when defining the problem(s) as you did?

1. That the teacher did not know the child well and did not recognize any existing problems. That the problems were not obvious in the child's observed

behavior. That the school was not a particularly threatening environment to her. That the academic activities were not the type that would reveal problem-solving inadequacies.

2. The assumption was that the problem may have resulted from the mother's behavior. It was assumed that the child's behavior was not atypical at school as the mother perceived it to be at home. It was assumed that the father either felt that no problem existed or that he was not concerned enough to talk to the counselor.

3. Despite an almost abysmal igornance of the complicated subject of child psychology in all and/or any of its manifestations, I would somehow whether by intuition, calculated guessing, luck, or divine intervention, be enabled to select certain relevant problems which might be, at least in a peripheral way, akin to those that might be selected by a *qualified* person!

4. I assume that Sally's behavior had been conditioned by past experiences and that, as a lawfully learned behavior, it can be manipulated by current contingencies.

5. Sally's overprotection made her feel that she cannot cope with new situations with peers. Shy behavior and temper tantrums can protect her from adults, while withdrawal protects her from her peers. She can hide her inadequacies. The mother needs more help to cope with the daughter's behavior and her own fears.

6. It was necessary to make assumptions concerning the cultural, ethnic, and class backgrounds of parents and the values held by their community and school.

7. Interpretations are based on a limited degree of training and experience and would lack the level of sophistication necessary in a realistic situation. Aware that interpretations of cases from unqualified personnel can be hazardous and that certain interpretations require a high level of clinical skill, interpretations were made with the caution and awareness that "a little learning is a dangerous thing." The questions were answered and recommendations made that, hopefully, would be therapeutic for any child; Sally had not matured socially to the level of her chronological age; and environmental factors could have contributed but were not necessarily the only cause.

8. There may be a relationship between personality deficiency and enuresis (some studies showed there is). The child's problem may be positively correlated with enuresis.

The more specific requirement of delineating what assumptions are necessary to make when defining the problems has lent itself to consolidation of opinion among the responders. There is now much more conciseness in the conceptualization of the analysis-synthesis process, where the focus is more one of cause and effect. If we have certain behavioral or attitudinal problems in a referenced setting, we therefore assume an underlying set of causes. Problems exist with regard to defining maladapative types of behavior, but this is but one level of the substrata of the review process. In the past, the child has reacted to certain kinds of relationship experiences and expectations. One responder simply accounts for all the labeled problems as "lawfully learned behavior." Others have inferred certain self-concepts for Sally based on the described behavioral pattern and the attitudes of certain people based on their perceptions of Sally. There is virtually no conceptualization of racial characteristic as a cause for the stated developmental pattern. Even statement J6 came from a no-color referenced protocol, with the implication that differences in

school and family values must be carefully acknowledged and juxtaposi-
tioned in planning.

K. *In order for your recommendations to be successfully implemented, what assumptions would be necessary?*

1. Behavior can be changed. The teachers, parents, and service people involved will cooperate, communicate, and coordinate their efforts to focus on a
school-home attack on the behavior that is undesirable. Group guidance with
procedures with others will provide a greater repertory of behavior for Sally. She
needs the freedom to explore and to make mistakes without having them pointed
out as "see what happens when you don't do as I say."

2. Teachers are competent in solving the problem and analyzing the development of the child. Overt behavior can be changed through environmental conditions. Gradual adaptation to the situation or problem situation would bring about
solution. The parents are willing to cooperate.

3. I would have to assume that the parents, teachers, and I could agree on the
terminal behavior goals for Sally, and these goals could be operationally defined
and therefore measured. The teachers and parents would have to be willing to
pursue my program faithfully. Also, I would have to assume that my program was
in fact responsible for behavioral changes on Sally's part. My basic assumption, of
course, is that behavior is lawful and that I have identified the reinforcers controlling Sally's behavior.

4. It would have to be assumed that my analysis of the problem, that the
problem is a family-connected one which manifests itself in school, is correct.
Obviously, the program of family therapy would be useless if it turned out that the
child had a defective bladder and therefore smelled, and as a result the child was
rejected by peers. This would mean that the child was rejected by peers instead
of rejecting peers. It would also put solution of the problem in a medical context
rather than a psychological one.

5. School personnel other than those in the guidance department are concerned about problems of pupils and will devote effort to solving the problems.
Problems such as Sally's are open to solution by persons who are not primarily
psychologists. The psychologist may and should play a major role in advising
teachers and directing efforts. The school should modify its usual routine if a child
can benefit from the change (possibly moving the neighborhood children into
Sally's class).

6. Each individual working with Sally has the same viewpoints (understandings) about Sally's behavior and likewise was fully cognizant of the case history and
recommendations to improve Sally's social skills and problem-solving techniques,
and was willing to carry out the recommendations (hopefully, each concerned
worker had played a part in developing the recommendations). It is assumed that
the full cooperation of all concerned would be forthcoming and that not just Sally's
behavior patterns are changed but the behavior patterns of others involved in the
case.

7. A technology of evaluation should be vigorously pursued and made opera-
tional as soon as possible. A comprehensive and unlimited program of services
should be made available to all students. Appointment should be made of a liaison
person properly qualified to take ultimate charge of program coordination between all services offered and reevaluation of the programs that have been implemented by all persons who of necessity must assist. My present position is in a
research-oriented environment. My philosophy concerning research and evaluation is dogmatically similar, and I view the difference between their practical

meanings as zero. My attack on this particular case analysis is an outgrowth of what I believe and hold is true in my own mind. By realizing the necessity of change in educational behavior, I find the following fault and I should use it to summarize my written opinion. When the evidence produced by any scientific concept or technique continually fails to affirm experimental observations and theory arising from that observation, the technique may itself appropriately be called into question.

8. The enrichment program was a heterogeneous group and not for slow learners. The parents would come in for counseling. The teachers would carry out behavior modification.

Except for the next to last statement in this section, there are several fairly consistent expectations with regard to the assumptions needed to successfully implement the recommendations. The responder in statement K7 sends up a verbal smoke screen, in apparent compensation for his inability to grasp even a rudimentary understanding of the case materials. The responders as a group assume that behavior patterns are learned and can be changed by virtue of creating different conditions for learning. Differences among the needed changes in the learning conditions are associated with the various ways in which the problems were defined. There is a second general assumption—that certain significant people, either individually or in cooperation, are the primary agents to create the conditions for change. Cooperation is the preferred modality of social and personal change with the personnel expert working in a coordinating role.

CASE STUDY: A PREJUDICED RESPONDER

Among the 48 protocols that were collected and analyzed in the evaluation of Sally, half of the responders were informed that the student was a black child. Only one of the 48 responders dealt with the information as though blackness was a fairly significant factor in and of itself. A review of this individual's protocol might be of interest to the reader.

The responder, whom we shall name Mr. Sanford, is a Dean of Students for a large metropolitan high school with approximately 7800 pupils. He is in charge of student admission, transfer, retention, and discipline, according to his report. He perceives his main job role as providing the necessary atmosphere for the accomplishment of goals established by the institution for which he works. He is interested in helping individual students obtain maximum benefit from the educational experiences offered by the school. In the future, he hopes to obtain employment as the Vice-president of Student Affairs in a small, state-supported college. His educational background includes an undergraduate emphasis on speech and sociology with graduate work in student personnel work.

In his reactions to the case information, Mr. Sanford lists the child's being a Negro as the first of six significant factors. He also reports other significant factors as her age and the age of her parents, the mother's appearance of being very protective, the child's appearance of over-dependency, and the child's fear of taking risks. In the educational setting he feels that risk taking is an essential part of performance (and progress and development). If Sally does not learn to take risks, she cannot progress. At first, she must be encouraged to take risks, which will have low negative consequence with relatively large positive reward for the taking of the risk. In his discussion of related problems, Mr. Sanford points out that Sally is a member of a minority group, which hardly encourages one to become very adventuresome. The negative consequences or risk taking are likely to be more dramatic and painful. He ties this in with the mother's attitude, which discourages Sally from venturing out on her own. Mr. Sanford is uncertain how much Sally's behavior can be attributed to her age level, but he suspects a great deal of it may be simply an age factor. (It is of interest to note that Mr. Sanford's stereotyping extends from one of racial condition to an oversimplification of age-related types of behavior.)

In reporting his own emotional reactions to the situation, Mr. Sanford indicated he would not personally feel uncomfortable working with this type of problem. However, he might feel very frustrated knowing that he could do very little about the negative influences Sally would probably be encountering because of her color. In contrast, he doubts that Sally views being a black as much of a problem (except when placed in a situation where she must participate in an activity unfamiliar to her). Thus, at this point he sees Sally's racial status as essentially a white problem.

Mr. Sanford reports that the mother feels that being a Negro is a problem, so that it is likely that in the near future Sally will also feel she will be different from other children in some negative way. He assumes that self-defeating racial attitudes are a product of cultural influences. Inasmuch as the mother feels intimidated by her racial status, her daughter will probably develop the same prejudices.

In discussing alternative ways of solving the identified problems, Mr. Sanford believes the mother must understand that Sally will have to learn to take risks. She must allow Sally to be more adventuresome. He would start his work with the parents by having an open discussion, especially with the mother. She must understand the problem through her own insight, not through some pronouncement by the counselor. The mother has become overly concerned.

In terms of additional information, the Dean of Students would request a test of hearing, more teacher observations, more information about the mother-daughter relationship and "it might help a great deal to talk to Sally."

It is interesting to note that the first assumption Mr. Sanford has made is that the case information reports were not biased. He also assumes that the problems are Sally's and not her mother's, and that the significant information was available. By assuming accuracy of the reports, he feels that he is qualified to define problems of this nature. To carry out his plans successfully, he assumes that the mother is genuinely interested in her daughter and would accept the counselor's recommendations. Sally must be encouraged to take risks. He believes that appropriate plans could be established, since he operates on the premise that her behavior is learned and, therefore, can be changed. This conclusion seems to contradict his earlier statement that he would feel frustrated knowing he could do little about the biased experiences Sally would have because of her black skin. Perhaps by applying his techniques of behavioral change, Mr. Sanford is able to mask his own racial prejudices.

Does Sally *have* to feel different if she has black skin? The reader may now be wondering whether Sally really is a black child or a white child or somewhere in the middle. The authors would answer by asking you what difference does it make anyway?

EPILOGUE

When Sally and her mother were originally seen for consultation, the general problems of maternal overprotectiveness and resulting dependency in the child were openly discussed. Suggestions were made for child-rearing practices with the parents. The problems were defined as emanating from the family interaction, on the assumption that substantive changes in the family pattern would influence the child's adaptiveness in other encounter situations. Consultation was provided the school to encourage more socialized learning experiences for Sally. A follow-up interview with the mother several months later revealed marked improvement in Sally's adjustment both in the home and school. No further service was requested.

CASE NO. 5 Tom
(Grades 9 through 12)

A longitudinal picture of Tom primarily involves a series of self-depicting essays he wrote in the ninth through twelfth grades. He is a young man who has overcome severe physical and personal-social difficulties in his early childhood and projects himself in a political career, maybe even President of the United States.

Tom's story begins when he was 14 years old and continues into his eighteenth year. This actually is his story because he wrote most of it. In the ninth grade and each successive year of high school he completed an essay as part of his school's counseling process. These essays were retained and are presented here in generally unedited form. Seldom are students found who present as clear a picture of themselves as these four essays portray. Partially as a consequence of the essay experience, Tom's counselor wrote a report on him and distributed it to his teachers. These case materials are presented alternatively—essay, report, essay, and so forth—in order to provide a longitudinal picture of his growth and development through the adolescent years. When reading these materials the reader should attempt to put the picture together in terms of what the future holds for Tom and what his experiences might mean for others who will go through the same school system.

CASE STUDY MATERIALS ON TOM

Freshman Essay

Instructions given to the student:

You will be given this hour to write an essay about yourself entitled, "The Dominant Forces That Have Directed My Life." Perhaps it would help if you keep the following questions in mind while you write.

1. In what ways have certain persons influenced my life most?
2. What other factors have caused me to be the person I am?
3. How will the above two factors aid or hinder me in attaining what I hope to become?

TOM'S ESSAY. I think that the forces and factors which have most profoundly influenced me are the unfortunate events of my family life, Mr. Jack Smith and Mr. John Jones, the time and general environment in which I was brought up, and the fact that I was handicapped as a result of a birth defect.

In discussing the effects of several unfortunate events upon my life I think that one thing that I have gained as a result of them is a personality that is able to withstand severe pain and strain. My life up to the time of my mother's death was largely uneventful, except that in this time surgical operation, orthodontic treatment, and speech therapy helped me to begin to overcome my birth defect—a cleft pallet. At the time of my mother's death I think that I gained a great deal of faith in God. The remarriage of my father several years following the death of my mother I think of as a transition period in which I learned all about the great happiness of marriage. This marked a period of "relative happiness," which ended just recently with the divorce of my father and stepmother. I then lapsed into a period of depression. The only really good thing to come out of the whole situation as that I am presently stronger, more flexible, and better equipped to adjust to unfavorable and unhappy situations. As a result of this I think that I have learned how to accept disappointments in stride.

My understanding of the responsibilities of leadership and the workings of a democracy has been furthered greatly by the Student Council Advisor, Mr. John Jones, and Principal, Mr. Jack Smith, of Smith Jr. High. I have learned many object lessons from these two men. From Mr. Jones I have learned how to be subordinate, that there are times when nothing is said, and the necessity of cooperation and good rapport between all parties involved in an issue in order for anything to be accomplished. I believe that Mr. Smith has taught me the meaning of patriotism and the meaning of the phrase "Never give up." Together, in summary, I would like to say that these men have shown me how to respect authority.

Obviously my family background would tend to have a profound effect on my thinking and my set of morals and values. My thinking, by virtue of my background has given me a tendency to dislike labor unions and favor management, to support the Republican Party, to hold conservative views, and to be outspoken—to stand up when the situation demands it—at times.

My birth defect, already having been discussed in a previous paragraph, is the last major factor which has greatly influenced my life. It has been a handicap to be sure, but in another respect it has given me something to work for. It has given me something to prove—that I can lead a normal life and that I can excel in anything I desire regardless of the defect. It has further helped in understanding the problems and goals of others.

Freshman Counselor Report

I think that the forces and factors which have most profoundly influenced me are the unfortunate events of my life. . . . I think that one thing I have gained as a result of them is (the ability) to withstand severe pain and strain. . . . I am presently stronger, more flexible, and better equipped to adjust to unfavorable and unhappy situations. I think I have learned how to accept disappointments in stride.

This above is quoted from the essay Tom wrote this year. At first sight, these remarks may seem to reflect a rather gloomy outlook. Very few students choose to focus on the unfortunate events in their lives—and indeed very few have many misadventures to focus on. Tom has. What is singular about him is that he is able to see the advantage in disadvantage.

Tom seems determined to derive profit and positive growth from his experiences, be they good or bad. He organizes his activities so as to provide himself with experiences he feels he needs in order to develop in directions he desires. When events occur over which he has no control, he accepts them also as experiences with developmental possibilities.

If Tom tends to overload himself with too many activities, it may be because he is strongly driven to show himself and others that he can master his handicaps and improve in spite of them; as he says, "I can lead a normal life and . . . excel in anything I desire." Many of the past events in Tom's life must seem to him to have been beyond his control. If he is a person who wants to get involved in things, who does not like to lose, who shows meticulous concern even for small points, or who gets frustrated when his work does not go as well as he would like, perhaps he is this way because of his intense motivation now to learn to exercise control over his present and future.

Sophomore Essay

Instructions given to the student:
    The purpose of this assignment is to make you aware of the variety of things that influence us in our "growing up" and in developing plans for our future. Besides being an assignment in writing about a very interesting person, YOU, the autobiography will help you decide "What kind of person am I?" "How did I get that way?" and "What do I hope to become?" Keep these three questions in mind and write freely about yourself. Include anything that you feel helped make you what you are. You will have about an hour to write.

TOM'S ESSAY
    I was born on a wintry December morning with a hairlip and cleft palate. An operation was attempted but due to complications (I cried too hard), it was unsuccessful. About four years following my uneventful birth, one week before Christmas 1948, an operation corrected my condition so that I no longer needed to wear my "little plate" to block the hole in my palate.
    I am still suffering from aftereffects of this birth defect, and my diction still shows serious flaws. However, I am largely over this.

Secondly, having inherited oily skin from my father, I have an acne problem, which has resulted in adding ugliness to ugliness. On the bright side, it has kept me modest.

Thus I have brought out one overpowering-physical trait: moderate ugliness which has resulted in a somewhat modest temperament.

The second outstanding trait of my character is "competitive spirit," or as someone said the other day (jokingly, I hope) power hunger, or perhaps even more completely a drive to be liked, accepted, and respected.

This I feel is a result of a desire to prove myself—that I could rise above my birth defect and secondly to give my mother and grandmother (were they still living)—something to be proud of. This is my only explanation for these "phenomena," if you wish to call them that, that I am able to explain.

I can only say that manifests itself in a number of ways. The best example is perhaps formed in racing. I can run myself sick before I will let anyone beat me—but this seems to be "wearing off" somewhat in that I am succumbing to the impulse of our society toward mediocrity.

Though very few of my "friends," if I truly have any acquaintances meriting that destruction, would say I am either shy or reticent in any sense of the word, I believe the "real me" is very introverted.

I will never really know what made me run for student council in eighth grade but I did and won by a mere vote. This one election transformed my whole life, I believe, for it was a stepping stone to the presidency of my junior high. This I feel gave me a taste of power—and apparently I liked the taste and went back for more. This liberated me from shyness to some extent and built the foundations of my very indefinite philosophy.

My inner personality was a result of self-consciousness about my lack of "beauty" and lack of good speech and diction. Since I am gradually overcoming this self-consciousness, I am gradually overcoming this product of my home life. I don't think that it will ever completely disappear.

Another product of my home life is a thorough Republican mind. It is this state of mind which influences me on all issues confronting our nation today.

In conclusion my dominant character traits are a modestness resulting from subconsciousness about my ugliness, competitive drive, and Republican sense of values.

Sophomore Counselor Report

Tom continues to exhibit the very strong motivation he displayed during his freshman year. He is very determined to overcome all traces of his speech handicap. He undertakes activities which he feels will afford him the opportunity for self-development in areas in which he has previously felt inadequate. Debate and forensics give him experience with his speech. Student government puts him in contact with people and places him in a position of responsibility and respect.

Tom is a good scholar, partly because he is accustomed to being so. Before Grade 8 he was a very lonely boy, and he found books and study his main sources of happiness. He now know that he does not want to concentrate on superior scholarship to the exclusion of other important aspects of life, but he has had the experiences he needed to continue to be an outstanding student even though he now devotes much of his time to activities other than class work. He is extremely well read, and he appreciates the many experiences he can gain through books.

It is unusual to observe concrete evidence such as Tom gives to show how meaningful reading experiences can be in terms of one's own deepest personal values and problems. As a result of his reading *Idylls of the King*, Tom has drawn a parallel between himself and the knights who searched for the Holy Grail. He realized that there are some people who can be content with themselves without driving for proof of their worthiness, whereas there are others who must constantly search for such proof. He wonders if he might be one of the latter type. He suspects that he may be "out to prove something." If he is, he wants to be sure whether his real motives are to furnish proof to himself or whether they are to prove to others that he is a worthy individual.

Tom is perhaps going through what all adolescents go through sooner or later: he is struggling to decide exactly what kind of a person he is and should be. He differs from many other youngsters in the sense that he shows remarkable ability to put into words his own deepest questions. Possibly, his past misfortunes have led him to do more thinking than is ordinarily the case for one his age. Possibly also, his very strong verbal ability facilitates this type of introspection. Whatever the reason, his writings and conversations reflect unusually well-organized thoughts concerning self-identification issues. It is expected that Tom will work these problems through with but minimal outside help.

Perhaps few of us will ever really appreciate the courage of this boy. Few of us have or will be put to the tests he has already experienced. Probably few of us given the same series of experiences, would show the resilience Tom has shown. It surely must be to the credit of his mother and father, at least in part, that he has learned to accept life as it comes and to look for the lesson in any new experience, be it good or bad. His teachers and classmates, too, deserve perhaps more credit than they realize. Perhaps his election to student government while he was in the eighth grade will be looked on later as a major turning point in his life. It is certainly true that some of Tom's most valued rewards have been the reactions of his teachers and classmates to him.

If Tom tries to undertake too much, especially in student activities, perhaps this tendency can be understood in the light of the above. It is in school activities that Tom has learned one of the most important lessons of his life—that he is regarded as worthy by others and that he has competencies and the potential for competencies that will be valued by others. If he tends to "overdo" in activities, it is because they have had enormous consequences insofar as his own self-concept is concerned. He may need to learn to pace himself and to help provide others with the important opportunities he has had. As one of his teachers said, "Tom, at times, can be a follower." He does need enough experience as a follower to know that function. He may also need to learn that by spreading himself too thin he can dissipate his energies without accomplishing his goal. But those who would teach him this lesson must teach it gently.

Junior Essay

Instructions given to the student:
   You will be given 45 minutes to write on the question, do you think you should be permitted to make more decisions?

TOM'S ESSAY

First I would like to say that I have nearly all the latitude I could wish for. I remain not far from the thin grey line which separates complete freedom to do as I wish from limited freedom. My father simply holds me there under my own recognizance. Thus, I have the power to cross that line but rarely betray the trust my father places in me.

Our most common disagreement is over the interval between my haircuts and the length of my hair, but this is a minor problem which creates no lasting disagreement, only a momentary argument.

I still maintain it is my right to decide how I want to look but it doesn't really matter anyway, because I can have unlimitedly long hair when I attend college.

It is not a question of being permitted to make my own decisions; I generally resolve my own problems. I am restricted in my affairs only by the good sense instilled in me by my father.

What I would like to discuss in connection with my self-restricted freedom is that I have a serious problem of self-discipline. I am unable to meaningfully control my desires. I tend to do not always what is best, but what I happen to feel like at the time. My judgment is not yet as mature as it should be, though I usually do not do ill-advised things. I may make undue sacrifices on my long-term best interest to fulfill my immediate desires.

This conflict comes out of a three-way collision among a desire for social acceptance in high school, a desire to be intellectually superior to the conformed masses of America, and a desire to live a meaningful life.

To accomplish or achieve a maximum of all three, I must acquire a strong sense of self-discipline that will enable me to put each problem and each new situation in its proper perspective. I must then stick by my decision rigidly.

I must in a sense compose a time table so that I can in part have my cake and eat it, too: be able to enjoy my immediate life, while also acquiring knowledge and experience to draw upon in order to live a meaningful life that will fulfill my thus far nebulous ambitions for myself.

Dr. Norman Vincent Peale once said that the only ones who are without problems are the dead. Thus, I must learn to wrestle with any problems and resolve them by looking at them in proper perspective.

The limited freedom I have enjoyed has in large part prepared me for such problem solving, but I am in desperate need of a greater degree of self-discipline to allow me to resolve life's problems with intelligent decisions.

Junior Counselor Report

Although a series of operations has completely corrected the cleft palate with which Tom was born, the matter continues to be of great importance to him. For many years, he was troubled by the gnawing doubt that this "ugliness" would ever allow him to lead a completely normal life. It was this doubt, possibly, that has led him in the past to devote so much time to books and learning, an area in which he could successfully complete. And it might well be a partial explanation of why Tom today engages in a myriad of activities— activities from which he so long felt barred.

Ever since the eighth grade, when he was elected to the Student Council, Tom finds that he has made steady progress in developing relationships with others. This year, he says he has made a special effort to put himself over socially, and has been largely successful. He does not feel that this has been an unmixed blessing, however. While subscribing outwardly to "the code of teen-age society" for the sake of acceptance, inwardly he does not find satisfaction in it. He finds it difficult, for example, to find in his peer group those who share his delight with books and ideas. Intellectually, at least, Tom seems much more mature than the majority of his age group. In this regard, he may prefer the company of his teachers or college students.

Tom also seems to feel that the energy which he is presently pouring into activities and athletics may be costing him something in his enthusiasm for his school subjects. Although this seems to be a matter of concern for him, it does not seem to have affected his grades so far, with the possible exception of German. Although he may try to do too much, his recent successes in the social realm may have taken some of the pressure off Tom to succeed in academics. His teachers may find that they must use new and imaginative techniques to keep this unusual boy challenged.

If his election to Student Council in the eighth grade helped him to start developing socially, Tom feels it also awakened two interests in him, public speaking and politics. His oral expression seems good, but he is interested in improving it by attending the Summer Speech Institute at Northwestern. He is particularly interested in developing his skill in speaking extemporaneously. In regard to politics, Tom was able to speak knowledgeably about the Johnson-Goldwater campaign, and reported having read *The Making of the President, 1960* and *The Making of the President, 1964.* He feels he may want to study political science in college.

Senior Essay

Instructions given to the student:
  You will be given one hour to write on the following topic: "The Future as I See It and My Place in That Future."

TOM'S ESSAY I have had but a small taste of leadership, but I still savor it. But before I will be prepared for the challenges of megapolis problems, I will have to subject myself to the acid test of time. Politics is intriguing. I believe that I have the ability to serve and a very real need to serve. This career would be both rewarding and stimulating.
  In the midst of an impersonal society I hope to achieve truly personal relationships.
  Before entering politics I hope to either practice law or work in accounting or banking.

Senior Counselor Report

  Tom elaborates on any topic at great length and it is difficult to distill what is of importance from the amount he produces. Throughout the interviews one gets the impression of an exceptionally strong desire to succeed, high goals, and a willingness to work for what he has set out to achieve. It appears now that he has high political ambitions which he thinks he can achieve by attending Dartmouth, followed by the study of law (or perhaps business) at a major university, and then on through the usual political steps to becoming a member of the United States Senate.

Since Tom seems to have a suitable plan for the immediate future and, since his school program seems to be satisfactory, it is difficult to make suggestions to the school staff other than the recommendation that they continue the good work that is being done.

REACTIONS TO THE CASE OF TOM

To most of the persons who read the above case materials, Tom seemed to be very articulate and frank. Yet, it is interesting to note that several different facets of his personality seemed to appear. One was a generally positive picture of Tom as a striving young adult who was overcoming obstacles in a mature manner. The second picture was a generally negative view of Tom. This second Tom was a young man with a strong ego drive, apparently so strong that he might be a person to fear rather than applaud. A third picture is somewhat in between but suggests substitutes. In order for the reader to observe these, five complete sets of reactions to the case information in the form they were received are given here. We suggest that you compare your reactions with those below, and when making comparisons, check to see if your reactions came through with either a positive, somewhat negative, or substitutive view.

Positive Reactions

RESPONSE A

A. *From the available information, what in your opinion are the most significant aspects of the case?*

   a. That Tom appears to be a very capable young man.
   b. That he has adjusted well to his handicap and even discovered ways to help overcome any remaining disadvantages.
   c. That he has a mature (at least for his age) approach to viewing any problems he might have.
   d. That he seems to have his immediate goals well in mind and has considered the pros and cons.

B. *What, if any, do you perceive as the main problems in the educational setting?*

   I don't really see any. It appears that Tom has had the opportunity to be stimulated both academically and in extracurricular affairs as well. Either he has pursued all available avenues well by himself, or he had good guidance into the proper channels.

C. *What, if any, do you view as the related problems?*

Again, I see no major problems. He himself saw a need for more peer interaction and acted upon this need. He must have a very good relationship with his father, and even the event of the divorce, which apparently he regretted, he accepted with equanimity far beyond his age.

D. *What would you be likely to feel about this situation?*

I would say this was a remarkably well-adjusted young man who is aware of his own shortcomings, however minor, and is attempting to deal with them in a very realistic fashion. He appears to be the type of student who will get the most he possibly can out of college, has set reasonable goals for himself, and will perhaps even be happier in a more academic setting than he can possibly find in college.

E. *How would the student probably feel about this situation?*

I would say he probably enjoys life and is attempting to get the most he possibly can from it. He has obviously felt some concern in the past about his handicap but has compensated for it effectively, and I don't feel at this time he is unduly concerned about it at all. Perhaps this earlier concern has led to his overcompensating by achieving in other areas, but since he is apparently able to do this effectively—more power to him!

F. *What would be your suggestions or alternatives for solving or improving the problem situations you identified?*

The boy obviously likes to read and enjoys stimulating mental activities. Perhaps also, if the boy's home is situated in a community where he might attend college classes, he might possibly be permitted to attend some of these for enrichment experiences and also a chance to relate to students who might give him a little more challenge.

Possibly, since he feels he is interested in politics, he might try to get some personal contact with a lawyer or politician who could give him some additional insight into these areas.

G. *How would you go about implementing your suggestions?*

I would attempt to promote a "great books" or some other type of discussion group with selected students as an enrichment program within the school.

If a college were nearby, I would try to establish some sort of liaison between the high school and college whereby gifted students could be accelerated if agreeable to both schools.

If the boy was interested in a personal contact with a lawyer or politician, I would attempt to locate such a person locally who would also be interested in such a contact and who could stimulate this interest or at least give him insight into the actual operations involved in these activities.

H. *What additional information would help you in developing possible solutions to these problems?*

Perhaps a little information about whether he has completely or effectively overcome any speech handicap he might have had would help in assessing his potential as a lawyer, but there is no indication here that he hasn't overcome this, so perhaps we can assume that he can speak effectively.

Also, information as to whether his family can afford to send him to Dartmouth or if he will be likely to be accepted would be useful in assessing his goals realistically.

I.   When reviewing the information available on this student, what assumptions did you have to make?

I assumed that he was an outstanding student.
I assumed he had a great relationship within his family of some type.
I assumed that his school was providing the necessary academic background compatible with his goals.
I assumed that he had effectively overcome his handicap.
I assumed that he was actually as mature as he sounded on paper.
I assumed that he was an effective speaker and leader.

J.   What assumptions were necessary to make when defining the problem(s) as you did?

Perhaps the only assumption made here was that he related as well to his peer group as he seemed to from these reports.

K.   In order for your recommendations to be successfully implemented, what assumptions would be necessary?

There would be people willing to go that "little extra way" at both the high school and the college (if one exists nearby) to implement an enrichment program for people like Tom.
Also, the counselor would have the liberty to present such ideas for consideration and be allowed to follow them through.
There is effective communication between the school and the community, so that an outside-of-school contact could be effectively made.

RESPONSE B

A.   From the available information, what in your opinion are the most significant aspects of the case?

Most of the important aspects of the case are easily recognized by the fact that they are mentioned by Tom in more than one of the essays. The factors are:

    a. Broken home.
    b. Birth defect.
    c. Election to student council.
    d. Well read.
    e. Resilience to depressing personal problems, that is, birth defect, death of mother, divorce of father.
    f. Love of leadership role.
    g. Extremely strong driving force to improve himself and gain usable knowledge from all experiences.

Tom seems to be a very honest, open, and insightful young man who has gone through a lot of difficult experiences. What really strikes me is his strength in bouncing back from his tragedies and his realizing that he could use them to his advantage in making him a stronger person. He does have a very strong drive to excel and does pile up his activities and work possibly to overcompensate for his "moderate ugliness," but, as the counselor said, he needs this now to prove himself. Yet he is realistic and insightful enough to recognize why he does these things—for social acceptance, intellectual superiority, and the desire to live a meaningful life. He does seem to have problems with his peers which may come from his inferiority complex and/or his advanced maturity in terms of his reading material and perceptions of life. He is searching for his place in society and wrestling with his sense of identity, and I feel that he will find himself.

B.   What, if any, do you perceive as the main problems in the educational setting?

Tom's unusual preoccupation with exploring and discussing ideas is not a common characteristic of most adolescents. Because of this, Tom's main interest cannot be shared with his peers to the degree that Tom would like. Tom probably enjoys talking to teachers and other adults rather than his peers. However, in Tom's case there seems to be no pressing problem because of his curiosity for ideas.

Tom also has a problem he labels "self-discipline" because he spreads himself too thin in his activities.

C.   What, if any, do you view as the related problems?

Tom may be a problem to some teachers who seldom give him challenging assignments.

D.   How would you be likely to feel about this situation?

As a counselor it would be refreshing to have a student like Tom. He is a student who could give nightmares to teachers and fellow students if he so desired, but instead uses all his skills and knowledge for the "good" of himself and those around him. I would want to make sure that the school did as much as possible to keep up his enthusiasm, while giving him a realistic appraisal so he could chose wisely from alternative positions.

E.   How would the student be likely to feel about this situation?

Tom seems to be very satisfied that he understands himself and his actions as well. I think Tom feels that he has gotten support and encouragement from his classmates (election to student council), faculty, and advisors. He might also feel that he needs to prove himself to the point of excellence, and must rise above the masses. He will probably constantly keep on searching for this proof. I also think that although he does dwell on his limitations (physical and need for self-discipline) that he does believe he has good potential and has set his aims high.

F.   What would be your suggestions or alternatives for solving or improving the problem situations you identified?

a. Possibly encourage Tom to find others (peers) who are interested in reading and exploring ideas and initiate a club or supplementary class (in place of study halls).
b. Let him enter a self-study program if one exists.
c. Talk to his teachers and see what they are doing with Tom. Possibly

recommend that they give special assignments to him, such as oral reports to the rest of the class on academic-related subjects.

G. *How would you go about implementing your suggestions?*

Self-explanatory and possibly talking to his teachers.

H. *What additional information would help you in developing possible solutions to these problems?*

I guess I don't really see any problem of magnitude and therefore would not need additional information. However, since Tom is interested in law and politics, I *might* try to arrange for him to talk with some lawyers.

I. *When reviewing the information available on this student, what assumptions did you have to make?*

a. That Tom did not fantasize when writing of his personal life.
b. That Tom is happy and self-satisfied to the extent that he takes pride in knowing his strengths and weaknesses.

J. *What assumptions were necessary to make when defining the problem(s) as you did?*

a. He does not have a lot of intimate friends.
b. He does not find class work as challenging as some other activities, but does get rewarding knowledge from class.

K. *In order for your recommendations to be successfully implemented, what assumptions would be necessary?*

The school system is very flexible and is essentially student-oriented as opposed to hard fast rules to traditional education and no exceptions made.

Negative Reactions

Responses by the two individuals labeled A and B were quite optimistic. Now we will present the responses of individuals C and D, which in their entirety are quite different.

RESPONSE C

A. *From the available information, what in your opinion are the most significant aspects of the case?*

a. The boy's physical defects.
b. The boy's high motivation drive.
c. The acceptance of the student body toward the boy.
d. The boy's willingness to make the most of a bad situation.
e. The boy's inner awareness or insight.
f. The boy's desire to prove himself to himself and to others.
g. I detect bitterness in the boy because of the handicap.
h. I get the feeling that he is saying what his counselor wants to hear and not what he really feels sometimes.

i. I think that he has done a lot of reading, has learned a lot of $2 words and uses them, but he doesn't know how to spell them and he doesn't always use them correctly.
j. I don't think the boy is as intelligent as the counselor's report leads on.
k. His feeling of unworthiness shows up in the way he talks about his uneventful birth and so on.

B. What, if any, do you perceive as the main problems in the educational setting?

The curriculum does not seem to be challenging enough. I get the feeling that the counselor is overwhelmed by the boy's accomplishments and is not facing his weaknesses, so he is not able to help the boy overcome these weaknesses.

C. What, if any, do you view as the related problems?

Interpersonal relationships. He still seems to find it difficult to relate to people in a very personal and real way. There is no evidence that he relates well to his father. He seems to be indirectly blaming his father for his misfortunes. He seems to be competing with everybody, so he cannot work with them. He himself mentions the matter of self-discipline and the counselor alludes to it.

D. How would you be likely to feel about this situation?

I don't know what this question means. I take it to mean, How would I as a counselor feel about a student in this situation?

I would feel concerned that the boy's aspirations are too high for his ability and level of adjustment. With his present desire for power, I would be afraid that if he got into a high political office he would do more harm than good. On the other hand, if he did not reach this level he would be a very frustrated and dissatisfied individual. I would hope that his adjustment would become such that he would learn to accept himself at a lower level of attainment.

E. How would the student be likely to feel about this situation?

I imagine him to be a very unhappy, very frustrated individual. I think that he has learned to manipulate people; he has won their sympathy; he has given the counselor a snow job and the counselor has fallen for it hook, line, and sinker. I (and three other counselors agreed with me) detect a controlled hostility throughout this boy's paper.

F. What would be your suggestions or alternatives for solving or improving the problem situations you identified?

I think that he needs to join organizations where he is a member and not a leader in the organization.

G. How would you go about implementing your suggestions?

I think I would suggest a project opened to students of high academic and leadership ability where his chances of failure are equal to his chances of success. He has learned to accept hardships; he has learned to accept success. I am not sure from the evidence given whether he has learned to accept failure. I get the impression from what the counselor says that the boy wants to have things his way or not at all.

H.   What additional information would help you in developing possible solutions to these problems?

I would like to know the size of school that the boy attends. Is he the best in a small school or is he the best in a large school where there are many quality students? (By best, I do not mean the number one student scholastically, sportswise, and so on—I just mean a high attaining student compared to the others.) I would like to know whether the counselor is really realistic about the boy's ability or whether he is blinded by sympathy for the boy. Sometimes the counselor's report reads like a romantic novel. I would like to know the boy's level of intelligence in comparison to the other students in the class. I would like to know whether Mr. Smith and Mr. Jones are Republicans. The boy stressed his "Republican values" (whatever those are) and I wondered what all this meant.

I.   When reviewing the information available on this student, what assumptions did you have to make?

I had to assume that what he is reporting and what the counselor is reporting is accurate, unbiased information. I found it very hard to buy this.

J.   What assumptions were necessary to make when defining the problem(s) as you did?

I guess that I assumed that he would feel as I would feel in a given situation. I assumed that the counselor would react to him as I probably would react to a student in a similar situation, and I assumed that the teachers and the student body would react to him as I have reacted and have seen other teachers and students react to boys and girls in a similar situation.

K.   In order for your recommendations to be successfully implemented, what assumptions would be necessary?

I assume that there would be cooperation from the teachers in setting up some sort of club or organization. I assume that he would be willing to cooperate.

RESPONSE D

A.   From the available information, what in your opinion are the most significant aspects of the case?

Tom, I believe first of all, would have the same problems even if he didn't have his birth defect. He is trying from his freshman essay all the way through school to be an image his mother would approve. I think he contradicts himself in almost every situation, such as when he says "my acne adds ugliness to ugliness. But on the bright side it still keeps me modest." I also think it abnormal for a child of this age to want to continue to please his mother and grandmother even though they are dead.

B.   What, if any, do you perceive as the main problems in the educational setting?

He wants to be a speaker even though he has had a speech problem. I think he may have self-persecution. He needs friends in his own age group. He is striving to impress only adults and does a good job of making adults, especially this counselor, believe that he is really interested in politics, law, and attendance at Harvard or any other big university. Tom should be more acquainted with the counselor. I don't think he really *knows* Tom as he really is.

C.   *What, if any, do you view as the related problems?*

I think he uses his birth defect as a crutch. He really doesn't care for his father, and I doubt that he really liked his mother—or as much as he put on the big act to indicate that he did. He acts as if all his problems are solved—that he has worked out all of the solutions. I think he feels very insecure because he always has to prove to himself that he can perform a certain task, such as his election to class president of his Junior class.

D.   *How would you be likely to feel about this situation?*

Tom would be a happier person if he would do what he wants to do. He needs good counseling and a set of young adult friends. He lives to please or pretend to please adults that are close to him. I think he is really lonely and depressed a lot and reads to substitute for friends that he probably really needs.

E.   *How would the student be likely to feel about this situation?*

He really knows that he doesn't feel the way he pretends. He is constantly aware of his birth defects and acne but he still gives a reason why he is happy or able to overcome his problems.

F.   *What would be your suggestions or alternatives for solving or improving the problem situations you identified?*

a. Having an interest in things other than himself and school.
b. He has never mentioned girl friends.
c. Share his spare time with others.
d. Be concerned with other people and their problems instead of dwelling only on his own troubles.
e. Do not always try to be a leader and try to be a follower for a change.

G.   *How would you go about implementing your suggestions?*

a. Enlist the aid of professional people.
b. The counselor should take more time with Tom and try to understand what he is trying to do and say.

H.   *What additional information would help you in developing possible solutions to these problems?*

a. Possibly talk with Tom's father or minister.
b. Look over his medical history and school records.

I.   *When reviewing the information available on this student, what assumptions did you have to make?*

I think Tom will always be selfish and try to be the best or first at all his undertakings. I think it will be very difficult for him to accept defeat. He definitely uses his mother's death, his birth defect, and the divorce as a crutch or an out instead of being what he really wants to be or the kind of person he wants to be.

J.   What assumptions were necessary to make when defining the problem(s) as you did?

He expects always to have problems because he mentions them almost in every paragraph. He repeatingly talks about his birth defect even though it is corrected. He also talks about his lack of beauty and ugliness, which wouldn't necessarily be true of anyone with acne.

K.   In order for your recommendations to be successfully implemented, what assumptions would be necessary?

    a. Take an interest in other than his immediate adult family.
    b. Recommend that eventually he will overcome the need to use his defect as an excuse for not doing and being himself.
    c. He may overcome the need to be always the leader and accept second best.
    d. Maybe he needs someone to make a few decisions for him. He always has more or less been able to make it his own rules and decisions.

This study never mentions Tom's ever being disciplined by his parents, except for his father's displeasure over his long hair.

Other Reactions

RESPONSE E. Hopefully, the two positive and two negative views were evident in the above case reactions. There were many other expressions about the case of Tom, but only one more will be presented here. This responder was more on the positive rather than the negative side but is included here primarily because of the substitutions suggested. In this case, the main substitution seen for Tom was athletics.

A.   From the available information, what in your opinion are the most significant aspects of the case?

Tom had two strikes against him when he came into the world, having been born with a cleft palate and having lost his mother at an early age.

He had many handicaps and disappointments early in life, but these tend to make him more determined to become stronger. His speech defect and acne problem added to his shyness.

I would assume that Tom was an only child, that he had few close friends and playmates early in life; because of his loneliness he turned to books and reading as an outlet for comfort and pleasure. One of his few happy moments, his father's remarriage, ended in sadness when they were divorced.

Tom was a brilliant boy, very mature, certainly not easily discouraged and he wanted the respect of his peers.

Tom respected his father, and he had a good family background, but I doubt that he and his father had much in common.

Tom's "big moment" was when he ran for, and was elected to, the student council in the eighth grade. He is self-disciplined and a leader.

B. What, if any, do you perceive as the main problems in the educational setting?

Learning ability will be no problem for Tom, and I feel that he has no financial problems; however, I feel that he may have fallen short in athletics; sports; and perhaps music, art, and drama.

Maybe, if he had been encouraged in athletics and sports, he would have found something in which he could have excelled. He needed this.

C. What, if any, do you view as the related problems?

If Tom had engaged in athletics and sports or perhaps in hobbies, he would have made more friends and new friends. I believe, too, that he would have gained the admiration of his friends in these fields because with Tom's determination to succeed in anything that he attempted, he would probably have gone far.

Tom needed more than just books.

D. How would you probably feel about this situation?

If I had known Tom and could have encouraged him to get involved in sports such as softball, tennis, soccer, basketball or swimming, I would have done so. I feel that he needed to be encouraged to be with people. His reading is good and I would certainly want him to keep it up but he also needs involvement with people.

E. How would the student probably feel about this situation?

Since there was no indication that Tom was involved in athletics or sports, I would assume that he simply was not interested in this type of activity. That being the case, it would probably be quite difficult to get him involved—and maybe impossible. He is very determined, and what he does, he does well. He might feel that too many activities would not be good.

Perhaps Tom would choose to devote more time to politics than to athletics and sports.

F. What would be your suggestions or alternatives for solving or improving the problem situations you identified?

Since Tom seems to be a boy who could not be easily influenced, I think this problem would have to be handled tactfully.

Perhaps Mr. Jack Smith or Mr. John Jones could convince Tom that participating in athletics and sports could prove to be quite fruitful for him.

Perhaps Tom's father could influence Tom to become involved in sports if he, too, would participate in some of them. Even if Tom felt that his father was supporting him, it would help.

G. How would you go about implementing your suggestions?

I would suggest that Tom's father take him golfing, swimming, or out for a game of tennis.

Since Tom has a drive to be liked, accepted, and respected and a desire to prove himself, I think his father should be the one to encourage him to fulfill his desires.

If Tom thought he had the complete admiration and support of his father and friends, he would try just as hard as he did at racing.

H. What additional information would help you in developing possible solutions to these problems?

It would be helpful to know if Tom really did not care for sports or if he had never been encouraged to participate in them.

Tom referred to his ugliness and his lack of beauty. If Tom is an ugly boy and he does have an acne problem, he could be helped by a dermatologist and then he would not be so self-conscious. It would certainly be interesting to know what, if anything, has been done about this problem.

I.   When reviewing the information available on this student, what assumptions did you have to make?

Tom was an only child.
He did not participate in sports.
He had none or very few hobbies.
He had few, if any, close relatives with whom he came in contact.
He respected his father.
He and his father were not close and may have had very little in common.
Tom was quite fond of his stepmother.

J.   What assumptions were necessary to make when defining the problem(s) as you did?

I assumed that Tom had never been interested or active in athletics and sports.
I assumed that he had no hobbies.
I assumed that financies were not one of his problems.
I assumed that he will probably go far in the political field.
I assumed that Tom could not be swayed once he had made a decision.

K. In order for your recommendations to be successfully implemented, what assumptions would be necessary?

It would be necessary to assume that Tom's father is very much interested in his son's success and happiness and will cooperate 100 percent.

I would have to assume that through engaging in a wider field of sports Tom would gain more confidence in himself and would be less conscious of his ugliness, while I can't feel that this should hinder his success in life.

SYNTHESIS

Problems for Discussion:
1. After reading the five reactions to the case of Tom, plus comparing them with your own opinions, how would you reevaluate your reactions to the case materials?
2. Is one of the approaches presented better than the others and, if so, which one?

The above questions were raised, (1) to reemphasize the need for modification and compromise in pupil personnel work where appropriate and (2) to bring out the point that sometimes you must hold to a professional opinion. Although alternative approaches that may strengthen the analysis to follow and continual reevaluation are always necessary, we hold that the positive approaches were the most appropriate ones for Tom.

In a very real sense one of the functions of pupil personnel specialists is to provide for individual differences of students—for all students, but especially for high performing students like Tom. When such students do have decided strengths, the role of the pupil personnel specialist should be to build upon these strengths. In a school setting, this effort may take the form of altering the school environment to work to the advantage of such students. Some possible examples of ways in which students can be encouraged are as follows:

1. Students participate in independent study programs in which they enroll for credit with a teacher, but for which no scheduled classes are held.
2. Students who demonstrate superior proficiency in a subject are excused from taking certain courses, so long as they take other more advanced work.
3. Students use facilities outside of school during school time when their class work is satisfactory.
4. Students participate in symposia, workshops, institutes, and other short-term (less than one semester) programs designed to introduce topics not ordinarily covered in course work, or to explore in greater depth topics that are introduced in classes.
5. Students enroll in semester or year-long seminars that encourage greater depth, scope, and originality in subject matter lines.
6. Tryout vocational experiences are arranged for superior students interested in particular occupational fields.
7. Summer courses or other activities are offered by the local schools specifically for enrichment.
8. Students attend college summer academic institutes.
9. Students enroll in two full-credit classes that meet at the same time, and attend alternately or as arranged with instructors.
10. A student who has a study hall and another activity (such as physical education or drivers' education) on alternate days audits a class instead of going to a study hall.
11. Students enroll in classes that go beyond usual high school course offerings.
12. Students participate in the Advanced Placement Program of the College Entrance Examination Board.

13. Students take high school or college-level courses by correspondence.
14. Students take college courses at a college while still in high school.
15. Students enter college under early admissions plans.
16. Students complete four years of high school in three years or less, and receive their high school diplomas.*

With this list of practices in mind, let us again consider how Tom, and other students like him, might be helped in an educational setting. To do this, we first look at some additional reactions to the case materials and then add some of the actual suggestions made by Tom's counselor that were not included in the case materials. In this attempt to put things together, synthesis, let us concentrate on the responders' perceptions of the main problem in the educational setting. According to a high school physical education teacher who responded to the case:

The basic problem is challenge. There was not enough of it in the school setting. Tom seemed to be very intelligent and there was not enough offered for him.

A fifth grade teacher said:

Provide stimulation and challenge for his creative talents and his intellectual abilities. Make his education meaningful and significant. Give him responsibility equal to his abilities. Reward him realistically for his efforts.

A second grade teacher said:

Tom needs to be in classes where the teachers try new and challenging techniques. Intellectually he is much more mature than the majority of students his age, so extra things must be given to him so he won't get bored with school.

A counselor in training noted:

The only problem I can see would be in agreement with the counselor's suggestion that the teachers must be sure to provide sufficient challenge for Tom to give him the most educationally that he can get from high school.

All of these reactors again pointed out what Tom's counselor had noted, the need to challenge him. It was disappointing, though, that reactors to the case were not more specific as to the type of challenge. Consequently, we have returned to the counselor reports for more specific points. Attached to the Freshman, Junior, and Senior Counselor Reports were suggestions that were not included in the case materials because they "gave away" the types of help we felt Tom needed. In reading suggestions that follow, the reader should attempt to relate them to the

*Each of these practices is elaborated in the booklet by John W. Rothney and Marshall P. Sanborn, "Identifying and Educating the Superior Student in Wisconsin High Schools," Research and Guidance Laboratory for Superior Students, University of Wisconsin, Madison, 1967.

list of possible activities of superior students and should also consider what other activities might be appropriate for Tom.

Freshman Counselor Report Suggestions

1. Several teachers commented that Tom may "spread himself too thin." He does seem to have that tendency. Maybe his teachers will want to help him avoid "going off in all directions."
2. Tom's communication skills are unusually outstanding, except for his writing habits. Would learning to type be important for him? Many of the mechanical errors he makes may be functions of careless penmanship.

Junior Counselor Report Suggestions

1. *Possibly Tom might profit from working in the forthcoming congressional campaign. Is there anyone in the school who could help him with the contacts necessary to get involved?*

2. *Could Tom be encouraged to continue his efforts in good writing?*

Tom is one of those perceptive people who can express himself well. His writing reveals a degree of introspection and maturity that is rare for a high school junior. This, combined with his imaginative use of words, results in a unique and interesting style. He seems to be at his best when writing about his own experiences and feelings, but he is seemingly impatient with the mechanics of writing, often making errors of punctuation and grammar.

3. *Could someone be of assistance to Tom in his German course?*

Tom is presently taking German by correspondence and finds it quite difficult. He says that part of the problem lies in motivating himself, but also that the material is hard. He seems to think that the more frequent presence of a teacher or tutor would be encouraging and helpful.

Since Tom is interested in taking German again next year, perhaps the school would be interested in investigating the possibility of having him take it at a junior college rather than by correspondence.

Senior Counselor Report Suggestions

1. *Can time be arranged so that Tom can do more reading?*

In many schools, reading clubs stimulate reading. With a teacher or combination of a teacher and librarian as sponsors, the members of the club select a book which they all read. Once a week these students meet in a separate room and discuss the book during their lunch period. Senior English groups might do this, even if no special club were formed. Such procedures seem to encourage the reading that very busy, bright students tend to neglect. Tom likes to discuss ideas and there may be many others who would like to do so, too. The reading group would provide another opportunity for Tom and others to debate and discuss the ideas they get from good books. He needs to be stimulated so that he will not miss this important phase of his education.

188 Case 5: Tom

188   *Case 5: Tom*

2. *Tom is a good learner of what is presented to him. Could steps be taken to see if he can be creative?*

Tom has become adept at taking tests when they are in multiple choice forms, and when they call for recognition and recall. Instead of testing for knowledge, could he be given more assignments in all areas in which the answers cannot be found readily by looking them up in a book or by recall? What can he do when he is encouraged to come up with new twists to old ideas, and to produce his own rather than reproduce others' ideas? Tom, and many other bright students, might profit from more problem-solving assignments in addition to, or in place of, information-getting challenges.

3. *Can Tom be better prepared for the long-term, independently done assignments that he will be required to do in the high level of college he wants to attend?*

Tom rejected the independent studies idea largely because he likes to discuss matters with others. He prefers classwork to independent study, but he will be required to do assignments covering a long period on his own in college. Despite his reluctance, it may be desirable to encourage him to do some independent study. He might be willing to try it if it were related to politics, and all of his current studies have political implications in one form or another. He thinks, for example, that mathematics is too abstract and that "it would be more meaningful if practical applications were stressed." Practical applications related to politics could be found in taxes and budgets. Physics, Tom thought, would be more interesting if the material were studied "in depth." An independent study project would permit depth of study in at least one area. Such study should be in place of, rather than in addition to, his current work.

4. *All of us need to consider with Tom at future occasions the matter of trying to do too much.*

Although Tom indicated that he was having some fun and finding some recreation, these matters seemed almost forced. Sports didn't seem to be fun for him but a matter of keeping physically fit to carry on more serious pursuits. Playing cards is not so much a matter of fun but a means of learning something about others that would be helpful in pursuing a political career. He seemed sometimes to be almost too intense and too concerned. Does he have any sense of humor? Can he relax? Does he ever have fun in the sense that many teen-agers do? Would he profit from some reading of humorous books? Would he enjoy Thurber? Could he take part in humorous skits? In being so serious, he may defeat his own purposes. Can we get him to see that all work and no play may make Tom a dull lad?

Problem for Discussion:

3. After reading the above examples of recommendations that might be helpful to Tom in his educational setting, can you add some additional recommendations?

ADDITIONAL INFORMATION ABOUT TOM

Deciding what information will give the most complete picture of a student is often difficult. In this case, for example, a great deal more information was available than the essays and counselor reports. Since there was more information available, we went back through the 60 responder forms on this case and checked answers to the question, "What additional information would help you?" From this checking it appeared that four reoccurring pieces of information were requested.

1. Something about his friends.
2. The teacher's views of Tom.
3. A talk with his father.
4. A personal interview.

To provide additional insight into the case, we have added three types of information. Yet even this information may not be exactly what the reader or the other responders were looking for because some of this material is only notes from interviews. The reader should try to answer the following four questions before reading the rest of the reports.

1. How would information about Tom's friends help you understand him better?
2. How would you go about getting information from his teachers, and what type of information would you like to have?
3. If you had the opportunity to interview Tom's father, what would you ask him?
4. What would you gain from a personal interview?

The additional information is not longitudinal in nature as the essays and counselor reports were and it jumps from year to year. Thus it is probably more typical of information contained in school records. The first report is a series of anecdotal records by each of Tom's ninth grade teachers taken from his cumulative folder. These provide insight into how Tom's teachers perceive him, but also add, in some cases, how Tom performs with his peers. The second and third reports are a series of notes the counselor recorded after interviews with the father. The last piece of information will conclude this case: a transcribed tape recording of the first interview Tom and his counselor had during his senior year.

After reading these reports, the reader should review his notes on the case and see if he would change any of his responses.

Anecdotal Reports by Ninth Grade Teachers

Biology teacher's comments:

Tom is one of the hardest workers that I have ever encountered. He is very meticulous in his work and tries hard to improve his "weak" points. Sometimes I feel that his concern for little insignificant points may be hampering his overall progress.

English teacher's comments:

Tom is especially adept in oral expression, and his ideas and opinions are valued by his classmates. He isn't afraid to argue any matter about which he feels strongly, nor does he hesitate to question decisions, corrections, even authority if he feels it necessary; but he never loses his consideration for others in the process.

He is quick to grasp ideas and concepts and to analyze situations in literature. He is a thinker and an excellent writer, although his writing is a bit careless from the standpoint of mechanics.

Geometry teacher's comments:

Could be very good but he is spread too thin. Does not possess the keen analytical mind needed in math. If he would concentrate in this one area, it could easily be developed. The intelligence is there.

Gym teacher's comments:

Tom at times can be a follower rather than a leader—has to learn to lose along with winning.

Typing teacher's comments:

Tom shows a bit of frustration when his work is not going as well as he'd like. Possibly, his frequent tardiness because of student council work may have some bearing on his losing out on an A grade. He has an A average for this quarter thus far. (Tom did enroll in typing as a consequence of his counselor's suggestion.)

Counselor Interview with Parents (Junior Year)

Counselor's recommendation for discussion with parents:

1. *College and career choice. Has the father considered Tom's preferences in his thinking about the future?*

Father still talks of medicine. Believes Tom will like it once he's exposed to it. Also Dartmouth. Was concerned about Tom's conservative political views. Seems against Law or Political Science.

2. *Reading. Suggested several books Tom might enjoy reading for explanatory vocational purposes.*
Murphy, *Diplomat among the Warriors*
Anderson, *Both Your Houses*
Thurber, *The Years with Ross*

Father will get the books. Also had made tentative plans for Tom to spend a summer in Berlin. Has a friend there who might be able to find him a job of sorts and will put him up for the summer. "Just a way to get a little experience."

Additional comments. (Note particularly if promised to take any action on any area, so that a check can be made of the following year.)

Father appeared much more settled during this visit. Still seems to resent having done job of rearing four children. He gets good ideas, though, for providing them with experiences that money can buy. Will really attempt to get some good summer experience for Tom. Realizes he is too old now to loaf and play all summer. If the Berlin thing doesn't work out, will encourage a summer institute of some kind. Money seems to be no problem.

Parents' Interview with Counselor
(Freshman Year)

1. *Mother only.*_____ *Father only.*_X_ *Both.*_____

2. *If other than parents, explain.* Mother is deceased.

3. *Significant comments of parents on test interpretation.* None. Father was aware that Tom scored high on tests.

4. *Significant comments on activities of student.* Tom is very busy. Father listed many accomplishments outside school. Most recent was achievement of Eagle Scout award.

5. *Significant comments on vocational plans of student.* Father has thought he might encourage Tom to consider medicine. Does not show much knowledge of Tom's thoughts.

6. *Significant comments on educational plans of student.* Not crystallized. Father would prefer an Ivy League school.

7. *Any other significant observations.* Father says he has not really communicated much with Tom. Resolved to "get closer to the boy." Emotional—to the point of tears—during the interview.

SCRIPT OF FIRST SENIOR INTERVIEW
(Held during the Fall)

Tom: Well, first of all—ah—well, I'll talk about colleges.

Counselor: Yes, do.

Tom: I think that's probably something that comes up all of the time.

Counselor: Yes.

Tom: Right now I have applied for an early decision to Dartmouth. And ah—well I don't know—I flew from Milwaukee. We drove down in that terrible weather about 25 miles an hour all the way, and well, I had my interview and I think it went pretty well. I'm not sure that I made the best impression I could've but I'm sure it wasn't negative.

Counselor: Why do you have doubts here, Tom? Because you didn't speak well or—.

Tom: Well, I don't know. Ah, I—I don't think I'm ever really satisfied. I don't think that I can say there's one thing in my life that I've done the best possibly. And that's something I'd like to be able to do in college. I'd just do something and when I'm through be able to say to myself, not pay any attention to what anyone else says, that this is the absolute best that I can do and this is, you know—.

Counselor: Very interesting, Tom. I think I can share your feeling. [*laugh*] Even at my age there are so many things, and after you've written a book or an article or given a speech you have doubts.

Tom: Maybe I shouldn't have said this or maybe I shouldn't have said that or I should have done that better.

Counselor: But did you talk that way to the Dartmouth representative?

Tom: Ah—I—I can't really decide. I—maybe, maybe when I talked to him I was a little bit too—ah well—I don't mean to say absurd but—ah well—I may have stressed these activities that I, I mean too much to the point where he thought, well, I was bragging, but I think that—ah—when I left he had a positive impression of me. I know they grade these students on a five-point deal and I'm sure I didn't get the last two and I'm quite sure I didn't get the next one. I think it's either a matter of whether I got superior or can't remember the other ones.

Counselor: Well, I think I can help to relieve that concern, Tom. Right today I can get a letter off to Dartmouth.

Tom: I did tell them about you and they, well additional information and everything and—ah well, well—the deal is that Dartmouth is not a very big school. They have a freshman class of about 800 and of this 800 there are only 150 that are chosen under early decision, which I am trying, and I'm just wondering. Well, my techniques I don't think were—I think that they are—the strongest single factor in my favor—but ah—at times I become overloaded with these activities and I maybe haven't done quite as well in some courses as I should have. Especially when I didn't particularly care for the teacher.

Counselor:	I'll get a letter off today to Dartmouth telling them about you and your accomplishments here, and I think that will help. I am quite familiar with Dartmouth, Tom, and have spent a good deal of time in the Dartmouth area and know much about their selection procedures.
Tom:	I think that if I can go I'd just love it there.
Counselor:	How much do you know about it Tom? Did you investigate it?
Tom:	Well—ah—the reason that I was particularly interested in it was —ah—because my father went there.
Counselor:	Oh yes.
Tom:	And he went there for only one year and then he enlisted, and they sent him to Harvard and then Northwestern, but—ah—he finally graduated from Wisconsin.
Counselor:	Yes.
Tom:	And—ah—this is what I became interested in at first and then, well, we went out, the whole family went out East—oh, we went out there twice and then I went to Dartmouth and—I don't know. I just loved, I loved Baker Library, and ah—.
Counselor:	Great.
Tom:	Dartmouth Row or something with the—you know the white buildings——Well, we had dinner at the outing club and then we stayed at the Hanover Inn and we went to John Hopkins Center, you know. They were just finishing that when we were there.
Counselor:	It's all familiar to me. You did suggest that perhaps you hadn't done as well in your courses as you might. Does this mean that your grades are slumping?
Tom:	Well, I, I wouldn't say it's not, it hasn't been. I, I think my grade point is between 3.5 and 3.7. I know, I—to me it's a slump in one way. But I suppose it isn't as serious as I make it out to be. I don't know.
Counselor:	Yes, go ahead.
Tom:	Well—ah—there are two experiences I wanted to tell you about. Ah—first of all Boy's State and—ah, well—to me aside from what we've learned there the most exciting thing was just meeting all of these boys and well, I, I'll just tell you about some of them. I was deeply impressed with them. Well, this sort of relates back to the question of grades and one boy by the name of Peter. Well, he really had the same activities as I was in and was out for track.* Ah, well—he was a little better speed than I and—

*Tom was captain of the cross country team during his sophomore, junior, and senior years.

ah, well—he wanted to be good, good at skiing. He had a four-point average at school and this is something that I, I always felt that I could've done if I'd worked hard enough, but I'm not that hard a worker. First of all, I don't know whether it's important enough.

Counselor: Well, let's say that if you don't, if you haven't gotten below a 3.5, that's no real problem as far as getting into Dartmouth is concerned. So, I don't think that this is really a matter of concern for you. And they will look with a great deal of approval at the, the things that you have done, four years of Student Council, four years of track, three years of cross country, two of debate, two of journalism, and president, co-captain, captain. Those and the selection for Boy's State are enough to compensate for what you call slumping grades. So, I don't think you need be too concerned there. Whenever you do apply to one of the eastern colleges, it's always well to have a second choice.

Tom: Umhuh. Well, that's, that's another thing I wanted to talk to you about. Ah, well right now—when we took the Merit Test last year—ah, well—I, I had a 134 on that and that made me commended. And, well—I had it sent to Dartmouth and at the time I had considered Carleton College in north Minnesota. I, I don't know. At the time I was pretty hep on the whole idea and so they, they sent me without even my request—ah—the bulletin, you know, all this material. And I have the application forms all filled out. It's the preliminary one, at home, and I haven't sent it in yet because they, well they want $10, and I want to be sure that I want to make an application there.

Counselor: Did they inform you about when Dartmouth would let you know?

Tom: Well, they said before Christmas.

Counselor: Before Christmas. Now I think you will still have time should you not be accepted at Dartmouth to send this in to Carleton.

Tom: Well now, I was thinking maybe I should send it in anyway. I was to ask you about that.

Counselor: I think so.

Tom: I mean $10 isn't going to break me. And ah—for the insurance that it will give me. Then the other place that I, I've been thinking about lately is Pomona out in California.

Counselor: Also very fine.

Tom: And ah, this is, is close to Claremont College and this is—well, I've never seen it. But I have an uncle out in California that says very nice things about it, and I don't know if this should be the determining factor, but from what I've read about it—ah—and from what he says, I think I'd, I'd like it out there, too. So I sent for application forms.

Counselor: Good.

Tom: Now the nice thing about Pomona is—that the deadline for application is March 1st rather than the usual—ah well,—January. Yes, January. So, I, I definitely have time to get something . off to them.

Counselor: Well, when I look at these three—Dartmouth, Carleton, and Pomona—I see that you have focused on smaller colleges and private colleges. Does this mean that you have rejected the idea of the large public university?

Tom: Well, I don't have anything against public universities. In fact, I would like to do graduate work at Madison or I, I think I'd like it better in Ann Arbor. But, first of all, I'd like to get away from this big city atmosphere. I don't know. I think I'd probably be able to do it—but ah—there's something about getting these people that I don't like although I, I like a personal relationship with people.

Counselor: And you think that can't be achieved at a big university?

Tom: Well, I'm not saying it can't be achieved at a big university, but I'm just saying my chances of achieving it are much better at a small place. Not only between students, but between the students and faculty. And, I, I don't know. I might, I could probably get a very good education at a state university but I, I would also like to get out of state so that I—well—I become sort of independent of my parents.

Counselor: My question, of course, was raised because of the expense. You know that it's going to cost well over $3,000 a year to go to Dartmouth, and I see there are four children in the family and the question is whether the family can afford it. Your younger sister will be in college at the same time that you are if she plans to go—and ah—this would mean considerable family expense. The state university costs just about half as much as it would cost to go to Dartmouth.

Tom: Oh, I know that.

Counselor: Yes. But—ah—have you talked this matter of expense over with your dad?

Tom: Well, I haven't had a real—ah—a real good talk with him about it, but he was the one who urged me to go there in the first place and—ah well—while he isn't a millionaire, he does well enough and he told me that wherever I want to go it could be done.

Counselor: Yes.

Tom: And, my sister, I don't know—she might be interested in going to a public university—I don't know. But this remains to be seen when she gets older.

Counselor: In other words, it has been considered, and your father must have considered it fully.

Tom: Well, I don't know. He's the one that brought the idea into my mind to start off.

Counselor: Have you thought about applying for scholarship?

Tom: Well, my father—I, I don't know—I don't really know much about my father's finan—ah, you know, his financial state. It's not something that he talks to me about and well, he told, according to what he told me, he said just forget it because—ah, we don't need it. I mean it's not that he wouldn't appreciate the money, it's just that according to what he told me—ah—he said that it was a waste of time to go through all of that because —ah—we were in such a position where there'd be people that'd need it a great deal more than we would.

Counselor: Alright. Then it has been given consideration. We just raise it here because—ah—sometimes it is something that is over-looked.

Tom: The other thing—if this were a problem, then at Dartmouth, if you were accepted, they would give you all the financial aid you needed.

Counselor: And, if you are a good student, they won't lose you for financial reasons. Now ah—that seems to be well on it's way—and ah— I'll get a letter off today adding to your qualifications. And let's hope you hear from them by Christmas or soon after.

Tom: Maybe I'll even hear by my birthday. That's a week before Christmas. That'd be a nice birthday present.

Counselor: It sure would. [*Pause*] Now that this seems to be well under control, the whole problem of career should be considered for at least a few moments. We are not trying to twist your arm, so to speak, or to hurry you to make up your mind. But the more thought that you have given to it, the more likely that your choice will be a good one. And you have mentioned that you would go into law, which means of course that you have two, three years really, to make that final decision. Your first—well— really your first four years of college, are very general, and your first year of college will be much like high school. You'll be covering English, history, and some science, the usual kinds of things. But it does appeal, does it, to you? That is, probably politics or in some area that law would be a, a contribution?

Tom: Well, yes. This, this is what I talked to the political science teacher about. I talked to him about politics and we talked about, first of all, going in through business and going in through law. Ah—he said there are two ways that you can do this. You can make your, make a million dollars if you can, and run for governor or something like this, like this guy out in Pennsylvania did.

Counselor: Yes.

Tom: Well, he didn't make it, but for an unknown he did very well. And ah, well—you could do it this way—but ah—he said chances are, in something like that—ah—you might become too involved in business and never get out of it. Now, that is one thing he said. The second thing is—unless you start your own business—ah—chances are that you'd get caught up in this corporate bureaucracy.

Counselor: Yes.

Tom: Now, I certainly don't want to get caught up in a mess like that.

Counselor: You don't?

Tom: I don't think it'd be fair to myself or—ah—I, I don't think I could give my, my—ah well—the best years of my life to something like this. I just don't think it's worth it. Ah—money is nice, but I don't think I'd want to pay that price. So—ah—it probably would come down to going into something like law and—ah—going back to a place in—like here—I don't know whether I'd come back here but wherever I'd go and become involved in politics at the town level—and ah—when, say some candidate —ah—is running for governor, is after my support if I chose to support him and—ah—back this candidate in hopes he gets elected and when he gets elected, take an appointment from him. From this appointed position I could work my way up and eventually run for some offices.

Counselor: Ah—are you being a bit modest, Tom? Would you be thinking of—ah—senator?

Tom: Well, yes.

Counselor: President?

Tom: No.

Counselor: Why not, Tom?

Tom: I well, I wouldn't want that.

Counselor:	No?
Tom:	Ah—to me—ah well—I, I just wouldn't—I, I don't know—I, I've always thought of politics and—oh well—I think back in 1958 —I don't know if you remember—ah, Sen, when, when, yeah —Senator McCarthy died. Now, I, I don't want to discuss Senator McCarthy but—ah—the Senator and Governor ran against each other. And, well, I, I—ah—being a Republican, I was for the Governor. And at that time he—I think it first occurred to me that I would like to—ah—well, I'd like to be a senator.
Counselor:	I see no reason why this isn't a, a very reasonable kind of goal, Tom. And ah—the plans that you have laid and the ground work that you have done as a student and as a person—ah—I don't, I see no reason why you shouldn't set these as goals. Of course, while you're at Dartmouth, the more practice that you can get, Tom, being in student affairs—.
Tom:	Umhuh. Well see that's, well—I ah—the only thing I was worried about, in something like that was that first of all—ah—I, I maybe should wait until my freshman and sophomore years— maybe just spend time on, on the required course of study and get that down pat, and then if I have time when I'm a junior and senior—I can—well, all the time I would hope I would be making friends so that maybe when I'm a junior and a senior I can—ah —be in a position to run for something.
Counselor:	Fine. Maybe you'll find that you don't want to postpone it that long.
Tom:	Umhuh. Well, now this is that other thing. Ah—I, I've been very successful running for things so far in elections. I, I first of all, well in sixth grade, I think, I was class president or something and— ah, well—I always chuckle about it because the boys were always jealous of the girls because—well—it happened that the girls outnumbered us in our room and—ah—it worked out that the girls were always elected all the officers, so we had our, our elementary lesson in political strategy. We decided—well, this is what, what we'll do—we'll nominate three girls for each office and split up their vote. And ah, well the teacher found out about this and he was very disgusted about the whole thing but—ah —well, well I, I finally made it anyway even—I got enough girls' votes so I made it—despite this.
Counselor:	Did you go to South Junior High?
Tom:	Yes.
Counselor:	Umhuh. That was a big school.
Tom:	And well—.

Counselor:	Yes.
Tom:	I just wanted to say one other thing. And then—well, I—I lost in an election to student council in seventh grade and I've been on every council since then. And in the eighth grade, well, that's when I really got involved in student council. But then this summer I was at Boy's State and—well, I—I think I should've thought things out a little bit better than I did before going there. Ah— I, I decided to undertake the very ambitious project of running for governor at Boy's State and, to say the least, I was defeated in the primary. And ah, well—I think there is something you can learn by this. I don't think—well, now you take somebody like Bill. He happened to have been elected—ah—governor of Boy's State and well—ah—I, I just didn't go about getting the votes in the way I should have, but I, I did make quite a few friends, but the mistake I made was not going after the block work and that's what you have to do. And, well—first I was handicapped because I didn't come from Chicago.
Counselor:	Well, these are rich experiences and ah—.
Tom:	Well, it just causes me to wonder now whether—well, I suppose I tell myself I'd really had a better chance if I had—ah—if I'd handled myself differently. I think—ah, I don't think, ah—I'm comparing myself now to Mr. Smith who's just been elected to Congress. And ah, well—he's, he's quite a different type of person than I am, I think, in that first of all, he makes a better first impression. I think I need a longer period of time to make a good impression on someone.
Counselor:	Why do you say that?
Tom:	Well, I don't know. Ah, ah—I, I can't really explain it. But I have just come to that conclusion.
Counselor:	Really?
Tom:	Well, people may not be very particularly impressed with me initially, but I think after I get to know them a little better—ah, well—I think one of my very biggest assets is that I can sound very sincere and I think I am quite sincere. Ah—I think this is— ah—one thing I have, but—ah—it takes me a while and I, and this is my rationalization, if you will, for being defeated so severely. And in fact, I came out sixth in the, our, primary. And well—now the other, the other problem was that I should have had support lined up in advance and I should have just come out and said, "I'm running" and I should have had a speech prepared and some material and all of this kind of stuff. But, I didn't think about it.

Counselor:	You've learned, Tom?

Counselor: You've learned, Tom?

Tom: That's right. I really did intend to do it because—well—to tell you the truth. I was elected school president for my, for, all school president last June—or well—May, actually. And—ah well—it was a very tough campaign. And ah, well—there was a little muscling and the whole bit. And ah, well—it happened that the boy I went to Boy's State with was my opponent and at the time I felt very badly—well, not badly, but—I, I can't really say I felt sorry for him, but—ah—well, there has to be a winner and there has to be a loser.

Counselor: Yes.

Tom: And it happened that—well—I came out on top in that case.

Counselor: Do you think that you have learned to take a loss well? You ran for governor, you didn't make it—and, this is likely to occur again. I mean all of this—ah, losses—*do* occur. Do you think you learned to take it so that it wouldn't bother you in the process of moving up? You sometimes have said that.

Tom: Well, yeah—well, now you take someone like Senator Proxmire —.

Counselor: Three times!

Tom: Three times—and you have to admire a person who will get up again and again. And I think you, you gain something in every defeat you have.

Counselor: Do you think you can do that?

Tom: I don't know. I'd have—that's something I'll have to wait and see. That's why I want to be prepared—having something to fall back on—the uncertainty of politics. Now, well I don't know. Maybe my place in politics is the smoke-filled room, in the back room making some of these decisions. Maybe I'd like it back there rather than being out on the firing line by myself. Ah—there, there's plenty of room for people that—or strategists and all this, campaign managers and in a way—well—in a way I almost think I would enjoy being a campaign manager *more* than I would the—putting myself on the chopping board, you know. But I don't know. This is something I'll have to find out.

Counselor: This is a bit beside the point, but what's your reaction to all these demonstrations that are appearing? The university had one yesterday.

Tom: Yeah, well there's—in fact, I think they're expecting one today down at the Marine Corps Office. Well, I don't know. I, I think it's quite ridiculous. I, well—I take the point of view of Senator

Brooks in Massachusetts. Ah—he was on television the other night. And I was very impressed with what he had to say. I, I think there is a time and place for demonstrations. I think demonstrations can be effective in swinging public opinion but I don't really think I'm the one that should be out demonstrating. I think—well I think—if I believe in something I can do more by not creating this antagonism that always results.

Counselor: Would you tend to take the point of view that was expressed in the newspapers, at least, of Governor Reagan, who said that if you come to the University, you like it or you get out? You don't demonstrate. You don't disturb the University. Would you tend to go in that direction?

Tom: Well, I—I think—I think I would be more in that direction than I would be in—say that I would be more apt to say—let's not have a demonstration, let's do this another way. And I think that is—ah, given the effect of leadership, ah—on the Berkeley campus they couldn't have changed this restriction without all of those demonstrations.

Counselor: Well, this one is beside the point—but it—it's interesting because these are the kinds of problems that you will meet if you're a politician.

Tom: Yeah. Well, I think that definitely you have to make use of those demonstrations. You've got—you can have, ah—as a politician I don't think that, unless you're going to take a very conservative position, you can say you don't like these demonstrations because those people who are demonstrating would not be demonstrating for the cause, whatever it may be, if they did not believe in it. And you've got to, well you've got to learn to deal with these—ah—people.

Counselor: Yes, this is one of the things that—ah—comes up in politics. There are many kinds of people.

Tom: Well, it seems to me that this is again aside from the point. I mentioned this too, I—ah—I worked as a bellhop this summer at this summer resort. And ah, well—I got to know very many different types of people. And ah, well—to me this just reinforced my—ah—my idea that I want to do something where I can be with people and try and understand people and—well, it's it's interesting because well—I suppose you shouldn't be too materialistic about the whole thing, but you see a guy walk up to the registration desk, you look at him and you stare at him for a couple of minutes, and you try and estimate in advance how, what kind of a tip you're going to get. And then—ah, well then, ah well—the other fellow and I used to make bets about what the tips were and then if it was more than what I guessed, then I would have to give it to him and if it was less he would have to pay me.

Counselor: [*Laugh*] How good were you?

Tom: Well, usually I came out pretty close. I intended to be conservative in my guess rather than—ah—rather than too liberal, but ah —. And then, then I'd make another guess in my mind while talking to him. And ah, well—the kind of people that I really liked were these people that came back about three times and well —ah, I don't, I cannot remember names real well but—ah—the faces were familiar and I can recall the name pretty well, if I thought about it for a while and—ah—these people were very impressed, you know, when "Well, nice to have you back," and so on . . .

Counselor: Yes.

Tom: I don't think you can just divide the occupations up in the four departments that there are, or the five departments—whatever there are in high school.

Counselor: Well, no, not exactly.

Tom: Well, I , I think it's only, that you're, you're able to do—. But for me to say that I want to do something in social studies or math or whatever. Now, one of the things that I've been considering lately is—ah—going into law and going into tax law and cost accounting—something like this. Ah—it'd mean taking a law degree and then getting a CPA. Ah—this is one thing I've been thinking about very seriously. And—ah—for this now, there'd definitely be math in there and I'm, while I'm not the best mathematician in the world, I'm not the worst either. Ah—I like, I, I like my math courses but on an SAT Test or something like that I never seem to do as well on math as I can.

Counselor: Well, there is this, Tom. In saying what you've just said, you're saying, "I don't want to be in a laboratory working day after day."

Tom: No. Definitely not.

Counselor: So, in a sense, we've excluded a whole area for you as a career.

Tom: Well, yes.

Counselor: Yes.

Tom: Except that, on the other hand, from the stand point of technology rather than pure science I might be interested in it. Ah —I've always had an interest in science.

Counselor:	But not to the extent of becoming an engineer?
Tom:	I don't think so.
Counselor:	Well, there's nothing in your record that suggests science as a career.
Tom:	Well, to that extent I think you're correct.
Counselor:	Uhuh.
Tom:	Except my difficulty is that I personally enjoy biology and I enjoy chemistry and I enjoy physics. I mean I have my moments that I wonder why I'm taking it. But ah well—I don't know. I'd almost have to say that I like it but I—well—I, I don't know. I found it fascinating, but I don't know whether—I, I couldn't be a research scientist. I know that for sure.
Counselor:	Well, the reason for these questions is to sort out and eliminate, and put in their proper place. You can be much interested in science and not be a scientist and—ah—also mathematics and not be primarily a mathematician.
Tom:	Well, now one thing that I had thought about is for a summer job—I had thought about—ah, seeing about—whether I couldn't take one of these brief courses in computer programming. I will have had enough math where I could—it would be a breeze for me to go through one of these eight, well, five- or six-week courses. And I think that this is something that—well, computers are here to stay and—.
Counselor:	Also, in your last two years of college it might be a good source of income. At Dartmouth they must have such a center—a computing center of some kind.
Tom:	Yeah, they have one at John Hopkins.
Counselor:	And we know of several students who are practically paying all of their college expenses—ah—by working at computing centers. And it isn't very time consuming without a purpose because the pay is at a high rate. So—this is something you might do. But you don't see yourself as being a computer programmer day after day.
Tom:	In fact, I think I would enjoy doing it for a while. I think for a summer it would be great or even for—ah—Saturdays or something.
Counselor:	Yes.
Tom:	Or part time. Ah—then the other area is foreign language. Ah now, I don't know. Ah—I, I, I think I need to take foreign language a little bit more before I can say. And the same—well, I

think I put that down for something else, too. I need, I need a little information about it—maybe take a course in it in college to decide whether I want to go into it.

Counselor: Yes.

Tom: So—do you have any questions? I can't think of any.

Counselor: Well I—ah—.

Tom: I've been sort of monopolizing the conversation.

Counselor: Well—and very interesting, Tom. And in a sense you've answered the kinds of questions I would be asking, you see. So, that's fine. Do you think that you have met any special problems because you have been a better-than-average student?

Tom: No.

Counselor: You don't see that as a problem at all? No name calling or—.

Tom: Well—there's always this resistance—egg head—that I can think of. But—ah, well—I, I, I've always tried—I've tried to be a good student and be a good guy at the same time. And this gets to be rather hard at times, but—ah—because of my other activities— well, track and so forth—people do not think of me as being as much of an egg head as they'd think if I weren't in these activities.

Counselor: That's right.

Tom: A lot of people who are better than average have a tendency to limit themselves to one field or one type of thing and—ah—this, is how I—.

Counselor: Well, we'll have to stop now, although I'll see you soon and go over your plans with you.

CASE NO. 6 Kathy
(Grades 9 through 11)

The case materials collected on this girl illustrate some of the feelings and attitudes of a brilliant student who completes high school in a three-year period. Some of her intellectual and personal characteristics seem to cut her off from the mainstream of adolescent life, yet she is certainly not sick and we should realize that many schools have a Kathy among the students for whom special planning is necessary.

In some settings the amount of information available in school records is extensive. This was certainly true of Kathy's cumulative folder. It was about two inches thick and provided one of the most extensive records of a student's progress through high school that the authors had ever seen. But the sheer volume of these materials presented some problems. One concern was that reproducing the folder for each of the case responders would have cost more than the money allotted to cover printing costs of the entire book manuscript. Another concern was that it would probably be difficult to get the responders to read all of the available information. This would make it difficult to determine what factors in the materials influenced their answers. A third, and probably the most relevant concern, was that much of the material was collected for specific purposes beyond the scope of this book. Our purpose in including materials on Kathy in this book was to provide a long-range view of a high-performing girl. One of the best ways to do this appeared to be through her own self-reports (primarily personal essays) and the general reactions of her counselor (as with the case of Tom). These are presented in a sequence of

205

essays, followed by counselor reports for the freshman, sophomore, and junior years, and end with a general review of her high school record and experiences.

CASE STUDY MATERIALS ON KATHY

Freshman Essay

Instructions given to student:

You will be given this hour to write an essay about yourself entitled, "The Dominant Forces That Have Directed My Life." Perhaps it would help if you keep the following questions in mind while you write.

1. In what ways have certain persons influenced my life most?
2. What other factors have caused me to be the person I am?
3. How will the above two factors aid or hinder me in attaining what I hope to become?

KATHY'S ESSAY

Many people have influenced my life. However, I think my mother has led me in this direction more than anyone else. I used to be able to talk to her all the time, but now that she is teaching, she spends most of her time studying and I have a limited time to discuss the "school and I" with her.

When I was very young I didn't have any type of religious background. When I heard my classmates talk about God, I wondered what it was all about. But mother didn't tell me that everything was thus and so. I was taught to keep an open mind about religion and find out facts for myself. In doing so, I came to the conclusion that miracles like God created Adam and one of his ribs was used for Eve's body, could not possibly happen in a world that is based on pretty much fact. So I looked for the alternatives. In doing so, I spoke too loudly, for my friends didn't like it when I disagreed with them. Ever since that, I've kept it to myself rather than discuss it in a small community where you can easily be an outcast from society.

My dad has always led me on the road to politics. Whenever the class would have a debate, I would be right there with the facts. I get up early in the morning with my dad and we spend about half an hour in the morning just discussing world situations. I really owe most of my knowledge to him. In grade school I had a teacher, who was most interesting when it came to world affairs. We had many special reports and debates to help us all be interested in campaigns, and so forth. Now, in high school, our teacher for social science believes in strictly no debates and he thinks we should be in a wider war over the Viet Nam situation. I argue with him in class because I believe that man's soul is the most important thing in the world. If we fight all over Southeast Asia, we may be saving some souls but on the other hand a nuclear war will kill about 700 million people. Yes, I believe there is no alternative to peace. But we can't have a debate, so the argument is closed and the teacher is right.

I've lived in the country all of my life. This, to me, is the best place for a child to be brought up. There are no worries of a big city. Instead, fresh air, plenty of room to play in, a few small responsibilities, and many animals to love. I own one bicycle to ride and a pair of legs to hike in our woods. That's all I needed when I was young. I also had one lamb which I played with constantly. The job of feeding and taking care of it gave me an early sense of responsibility.

But now, I need more than just a bike and a pet. Our world is more challenging now than ever before, and I am one of the many young people that will someday grow up to vote and be a part of the democracy. Therefore I must use the ability that I have as best as I know how.

I plan on attending the university and either major in guidance, teaching, or science. These are three almost opposite fields, but until I reach that point I'm not sure what I'm going to be. I have a large interest in science, but my mother thinks that I would do better in more of a social job where I could work with people. My dad wants me to become a member of the Peace Corps. Next summer I am planning on going to a work camp for three months. This again would lead me in the direction of working more on the social side rather than alone. However, my big problem that I should worry about now is getting through high school with good grades and to learn how to read and study more extensively.

Freshman Counselor Report

Kathy was very responsive in her interview. She is most interested in talking about her future plans. Already she seems to have done considerable thinking about her educational plans in direct relationship to her vocational choice.

Kathy appears to have a very positive attitude toward her friends, teachers, school work, and life in general. She articulates very well. In her writing of the freshman essay, she expresssed herself well and showed definite evidence of being able to do sound critical thinking. The thoughts or ideas that she expressed in the essay were substantiated by logical arguments. In addition, she has a fine respect for both of her parents and feels that they have influenced her a great deal. They were described in these terms, "I think I have brilliant parents." From her description of her parents, it appears as though they have influenced her educational plans, vocational plans, and value concepts.

Kathy states that considerable time is spent "talking over" politics with her dad. She feels fairly well versed in politics because of her dad's interest. They discuss world affairs for a period of about one-half hour each day. Because of this Kathy would like to go out for forensics and participate in debate and plays. She would like to be involved in these activities because, "I like to stand up in front of people and talk."

Sophomore Essay

Instructions given to student:

The purpose of this assignment is to make you aware of the variety of things that influence us in our "growing up" and in developing plans for our future. Besides being an assignment in writing about a very interesting person, YOU, the autobiography will help you decide "What kind of person am I?" "How did I get that way?" and "What do I hope to become?" Keep these three questions in mind and write freely about yourself. Include anything that you feel helped make you become what you are. You will have about an hour to write.

KATHY'S ESSAY

The main thing that influenced my personality is most likely my environment. We lived on a farm, and there always was a sense of freedom about us. Getting to know the animals (they really were dear friends) and hiking in the woods, I think, have all formed my personality. We didn't have to go to Sunday school so I never had any religious ideas until we studied how the earth was formed in science classes. This is probably why I take religion only factually and don't believe in god.

All through my life, my parents (Mom is a social problems, world history teacher, and guidance teacher. She has a Phi Beta Kappa key) have discussed economic and social problems with me, giving me different viewpoints as to world conditions. Most of these ideas conflict with those of the community. Practically no one agrees with me and it's hopeless to try to discuss anything with them.

My uncle has always been a very philosophical person and he always gives me such inspiring ideas to discuss with teachers and friends. My freshman social studies teacher liked to discuss many of the ideas, but I've never met anyone else in the high school that did. Actually, the reason why I like to talk a lot about world situations and religion, and so forth is probably because of my heredity. They say Lebanese people have very expressive minds. Look at Danny Thomas. In almost all of his shows, he makes a big speech.

Everyone in the community is German and they are very strong in the points of view in religion. I think I would take the first chance I had to live in a larger city. There everyone doesn't know everybody else, and there isn't such a small town outlook on life.

I also think there are a few prominent families in town and a new family coming in is never entirely accepted. My mother and I both were born in Missouri. (The rest of the family was born in Wisconsin. This includes Sally—10, George—12, Johnny—16, Jimmy —19.) These are four of my biggest problems. Every time I'd like to read a book or study French, and so forth, they've got to be arguing or banging pans together. Our house is never quiet enough to think straight in. I believe in having an active family, but this is ridiculous. However, we do have lots of fun together hiking, playing tennis (twice a week), and other projects. Many times, my dad, who is an *intelligent* farmer, gives us a spelling quiz. The reason why I say intelligent farmer is that people in our community, who depend upon the farmer for their living, think he is a very stupid person who can do nothing but slop hogs and plow. This presents another controversy which I would like to take up in a debating team. Unfortunately, our school doesn't have a debating team, but I have written an article in the paper introducing the idea and a few students have supported it. I have tried to get an article every week in the school paper as a column (weekly).

Some of the other extracurricular activities that I have are band (oboe), chorus, drama club, Girls Athletic Association, French club, and forensics. These are all interesting and a lot of fun. I think these activities take a lot of my time that I could be studying in but a person should have a well-rounded program. In the future I would like to be a million things but everything is undecided as of now. In other words, I'm completely mixed up!!

Sophomore Counselor Report

Kathy's ideas about the ways in which she views herself, home, school, and peer relations, differ from the usual, and these views may be basic to some of the problems discussed during her recent visit to the counselor. She feels strongly about looking for her place in the school situation, and states: "Most of these ideas conflict with those of the community. Practically no one agrees with me, and it is hopeless to try to discuss anything with them." She considers her father "very intelligent and knows a lot about the world situation." The respect that she has for both her father and mother is evident, and she added: "They are brilliant." A second problem that Kathy mentioned was "the noise of everybody doing everything at home. I believe in having an active family, but this is ridiculous." She said that at times when she would like to study, the activity in the house made it impossible, and that her sister and three brothers were four of her biggest problems.

Conflict between peer and sibling relations appear to be problems that Kathy needs to solve. She mentioned the possibility of going to a larger school, but she cannot solve her problems by running away or rationalizing that "it does not really matter." Since she enjoys biology, it might be profitable for her if she could be given an opportunity to talk to her biology teacher and continue to talk to her counselor about some of these problems.

Kathy enjoys the subject matter from all of her courses. Of French, she said: "It is challenging to try to speak it fluently." Of biology, she said: "It is thrilling to make discoveries. I especially like to investigate pond water to find one-celled animals." Of history, she said: "He tells everything in such a clear way." Kathy made straight "A's" on the five academic subjects and physical education that she is taking this year, but she said that "it is really not too hard to do it." She said that if she were given the opportunity, help, and encouragement, she would like to do special projects for her classes or to read and make reports. This seems to be an excellent opportunity for her teachers to enrich and supplement her work. The challenging schedule that Kathy is planning for her junior year in high school consists of six academic subjects.

Newspaper work, band, drama club, Girls Athletic Association, and French club are the activities in which Kathy is participating this year. In addition, she would like to join the student council because "it would give me a chance to help classes out and lead in projects," but she said that she could not participate because one "must be elected."

College is a goal that Kathy plans to reach. Although she said her mother does not think she could be a scientist because "I am too sociable," Kathy said that she was considering science as a possible future occupation. She also mentioned teaching French or psychology on the college level. Many of her ideas about these occupations are not realistic, and she would profit from examining in depth much educational and occupational information.

Junior Essay

Instructions given to the student:
    You will be given 45 minutes to write on the question, do *you* think you should be permitted to make more decisions?

KATHY'S ESSAY

I imagine all teen-agers, or for that matter, all people believe they should be permitted to make more decisions. As for myself, I usually make all the decisions that pertain to my own life with, perhaps, a little persuasion from my parents. However, they leave the major decisions up to myself. If the decision concerns me, I should be the person to decide yes or no. Many times when the decision concerns money from the pockets of my parents, it is best I let them know what I would desire, but leave the decision up to them.

One example could be the American Foreign Student Scholarship to Europe or Asia. Both of my parents think it is a wonderful opportunity for the advancement of education and a new experience in social environment. However, this new experience will cost $750 which my parents are obliged to pay in full. If this were my decision, I would say "yes," which would not have too much bearing on the trip since I haven't got $750. I do feel that my parents should consider my opinion when making decisions such as this, as it will affect my life.

Perhaps, my case is somewhat different from those of other students. In a decision that I would make relating to the college of my choice or whether or not to graduate in three years is usually of my own choosing. However, my parents always agree with the choice I make. Either this is the case, or they persuade me to arrive at the same conclusions they have already reached. Many other students might have a great deal of controversy between themselves and their parents, so that their decisions would have an effect on their future different from those decisions made by their parents. (Confusing, isn't it!)

If one were to relate my decision-making power to my school supervisors, I would insist on extended rights. As of the past two years, I have attempted to convince them that I should be allowed to graduate in three years. As of yet, they have hardly considered the suggestions unless I can muster up nineteen credits, instead of the usual sixteen required by graduates of the year I plan on graduating. Here is a case where I believe the decision should not be so much theirs as perhaps my parents and my own. Whether or not I graduate in three years will not at all affect them but myself. If I feel I would gain more by a year of university credit than a year of high school credit, then I can't understand why they should be able to say, "no, you can't be different from everyone else!" Actually, I feel the supervisor will win out in the end, but I believe it is a cause worth arguing over. It not only affects me, but will affect many students who wish to accelerate in the future.

In summary, the power to make a decision should be left up to the person most closely associated with the end results and who is most qualified to decide upon the matter. I realize I have only grown to the edge of maturity and am not fully acquainted with all situations. Many decisions would be more wisely made by an adult, in most cases my parents, who understand me and my problems. *Let me add, this is quite an achievement!*

Junior Counselor Report

Kathy seems to be very critical of nonintellectuals. She appears to have an inquiring mind that, although mature in many ways, has not achieved the part of maturity that would allow her to have more tolerance for those who do not seek the same things that she and her family feel important. Her intolerance of most of her peers and their reaction to her perpetual striving for a "serious conversation" has posed a problem for Kathy. She has, in her own mind, solved this by choosing to "go my own way and forget about it." It is suggested that Kathy does not "forget about it" and that she seems to interpret the existing relationship between her and her peers as more evidence that she is "different" from others. It is suggested also that this is not entirely displeasing to her.

She has great admiration and respect for her parents to whom she attributes much of her success as a student. Kathy finds both of her parents extremely intelligent and especially enjoys the many and varied intellectual discussions which she stated that they have.

Kathy, on a recent trip to the university, chose to visit a class in French literature. She was quite surprised with the amount of material covered in one hour and expressed a desire to be able to move as quickly in her own French class at school.

She has hopes of being accepted into the American Foreign Student's program for next year. If this does not become a reality for Kathy, she has chosen to attend the University of Wisconsin.

Although her vocational interests are varied and have fluctuated in the past, Kathy seems to prefer to be a French language teacher at the present time. She also has an interest in teaching history at the secondary level. Kathy commented that her parents feel that her vocational plans should be her decision but that her father had suggested that she consider the Peace Corps.

She is currently taking a correspondence course in English composition, which she believes to be extremely difficult. She feels, however, that she is learning a great deal because "the instructor is strict and doesn't give me good grades unless I really deserve them." Her stated reason for taking a correspondence course was because she felt a need to learn more about composition and to also earn credits so that she could graduate in June.

Kathy's most pressing educational problem, at this time, is centered around knowing whether she will be able to graduate in June or not. She stated that unless she took another correspondence course next semester that she would be three-fourths of a credit short of the 19 credits required for graduation. Is there a possibility that the three-fourths credit could be assigned to an extensive research paper that she might complete? It is realized that this is not common practice and that this counselor may not have all the facts involved in this particular situation, but it appears that some alternatives should be in order.

Review of School Record

Number of English courses taken and now taking. Give names of English courses if the names differed from the usual English 1, 2, 3, and 4. Circle honors courses. English 1, 2, 3, and Advanced English Composition by correspondence from the University.

Looking back at all the English you have had in high school, what comments would you make? (Try to think of the subject field itself, not about teachers.) It seems as though we accomplished more in grade school than we ever did in high school. Except for my correspondence course, which was really tremendous, I feel as though my English skills (grammar) have declined.

Would you choose an occupation in which high performance in English was the main requirement? No. *Why or why not?* I struggled through my composition course and have difficulty writing papers for any class.

Names of mathematics courses taken and now taking. Circle honors courses. Algebra I, Geometry I, Algebra II (Advanced Mathematics)

Looking back at all the mathematics you have had in high school, what comments would you make? (Try to think of the subject field, not about teachers.) This school stresses mathematics and science and I feel that all my courses in this area have been outstanding.

Would you choose an occupation in which high performance in mathematics was the main requirement? No. *Why or why not?* Math is fun when you have one assignment per night, but I'd go crazy working with numbers for the rest of my life.

Names of science courses taken and now taking. Circle honors courses. Physical Science, Biology I, Chemistry I.

Looking back at all the science you have had in high school, what comments would you make? (Think of the subjects, not the teachers.) They have all been very stimulating and challenging. I received my best background in science in seventh and eighth grade but became more curious in high school.

Would you choose an occupation in which high performance in science was the main requirement? Possibly. *Why or why not?* After my eight weeks session this summer of concentrated science I'll be better prepared to answer this question. That should be a real test!

Names of social studies (include history) courses taken and now taking. Circle honors courses: Civics, World History, American History in summer school at Central High School, Social Problems.

Looking back at all the social studies you have had in high school, what comments would you make? (Think of subject field, not the teachers.) Every teacher was a part-time coach and taught history merely as something to do in spare time. Central was tremendous but my coaches were so much involved in football they treated history like a goal post, something you just want to reach, not contemplate about.

Would you choose an occupation in which high performance in social studies was the main requirement? Yes. *Why or why not?* Probably because of my mother's and father's influence. I believe history in the past and at present is fascinating and ever-changing. A study in this field could never be boring.

Names of foreign languages taken and now taking. Circle honors courses. French I, II, III, Spanish H10—correspondence from the University.

Looking back at all the foreign languages you have had in high school, what comments would you make? (Think of the subjects, not the teachers.) French I and II were fabulous, but this year we hardly ever even speak French. We spend every class period just talking about fashions in English. However, I have read Voltaire's *Candide* in French and other short stories.

Would you choose an occupation in which high performance in foreign languages was the main requirement? Yes. *Why or why not?* Languages are so much fun to learn and to teach. With my semester of Spanish, I could even communicate with our Spanish AFS exchange student.

Review of School, Community, and Other Activities

Activities in which you participated	Number of years	Offices held
Senior Band	4	Oboe player
Mixed Chorus	4	Soprano
French Club	3	
Drama Club	3	Vice-president
Girls Athletic Association	3	
Science Club	1	
One-Act Play	3	Leading roles
Newspaper Staff	2	Columnist

List any special honors or activities.

Valedictorian of Senior Class—"Legislative A Scholarship"
National Science Foundation Scholarships
High honors every year
Scholarship to Summer Music Clinic

Looking back at these activities, what comments would you make? My activities actually made high school. Without them I would have been bored to tears. We never get homework. Any work done at night is extra credit.

Has participation in any of the activities influenced your choice of an occupation? Yes. *If so, tell which one and how it has influenced you.* All through high school I've had Music Appreciation in band, chorus and guitar, piano, and summer clinics so that I've developed a bit of an ear for music. I really love it and am certain I will continue this interest in some form or other.

About how many hours per week of nonrequired reading do you do? Seven hours per week.

Plans for the Future

What do you plan to do next year? After the NSF session at Purdue, I plan to attend the University of Wisconsin.

What steps have you taken toward your plan? I have applied for a scholarship there, applied for admission in a scholarship house.

What occupation are you planning to enter? I would like to teach languages or social science, either on the secondary level or college.

Why did you choose those? I haven't made any definite plans as of yet, and these are where my interests lie.

What other occupations are you considering? Perhaps, if I enjoy Purdue which is eight hours of study in science each day, I might enter that field.

Why did you choose that one? I don't know yet. I'm just curious about science and would like to know more about it.

Does your mother agree with your educational plans? Yes.

Does your mother agree with your vocational plans? Yes.

Does your father agree with your educational plans? Yes.

Does your father agree with your vocational plans? Yes.

Who, if anyone, helped you to make up your mind about the place you have considered for post-high school training? My mother, but myself mostly.

General Comments

Is there anything about your health that keeps you from doing what you would like to do? I'd like to eat crunchy popcorn but I have braces.

Looking back at your high school experience, could you suggest any ways in which it might have been made more valuable? If some of my teachers had been interested in history, more so than football or French, more so than personal tidbits, it would have helped. But on the whole, I got out of high school exactly what I put into it and if the French teacher didn't read the text, I didn't strain myself either. It's equally my fault in some ways.

More interesting?

What special problems have you met because you have been a better than average student? Being a better than average student was nothing compared to graduating in three years; then the trouble really began. Now I feel like everyone hates me: my teachers because they think I don't appreciate their help, the students because I think I'm too good for them, and so forth.

Are there any problems about your education or future plans that we should discuss during our interview? All I need is courage!

General comment about your school experiences over the past four years. (The use of this space is up to you. Use it or not in any way that you wish. You may write on the back of this page.)

Although I'm glad I'm graduating this year, I would never have traded these three years for some other paradise. I would have appreciated a larger school with more liberal minds and better teachers or just more academic interests, but the friends I've met and extracurricular activities I've participated in have been wonderful and valuable. So many people have gone out of their way to help me in some of my interests. The music instructors gave me extra voice lessons and, later, guitar lessons and took extra pains to improve my oboe tone. The science teacher has stayed after school nights to help me with chemistry experiments, just when they were extra experiments I was curious about. The Physical Education teacher let me teach trampoline for two weeks which was really fun. Of course, I couldn't even have graduated without the counselor's help. He also directed me to many scholarships and opportunities that he thought were valuable. This summer he will also attend Purdue University on a guidance scholarship by the NEA or something.

Actually, as far as academic achievement goes, I think I could have skipped from eighth grade to college with perhaps one year of concentrated high school. Next year I really have to begin working on studies for the first time in three years. Perhaps if I hadn't had the extra time in high school, though, I would not have developed so many interests in other activities, such as tennis, music, skiing, skating, debating, acting, and so forth. In college I hope I'll have the opportunity to really develop some of these interests.

Au revoir!
Hasta la vista!

REACTIONS TO THE CASE OF KATHY

The analysis of case materials can be viewed as a sorting out process. Decisions have to be made and conceptualized in a meaningful way. There are no limits on this process, and it can be successfully completed by the accomplished pupil personnel specialist as well as the beginner. For example, the analyses presented below to the first two questions on the case reaction form were completed by a 35-year-old curriculum director with 10 years of teaching experience and by a 22-year-old beginning elementary school guidance M. S. candidate with only student teaching experience.

CURRICULUM DIRECTOR'S ANALYSIS

A. *From the available information, what in your opinion are the most significant aspects of the case?*

The most significant aspects can be discussed under four topics:

    (a) Family:
        (1) Kathy's strong identification with her parents and their influence on her development.

    (2) Possibly some sibling rivalry—although this is only mentioned once briefly by Kathy.

(b) School:
    (1) Kathy's frustration and disappointment in her high school curriculum.
    (2) Her intense interest in academic pursuits.

(c) Social aspects:
    (1) Kathy's conflict with her peers concerning religion, politics, and so on.
    (2) Her intolerance for nonintellectuals.
    (3) Her awareness of being "different."

(d) Early environment:
    (1) Kathy grew up in a small rural community.
    (2) She developed an early sense of responsibility.

B. *What, if any, do you perceive as the main problems in the educational setting?*

(a) The unchallenging curriculum—the teachers' inability to provide motivation and stimulation.

(b) Insufficient enrichment activities for involving advanced students.

(c) Disinterest on the part of some teachers such as the Social Studies "coaches."

(d) Lack of a "gifted" or accelerated program.

GUIDANCE CANDIDATE'S ANALYSIS

A. *From the available information, what in your opinion are the most significant aspects of the case?*

(a) The student is obviously very bright.

(b) Kathy is perhaps more mature in thoughts and actions than her fellow students.

(c) Apparently her interests are not the same as most of the other students.

B. *What, if any, do you perceive as the main problems in the educational setting?*

(a) The courses she takes may not be challenging enough for her.

(b) Apparently there was difficulty about a rather inflexible rule on number of hours needed to graduate.

(c) Kathy is possibly more perceptive (or realistic) about the teacher-coach history teachers than the administrators.

The process of analysis and synthesis for responders is illustrated in the two above reactions. They attempted to put the materials together in terms of the questions asked about the case materials. For the authors the process was slightly different. We went through the case reactions and attempted to put these reactions together in a meaningful form. We would jot down notes to ourselves about the most consistent views about significant aspects of the case. Thus, after reading the curriculum specialists' views, we would try to compare and attach these with the next responders and so on. It is probably worthwhile to point out again that the persons we asked to respond to the cases may or may not have had systematic training in analysis of case materials. When reading the reactions of the Curriculum Director, we were struck by the logic of the presentation. The four headings chosen for the most significant aspects of the case, Family, School, Social, and Early Environment, seemed to encompass most of the major aspects we had identified. Our notes listed the following headings. Although the words and order of presentation we chose were different, the emphasis was quite similar.

1. School and curriculum problems.
2. Graduation in three-year-period of time.
3. Relationship to environment (home versus school).
4. Relationship with parents.
5. Relationship with peers.

As pupil personnel specialists all of these factors are of concern. However, because of the interrelationships between all of them, we will not deal with them separately but will concentrate on the area where a pupil personnel worker can probably have the greatest impact, that is, the school-related situation over a period of time.*

It is our philosophy that pupil personnel workers must be actively involved with students; with the data base gleaned from this source, they must work to improve situations for students. In most schools there will be a student like Kathy. Such students can provide valuable information about what is happening in the local educational system. This is not to say that pupil personnel specialists listen only to the bright students. Other cases in this text should illustrate that you get information upon which professional decisions must be based from the whole spectrum of students. In the present chapter, however, we will concentrate on attempts to alter the environment for gifted students like Kathy. A review of the case materials given so far is recommended before the reader considers the following discussion problems.

*On a short-term basis, the biggest impact is probably with people.

Problems for Discussion:

1. In the Freshman essay, Kathy presents some thoughts on discussing issues in classes. With these views in mind, how might you approach her teachers on this topic and what might you suggest the teachers do?

2. Kathy is taking forensics and, according to her sophomore essay, enjoys this activity. However, she would like to participate on a debate team. How might you, if working in Kathy's school, initiate a debate team or similar activity? In other words, without knowing the personnel in the school, what might be some appropriate steps to take to initiate such an activity?

3. In the sophomore report, by the counselor, he reviews some of Kathy's comments about her classes, for instance, for her biology class she stated that "It is thrilling to make discoveries." This same paragraph goes on and tells us that Kathy would like to do special projects for her classes or to read and make reports. Look over her school record review and think up specific activities which you might suggest to Kathy's teachers.*

4. Several places in the case materials are first indications and, later, definite plans for Kathy's college attendance. If you had had the opportunity to work with Kathy over the three-year period she was in high school, how would you have helped her through the college decision-making process?

5. In the junior year essay, counselor report, and also in the concluding comments about her school experiences, Kathy comments about her difficulties and thoughts about graduating in three years. What would you have done to come to her aid in this situation?

Now we continue with the reactions to the case by the curriculum specialist and the in-training elementary school counselor. Their comments to several questions are given in their entirety.

CURRICULUM SPECIALIST'S VIEWS

D. *How would you be likely to feel about this situation?*

Considering the situation as a whole, I would say that Kathy should perhaps have had more opportunity for individual study (she did do the University Correspondence Courses apparently by herself).

---

*Counselors are not specialists in all subject matter areas, but they should be knowledgable enough about classroom activities and curriculum to make *suggestions* to teachers about assignments or projects for students like Kathy after talking with them.

F. *What would be your suggestions or alternatives for solving or improving the problem situations you identified?*

Kathy should have been allowed time for individual study and research and to carry out educational projects in which she was interested.

If she felt that she was not benefitting from a course, she should have been allowed to discontinue coming to regular classes and be allowed to study the subject on her own, reporting every week or two to her teacher on her progress.

She might also have been given the opportunity to tutor other students if she wanted to. She did indicate some interest in becoming a teacher.

G. *How would you go about implementing your suggestions?*

I would suggest that the counselor discuss with her alternative plans for organizing her program of studies in terms of content, time, and so forth with respect to her interests and the need to meet certain requirements for graduation. Also, each of the teachers who might supervise her study or who have been her teachers could suggest to her and to the counselor specific information with regard to content, projects, and so on, which might be appropriate.

H. *What additional information would help you in developing possible solutions to these problems?*

It would be helpful to know to what extent Kathy's teachers would be able and/or willing to spend the time required to help her establish and carry out a program of individual studies, and the extent to which the teachers would cooperate with each other in maintaining some sort of balance in programs of this kind.

I. *When reviewing the information available on this student, what assumptions did you have to make?*

I had to assume that some of the information supplied by the counselor was correct and that Kathy was expressing what were her most important concerns.

J. *What assumptions were necessary to make when defining the problem(s) as you did?*

I assumed her writing indicated that some of her courses were a bit dull to her and thus not challenging. I assumed also that she was a bright student because of her accomplishments.

I also assumed that Kathy's view of the problem concerning the number of hours for graduation presented sufficient evidence to make the statement which I did make. I would have liked to have had the administrator's view on this particular problem.

THE IN-TRAINING ELEMENTARY SCHOOL COUNSELOR'S VIEWS

D. *How would you be likely to feel about this situation?*

I think Kathy has made a good decision in wishing to complete high school in three years. College may provide her with the academic challenge she is seeking and will acquaint her with people of similar interests and aptitude and expose her to new aspects of life. I would be concerned that she be very careful in selecting a college which would fulfill her expectations.

My main concern would be with improving the school curriculum, since I find it at fault, rather than Kathy's having a problem. If she had been raised and educated in a more challenging atmosphere, I doubt she would have felt the same frustration and boredom in her school work.

F.   *What would be your suggestions or alternatives for solving or improving the problem situations you identified?*

First, I think Kathy's boredom with education and her lack of friends with similar interests and motivation will be corrected by her attendance at a university. Being away from home and being exposed to a wide variety of people may weaken her dependence on her parents and lessen her intolerance for un-intellectuals.

The real problem in the school, however, must be dealt with through curriculum changes and improvement of the teaching staff.

G.   *How would you go about implementing your suggestions?*

My suggestions for Kathy can be implemented by helping her with her selection of a college and by discussing her intolerance and dependency.

Meetings with the school administration to point up areas of deficiency in the curriculum should be established. In-service training and workshops with the teachers may improve their teaching techniques and may point out the special needs of the students. A new program for accelerated students should also be considered.

H.   *What additional information would help you in developing possible solutions to these problems?*

In reference to Kathy:
  a. More extensive family background information.
  b. Remarks and observations by some of Kathy's teachers and friends.
  c. Test results referring to Kathy's mental aptitude and achievement.

In reference to the school:
  a. An outline of the present curriculum.
  b. Information of the qualifications of the teaching staff.
  c. Knowledge of the financial position of the community and the resource materials and services.

I.   *When reviewing the information available on this student what assumptions did you have to make?*

  a. Kathy was being truthful in the statements she made in her essays.
  b. There was no accelerated or honors program already established at the school.
  c. This was the only information available.
  d. The information had been reported correctly.

J.   *What assumptions were necessary to make when defining the problems(s) as you did?*

  a. Kathy was being truthful in the statements she made.
  b. The counselor's interpretations of her essays and conversations were reasonably correct and objective.
  c. Kathy was objective when criticizing her teachers and school work.

We felt that these two sets of reactions to the case were appropriate and very much in line with how we would have responded to the questions under similar conditions. Yet, there are still some questions as to how changes could be brought about for Kathy. Meetings with the school administration, in-service training sessions or initiating accelerated classes are all suggested methods with which we would concur. Yet, these would not be the crux of the initial procecure that should be followed. To extend the scope of the discussion on how to begin changing the situation, additional responses to the question "What, if any, do you perceive as the main problems in the educational setting?" and "How would you go about implementing your suggestions?" will be presented. When reading these suggestions, the reader should attempt to formulate a concrete method of implementation he would follow.

COMMENTS BY A BEGINNING MATHEMATICS TEACHER

I think that the educational setting was not challenging enough for Kathy. In her case, special attention would have been needed to do it, since Kathy sets her goals very high. Perhaps if instead of reading she could have prepared special reports for her classes, Kathy could have been encouraged to read and discuss with her instructors more about possible vocations.

I would try to find people among friends and acquaintances who are working in fields interesting Kathy and have them talk with her. If possible, show her where they work and some of the routine.

Here is a suggestion we would also encourage. In fact, exploratory experiences and discussions are greatly needed for high school students, but this suggestion does not include a solution for Kathy's main problem in the educational context.

COMMENTS BY A HIGH SCHOOL ENGLISH TEACHER WHO WAS TAKING EVENING COURSES TO PREPARE TO BECOME ACCREDITED AS A COUNSELOR

I feel that it is too bad that an accelerated program couldn't have been available for Kathy. In this program, she could have been given extra projects and encouraged to delve into extra subjects which interested her.

I would like to set aside special time when I could talk to Kathy and try to show her how developing socially is very important.

We would argue that it was too bad that an accelerated program was not available in Kathy's school. However, setting aside time to talk about developing socially, even though it might be of value to her, would not bring about the accelerated program.

COMMENTS BY AN ELEMENTARY SCHOOL COUNSELOR WITH TWO YEARS OF PRIOR EXPERIENCE AS A THIRD GRADE TEACHER

It appears that the community and school are pretty conservative and traditional in their views of education. Their curriculum seems geared toward only the average and makes little provision for individualizing instruction which can be damaging to students like Kathy. They seem to discourage outside work reports, reading beyond requirement, as well as sticking to traditional teaching methods. They also seem to hold policy as "sacred," that is, in their feelings about early graduation, and they don't seem prepared to be flexible when the situation calls for it. Kathy needs to learn and develop more tolerance and a realistic appraisal of herself.

I would want to review the school curriculum and policies to evaluate and look for strengths and weakness. If it were possible, I would want to institute some sort of teacher workshop where individualizing instruction could be discussed. This might include ways of starting study projects and encouraging these to be presented to the class. Also, I might bring up ways of making course content more meaningful. Possibly I might suggest a conference with the administration about evaluating teacher's qualifications (coach teaching history) and also school policy about early graduation.

This was one of the most specific suggestions we received and the type that we think pupil personnel specialists need to make. For contrast, consider the comments of two responders who had similar experential backgrounds: both were elementary school counselors and had taught third grade.

COMMENTS BY A SECOND ELEMENTARY SCHOOL COUNSELOR WITH TWO YEARS OF PRIOR EXPERIENCE AS A THIRD GRADE TEACHER

The educational system was not geared toward the gifted students that much. Although some of Kathy's teachers helped, I feel that much more could have been done, such as more advanced courses (possibly college credit) in the senior year, more extra credit and projects, and more open-mindedness on the teacher's part so that better and more inspiring relationships (and debate) could develop. Kathy felt she could have gained no more from high school; therefore, something was wrong.

I would explain to Kathy that everyone is different and no one is any better than anyone else. Tell her that friendships are one of the most valuable things in the world and one should try to get along with others. I would tell her not to push herself so much and that she can't always be surrounded by people who are inspiring, intellectual, and so forth. Tell her if she wants some things changed that she should make polite suggestions rather than pointing a finger. Also, I would try to bring about a more enriched educational setting for gifted students.

Reactions to this explanation of the main problem in the educational setting and means of implementing suggestions are left to the reader.

COMMENTS BY AN EX-PHYSICAL EDUCATION TEACHER TURNED COUNSELOR

Kathy does not seem to be able to receive the type of instruction that will satisfy her needs; she needs more advanced courses and courses that deal in more depth. The teachers don't seem to take their work seriously.

I might suggest that Kathy be given the opportunity to progress at the rate in which she is capable and explore in depth the subjects in which she is interested. I might try to establish an accelerated program in the school curriculum for people such as Kathy; or if that was not possible then I would suggest transferring her to a school that offers such a program.

I also think she needs some personal counseling to help her in her struggle for independence.

This counselor stated that he would attempt to do something for Kathy—start an accelerated program in the school. We believe that pupil personnel workers must be initiators of change and undertake alterations in such things as curriculum. This does not diminish the need for, or appropriateness of, counseling individual students, though. It is through counseling that you identify where changes are needed, while concurrently helping someone like Kathy in her struggle for independence.

Prior to a summarization of the approach we would take, one last set of reactions is presented. These come from a person trained as a counselor who is teaching high school American history. He wrote:

> One approach might be to change her environment. This solution seems to be a good solution, even though some people might view it as an escape from the problem. Having lived in two small communities and student taught in a third, I am quite aware of the attitudes that Kathy must have had to cope with. If the community was very homogeneous, she would probably be better off to leave.
>
> Another approach might have been to shape Kathy's attitudes and behavior so that she could be in greater harmony with her peers and the community, by encouraging her to be more tolerant of her peers' attitudes. Also, she might be encouraged to be less obvious about her intellectual abilities. However, one would have to be careful not to discourage her from achieving at her high level.
>
> I'd initiate No. 1 by helping her find scholarships so that she could attend a school in a community that she might be more at ease with, so that she might make acquaintances with people of similar attitudes and abilities.
>
> For No. 2, she might be reinforced to changing her behavior through a counseling relationship, or peers might be encouraged to be more tolerant of her attitudes and beliefs.

This last set of reactions was included because of the comments about small communities. Knowledge about small high schools and rural communities forms the basis of a set of assumptions we would have to make concerning Kathy's case. Among responders, the most commonly stated assumption was that Kathy's statements in her essays were representative of her true nature. This is certainly something necessary to assume, but the basis from which people react to the information usually goes beyond this. For example, one assumption made by a responder which would be similar to the type we would make was that most of the inhabitants of the community beside her parents were conservative and church-oriented people. In addition, we assume that there was an identifiable social system in the community based upon certain church affiliations. Kathy and her family have sort of cut themselves out of this community by their absence of a specified religion. Kathy has felt the social pressure and as of her freshman essay no longer talks about religion because, as she said, "in a small community . . . you can easily be an outcast from society." Another factor that might go right along with the religion is the cultural heritage. Kathy noted that "everyone in the community is German" in her sophomore essay. It was interesting to note that this statement came right after a discussion about her Lebanese ancestry. Thus we find that religion and cultural background as well as being a new family in the community (new families are never entirely accepted, according to Kathy) all serve to cut her off from the community.

Schools usually reflect community attitudes; consequently we would expect that Kathy would have the same social difficulties in school. If we wanted to alter the in-school situation for Kathy, there might be a need to generalize these needs for other students as well. This is based on the assumption that many teachers in her school are also from the conservative, religious German stock Kathy described in the community. Making exceptions for Kathy would not be viewed as the most positive method by the school staff. Take, for example, the apparent requirement that she complete more credits to graduate in three years than the number needed by a student in attendance four years. Therefore, we would attempt to identify two or three other high performing students in the school. With this group of students, we would spend the better part of an academic year collecting information and developing case studies. This amount of time is suggested because some schools, particularly those like the one Kathy attended, may not accept changes unless the needs and purposes for modifications can be logically developed and well documented. We would look for very specific programs that are needed, based upon the sample of students included in the case studies and documentation that they are needed in terms of comments and examples by students, teachers, and others in the school and community.* When the case studies have been developed, we would distribute them to the entire school staff. At this stage our next steps would have to be based upon our professional knowledge and assumptions about outcomes. For example, if there were a reasonable relationship with the principal and superintendent, a rather lengthy, say two-hour, appointment would be made in which we could explain the case studies, their implications, and possible plans for action. We might even arrange for the students involved to attend. Following this would be a staffing, or, if the entire school staff is small enough, maybe something like an in-service day.† Out of this should come some consensus about what should be done in the school for superior students. The suggestions made by responders, such as beginning accelerated or gifted programs or holding a series of workshops to encourage individualized instruction, might be the outcomes from staffings.

---

*See John W. M. Rothney's book, *Methods of Studying the Individual Child: The Psychological Case Study*, Blaisdell, Waltham, Mass.: 1968, for a thorough yet readable description on the collecting of information and writing of case studies in the vein we are presently suggesting.
†Many states allow school to be dismissed early a certain number of times per year to hold in-service training sessions, workshops, or institutes.

Summary of Part Two

Planning curricula to meet the multiple educational needs of each student as defined by the 1955 White House Conference on Education (Chapter 1) is a complex and challenging task. Difficulties occur at two levels. The first is deciding the what, when, and how of content and the other learning experiences to be provided. The second is matching the pupil's day-by-day skills and concept development, abilities, and personal-social factors with ongoing programs. If the student becomes overwhelmed and frustrated in the educational process, he *feels* alienated and becomes a psychological dropout. Dropping out psychologically has many forms, among them: daydreaming, loafing, rebelling, hating, selection of the easiest courses and activities, peer dependence, fear, anxiety, drugs, sex play, the defiance of authority, and overconformity.

The psychological habit of dropping out does not prepare the student to cope with, and successfully meet, the day-by-day challenges of his family, social, and vocational life. The psychological habit of failure in the school setting, at its worst, could be based on literally thousands of practice trails that led to failure, over the most formative years. Indeed, unless we can match the student to the learning experiences, the possible psychological consequences are disturbing.

When the student becomes a psychological dropout, he is not only a personal failure as an individual, he is a significant failure for the school *because* there may not have been an adequate understanding and matching of the student's needs, abilities, and personal-social factors with ongoing programs.

The psychological habit of success in the school setting has all the reverse possibilities of perceived failure. The student who has an array of learning opportunities appropriate for him at that given moment *feels* a healthy sense of self-acceptance, and he identifies positively with school and community values. Staying in school and graduating is the final act of a long series of personalized school-related successes. *Not* dropping out psychologically has many forms: alertness, ambition, optimism, critical thinking, and a personal sense of self-identity. The student who does not drop out may also be one who selects challenging courses, is goal-directed, forms significant peer relationships, has a sense of social interdependence and poise, views sex as an expression of love and a beautiful sharing relationship, and works for change effectively within the social mores.

The psychological habit of *not* dropping out best prepares the student to cope with, and successfully master, the day-by-day challenges of his school, family, and vocational life. Success in the school setting, at its best, must be based on thousands of positive learning experiences covering the widest array of significant information and activities throughout the formal years of education. Indeed, when we successfully match the student to his learning experiences, the possible psychological consequences are tremendous.

The authors clearly do not ascribe to a narrow Freudian view that personality factors are so firmly structured by age five or six that further maturity is less consequential. The whole process of developing positive attitudes, skills, problem-solving techniques, and social relationships is largely dominated by school-age experiences. The experiences to a vast degree are either provided directly in the school setting, in school-related activities, or in friendship patterns arising out of the school experience. Furthermore, we find it illogical to assume that the successful student is a product of the school, while at the same time assuming the school dropout is *not* a product of the school. If the student is successful *because* of the educational process then the student that fails is one who could not survive in the established system. The fact of the matter is that success as well as failure in the school setting are both an integral part of the system. Both success credits and failure credits belong to the school process.

Both student success and failure communicate to professional people in education how well the defined educational objectives are being carried out in the daily educational process. (Again refer back to the list provided by the 1955 White House Conference on Education.) The encounter between teacher and student is *interactive*. The products of perceived success and failure tell us about the effectiveness of the encounter. The perception of this encounter provides feedback all along the educational process; we need these results to help us assess our past effectiveness and to guide us into the future.

Major imperfections exist in the educational process because teaching is more of an art than a science; there are limited materials and professional resources; and not only do students vary greatly among themselves, but so do teachers. A good part of what the student learns is to cope with the teacher in a given situation at a given moment. The same might be said of the teacher who must cope with the student—and more often, a whole group of students.

One of the most trying tasks in education is understanding the student, and without relevant information and interpretation, the task of providing adequately for the student's educational needs is most difficult. This book has been designed almost solely for the purpose of helping the reader-participant understand the concepts of pupil personnel services and learn to use student information effectively in educational planning. The task is an enormous one because there is often a great deal of data to analyze and practically no one interprets it in the same way.

Pupil personnel services are a subjective and personal business. Almost everyone in the business of education is there because he cares about young people and has a genuine desire to help young people develop their human potentialities. Almost everything that occurs in the classroom and school setting has psychological consequences for the pupil as a person. The consequences of a successful day-to-day pattern of learning in all of its school ramifications are so important and so pervasive for the student that we are all impelled to be pupil-oriented and to share in the responsibility of pupil personnel services. Continued practice in this process will help sharpen professional judgment, which is the basis for implementing the services.

PART THREE

Case Studies for Discussion

T his book has one basic purpose: to help readers gain a closer understanding of the processes by which pupil personnel information becomes
an effective aspect of educational practices. All professional people in
education have a daily need for skills in pupil personnel work because they
are continually called upon to make judgments relative to a student's
school progress and personal-social development. Therefore, Part Three
is designed to take training beyond the usual academic setting to a school-
type setting. This will help the reader-responders discover how they
might best function in matters related to pupil personnel planning. In
short, this section is largely a training section.

The six cases in Part Three follow the same general format as the first
six cases, but these latter cases are not analyzed separately in the text. By

the time the reader gets to Case No. 7, on Tim, he should have developed some skill in responding to case materials. (These cases may also be used intermittently with Cases Nos. 1–6.) For these cases, a class as a group can practice the analysis and synthesis process used with the cases in Part Two. Various approaches are available for discussion of the cases, but one deserving special attention is the hypothetical case conference. This approach, as illustrated in Case No. 2, is one that the pupil personnel specialist uses frequently. Simulated experiences such as this should help the reader to prepare for actual case conferences.

CASE NO. 7 Tim

(Grades 9 through 12)

Tim is a rebel . . . bright, outspoken, erratic in his school pattern, and offensive to most people. He feels emancipated from cultural norms because of having lived in another country. In many ways, he acts out his parents' intellectualizations but without their sophistication or attainments.

Tim does not like school, his community, or his country very much. Many of his preoccupations are with the "phoniness" of others, especially the adults in his culture and especially his government. He rebels in his dress, his manner, and in his unguarded expression of feelings. Sensing his difference, though not acknowledging personal error, Tim has sought out the school counselor as a sounding board for his concerns with the "dishonest" others. His intellectual strength centers on social criticism to the exclusion of constructive alternatives.

CASE STUDY MATERIALS ON TIM

Tim was self-referred to the school counselor because he was having many problems in conforming to school standards and accepting assignments in his classes. In an effort to develop with him appropriate plans for helping him, the following information was obtained.

231

Family Background

Tim

Age: 17.

Father

Age: 60.
Education: B.A., M.A.
Occupation: Teaches industrial arts at a vocational technical school.
Health: Average.

Mother

Age: 56.
Education: Three years college.
Occupation: Housewife.
Health: Average.

Siblings

Brother

Age: 38.
Education: 12 years public school.
Occupation: Career Navy man for 17 years.
Marital status: Divorced. He has custody of his 18-year-old daughter.
Health: Good.
Address: West Coast.

Sister

Age: 39.
Education: 12 years public school.
Occupation: Assembly line worker.
Marital status: Divorced. She has custody of her two children.
Health: Good.
Address: Midwest.

Educational Background

Only secondary school records are available.

Academic Record: American International School, Middle East

Freshman:			Sophomore:		
English	C D		English	D D+
Biology	D D		World History	D D+
Math	D D		Algebra I	F C−
Speech	F D		Spanish I	D D
Drama	B+C		Driver's Education	
Grade Point: 2.375			Grade Point: 2.031	

Junior: English   D C
      American History   C C
      Business Mathmatics C C
      World Geography   C C+
      Grade Point: 2.2708

Community High School (entered 8/24/70)

Senior: Consumer Education   D   Second semester
      Machine Shop   C−   unavailable
      Civics   D
      Algebra I   E

Tests Administered:

1969 Preliminary Scholastic Aptitude Test (PSAT)

Verbal 44   Math 30
     77%   28%

1969 SRA National Educational Development Tests

English Usage   39%
Mathematics Usage   25%
Social Studies Reading   66%
Natural Science   66%
Word Usage   92%
Composit   62%

1971 Peabody Picture Vocabulary Test, Form B

Mental Age 18+
Intelligence Quotient 124
Percentile 92

School Report, Community High School

Attendance record. Regular attendance.

Special academic interests. Shop courses.

Special academic difficulties. Mathematics, social studies, biology.

Classroom participation. Very seldom. He is usually preoccupied with drawing or reading a library book. When he does participate, his views are anarchistic. Other students invariably disagree emphatically.

Social adjustment. He has few friends. Students make fun of him. His reaction is to do nothing, either verbal or physical.

Group participation. When he is with his acquaintances with whom he has something in common, such as long hair and using drugs, he seems to be a leader. In the school environment, he is withdrawn.

Student's response to authority. Well-mannered in a superficial way. He is never disruptive, but has a condescending attitude.

Student's physical appearance. He is quite thin and rather tall. His clothes are always clean although sometimes rumpled. He wears his hair shoulder length and has a droopy mustache and a goatee. He wears a single gold hoop earring in a pierced ear. For the last year, he has regularly worn a belt with a clasp made out of a hashish pipe.

Apparent health problems. None that are obvious.

Relationship between school and parents. Tim's father and mother are determined that they know more about what schooling their boy should get than does the school system. The father has upon occasion had rather heated discussions with the staff on that subject.

Transcript of Counseling Session with Tim

Tim: I guess the main problem I've had since I came back to the States last August (1970) has been with the attitude here toward kids my age. When we were in Istanbul (Turkey), a boy became a man when he started acting like one. I was really on my own a lot, and I got to the point where I could depend on myself instead of running to my old man and old lady for answers or to get me out of a situation.

[*We were talking about his feelings about different countries.*] I'm against our government. Everybody passes the buck, and what does get done is just for the benefit of the dopes that run this country. A couple of examples. When we were over there, I ran over a little kid with my chopper (motor bike). The Turkish government took my bike away from me, and the kid's parents sued my folks. The State Department didn't do a thing to help. They said it was out of their hands. Then several months later, the same thing happened to the son of a State Department employee. The guy ran over and killed a Turk. He got his bike taken away from him all right, but he got it back the afternoon of the same day. So my folks—my old man's the greatest—he put the screws on the State Department that same day and got my bike for me. Wow, talk about hypocrisy.

[*Tim was commenting on the attitudes of people.*]

Counselor: I have the feeling you really liked it over there.

Tim: I'd love to go back there. The people really appreciate other people. They all live so close to death; and everything is so honest and real, that if you do something for one of them (the Turkish people), they really light up.

Counselor:	You like people to be honest and to appreciate what is inside a person.
Tim:	Yeah. Take the dope thing. Over here everybody is really paranoid about it. People over there have been using hash for centuries. Nobody thinks anything about it. Right before we came back, we began getting a lot of real freaks from Nepal, kids from the States who'd been bumming off the people in Nepal until the government threw them out. They were really strung out; it was disgusting. If you're going to do dope, be intelligent about it.
	Another thing is sex. I've only scored with two girls in my life. In Istanbul, there was this girl. If I wanted to go to bed with her, I'd take her up to my room and turn the record player up. My folks were there. They knew about it. Here it's so dishonest. The only place it's acceptable is in the back seat of a car. To me that's a lie. You're being just as hypocritical as our government.
Counselor:	I'm getting the feeling that your friends here act differently from the way you act. Your actions are maybe more honest and real.
Tim:	My friends? Hah. What friends. Over there, the two guys who were my friends were in their late 30's. They were willing to live and let live. Here all you've got is a bunch of teeny bopper types. A chick goes out with a guy if he's in athletics and has a sharp car. Not one of them looks on the inside of a person. Sure I'm lonely. But if I started acting like they do, I'd be compromising my own beliefs. I'm really scared that there will be such constant pressure that my beliefs will break down.
Counselor:	The people here are pushing you into a corner as far as your beliefs are concerned.
Tim:	Yeah. A cornered rat. Next year, I'm going to an industrial school in Arizona. At least, there, I can take my chopper down into the Southwest, and just hole up sometimes. Just get away from all this paranoid hypocrisy.
	[*We were talking about his family environment.*]
Counselor:	Your brother and sister are a lot older than you.
Tim:	Yeah. My folks really raised me different from them. My folks are really the greatest. They let you be a man when you're ready to act like one.
Counselor:	I get the feeling you think you had an advantage being raised differently from your brother and sister.
Tim:	Oh man. Yeah. Both of them really got mangled in their marriages. I'm not going to make the same mistake. When I get married, it's going to be permanent—no divorce—never.

[We were talking about his appearance.]

Tim: You'd be surprised at the number of hypocrites in this town. All these teeny boppers "Oh-ing" and "Ah-ing" over their fake freaky clothes. And the funny thing is, you get close to them and they act like you're going to rape them. It's really weird. When we went to Istanbul, I was as straight as anybody. But then I started getting my head together. You know, I really liked my hair long and the grubbies (his denim bell bottoms and jacket). It was so natural. And the guys in the International School were sophisticated enough to be what they wanted to be, and people just left you alone. They accepted you. I was on real good terms with the straights there.

    Here in the States, the only people I really feel like I fit in with are the Hell's Angels.

Counselor: They're the only people who are real to you.

Tim: They're honest. None of this rotten lying. I'm going with this girl now. Her brother's an Angel. I know what they're like. They're free. The government doesn't tell them what to do. They can take care of themselves. They've got rules.

Counselor's Interview with an Acquaintance of Tim

[We were talking about Donna's circle of friends.]

Counselor: You mentioned that you know "Buck" and Tim.

Donna: Yeah. Buck is OK. Wow, that Tim is something else though. He's really gross anymore.

Counselor: He's not the same person that he was last fall.

Donna: You know, he used to have some manners. He's got sex on the brain anymore. I mean, last Saturday, a girl friend of mine had a tight sweater on. One of the guys made a joke about it. Tim chimed right in. We just avoid him anymore. Sure, I mean, some of my friends have gone to bed with guys, but he's just too gross. Last fall he was fun. He always knew when some dope was coming in, and I don't know, he was just fun then, and he's not anymore.

Two Teachers' Perceptions of Tim's Behavior and Academic Work

ENGLISH TEACHER'S COMMENTS   (Noncredit English for seniors)

After having had your client in my English class for almost nine months, I think I may be the wrong person to ask for this report on him. I identify rather closely with his attitudes toward our society and toward what I would call the Protestant ethic of "work, work, work."

His work for me has been uneven in quantity, but the quality is good. His ideas are unhampered by social mores, and he shows evidence of thinking deeply. He recently did a critique of *The Naked Ape* and *The Social Contract,* in which he brought in the philosophies of St. Thomas Aquinas and Martin Buber. The structure was good and it was a very rational paper. This was, however, a paper he wanted to do. When he is not interested in some assignment, I might as well forget about his making it up. His stock reply when I ask him about overdue papers is a quiet and very final statement, "It wasn't relevant."

I would like to see him contribute more in class, for I believe he has much to give. But my only question is whether our school (and our town) are ready for his rather uncomfortable, "honest" criticisms of our society.

SOCIAL STUDIES TEACHER'S COMMENTS

Tim is a strange boy. I know he has ideas on government, but he never volunteers in class anymore. He had been getting increasingly reticent, mainly for two reasons. The students in his civics class come from good, patriotic families and they challenge him when he *does* speak up. His outlandish dress and long hair and that one earring dangling from a pierced earlobe probably get to them. He wouldn't be a bad looking boy if he would cut off that hair and shave.

His work in class is poor. He hands in all out-of-class assignments, but his ideas are always idealistic. There is never anything practiced and down to earth in his written reports. A month ago he handed in a paper on some required readings on the Pentagon. It was a diatribe against Senator John Stennis.

He refused to take part in our mock elections last fall and the Little United Nations we had in the classroom, saying that our government in his words, is a "self-serving bureaucracy that does things for itself first and for the nation second."

His exam grades are very low. I had a conference with him, in hopes that a pep talk would do him some good. There was a wall between us that I couldn't break down. He was very mannerly—he always is—but he really didn't seem to be listening to me.

He did mention to me that he is going to a technical school in Arizona next year to learn to repair diesel engines. This might be a fine thing for him. By the time he gets a degree from that school, some of his attitudes will hopefully have matured.

Statement by Tim's Father

Tim is much more mature than the students with whom he goes to school. We've always known he is above average in intelligence, so we reared him permissively. He's never disappointed us. We've been in some scrapes because of Tim, but we've always stood behind him.

We do a lot of things together. We both like to work on cars, and I taught him to take the motor bike apart and repair it. We all read a great deal, and none of us thinks very much of our government.

Tim isn't getting grades in school that really reflect his ability. The kids give him a rough time, because he has the guts to look like he wants to look. The teachers are just reflections of our materialistic society. They really don't try to get to know him.

CASE NO. 8 Sharon
(Grades 9 through 12)

Sharon's case is a combination of self-report forms and counselor reports that cover the last four years she was in high school. These materials bring out a lot of typical problems of the adolescent years. Such problems should not be minimized, but the case of Sharon is specifically included for consideration of career development.

Various types of information are kept by schools for pupil personnel purposes. The materials on Sharon reflect the extensive use of student self-report information. Repeating the same questions over a period of time, in this case for the ninth, tenth, eleventh, and twelfth grades, provides for a developmental picture. The self-report information forms are coupled with a counselor report, emphasizing suggestions to the school staff. The purpose of these reports was to provide an opportunity for the school staff to better meet the needs of these students. By concentrating on selected students, like Sharon, the counselor hoped the school staff might generalize this attention and thereby better meet the individual needs of more students in the school.

The materials and counselor reports on Sharon bring out a lot of typical problems of the adolescent years. These problems should not be minimized, but the case of Sharon was specifically included in this manual for consideration of career development. The reader should attempt to identify those aspects that would be important when assisting high school students in their educational and career planning.

238

CASE STUDY MATERIALS ON SHARON

Freshman Year Information

1. *Are you living at home with your father and mother?* Yes.
2. *How many brothers and sisters do you have?* Two. My sister is 20 years old and in her junior year in college. My brother is 16 and is in his junior year in high school.
3. *Does anyone else live with you?* No.
4. *What is your father's occupation?* Federal Bureau of Investigation.
5. *How much education did he have?* Through a master's degree.
6. *Does your mother work outside the home?* Yes—school teacher.
7. *How much education did she have?* She is working on her master's degree.
8. *Is there anything that you consider to be special about your family?* My father has had two nervous breakdowns.
9. *If I were to ask your friends what kind of person you are, how do you think they might describe you?* Most would probably say nice, because they might think it would get back to me. But they would probably want to say "different."
10. *What do you do when there is nothing that you have to do?* I enjoy reading; or sometimes I'll play the piano till someone makes me stop.
11. *What do you do during the summer?* Moved from Minnesota here. I went to Detroit for a week. The rest of the summer was just regular.
12. *What courses are you taking at school this year? What were your grades at the last marking period?*

Latin I — B	Biology — B
Algebra I — A	Civics — A
English — B	Choir and Physical Education — A — B

13. *How many study halls per week do you have?* Two.
14. *If you could spend all of your time on one of your current subjects, which one would it be and why?* Biology. Because to get the most of it you have to spend more time than available in class on it.
15. *Second choice?* Latin. Because it is hardest of all my subjects for me to get.
16. *If one subject were to be dropped from your current high school program, which would it be and why?* Choir. Because that is not necessary to get into a college.
17. *Second choice? Why?* Physical Education. Because it is not a necessary part of schooling which is needed for college entrance.
18. *What courses are you planning to take next year?*

English	World History
Latin II	Typing
Chemistry	Physical Education
Algebra II	

19. *In what group activities—school, church, or community—do you partici-pate? (Consider activities of last year if this is early in the school year.)* I'm in Pep Club; I'm the Treasurer of my home room. I enjoy dances and parties where there are lots of people. Piano lessons (Job's Daughters).
20. *Any offices in these activities?* Treasurer in my home room.
21. *Is there anything about your health that prevents you from doing any-thing you want to do?* No.
22. *What occupation are you considering most as a career?* Working with mentally retarded children.
23. *Why are you considering it?* Because it would be helping someone who really needed it.
24. *What other occupations are you considering?* Laboratory technician.
25. *What has your father said about your plans for the future?* He encourages me.
26. *What has your mother said about your plans for the future?* She also encourages me.
27. *If you could do as you pleased, what would you like to be doing 10 years from now?* Working in a special home for the mentally retarded.
28. *If you were given the opportunity to finish high school in three years by doing extra work, would you take it?* Yes.
29. *Why or why not?* Because then I would be able to get college over with sooner and be able to reach my goal.
30. *Would you like to be in classes composed only of better-than-average students?* No.
31. *Why or why not?* Because it would be too much pressure all of the time.
32. *If you could have any three wishes, what would they be?* To get my mom a really good home. Send my brother to a boarding school. And to be able to play the piano without having to practice.
33. *Any additional information which you think will help us know you better?* When I was little, I never really got along with other kids. I always want them to follow me, always to be the leader.

Freshman Counselor Report

1.   All of Sharon's teachers and counselors, as well as other members of the faculty are in a position to know her as an individual and to help her gain the self-confidence, security, and acceptance for which she is striving. Knowledge of her background may be useful if situations arise in which her behavior varies from the usual.

Sharon has been showered with many more enriching, as well as discomforting, experiences than the typical ninth grade student. Her travel record, which is comprised of moving to approximately seven different places and attendance at approximately four different schools within nine years, was most likely caused by her father's position with the FBI. This frequent shuffle was accompanied by the many adjustments that Sharon had to make to new settings and friends. She has never had a definite opportunity to establish roots in one place. This diversified pattern has also been complicated by her father's illness.

Sharon belabored the word "different" in referring to herself as well as others. She thought that her friends would describe her as this kind of person: "Most would probably say nice, because they might think it would get back to me. But they would probably want to say 'different'." When questioned about her terminology, she alluded to previous experiences in which she tried to assert her leadership potential and to the fact that she stated she was a quarter Indian. Also, in her essay, this expression is used in this fashion, "My family, I feel, has always been different from other families. This may not be true, but it just seems that way to me." Sharon feels that because her mother works outside of the home, she does not have someone to come home to after school; hardly any of her girl friends' mothers have to work. This interviewer questions the attitudes displayed and wonders if Sharon, perhaps for many years, has been striving very vigorously to find security and social acceptance and at times just overdoes it. Sharon added this information, "When I was little I never really got along with other kids. I always wanted them to follow me, always to be the leader."

2. *Is it possible for Sharon to take an active part in helping to organize a Latin club or a debate group on the freshman level? She seemed to be enthusiastic about these two ideas. She needs to become more involved in activities from which she can gain confidence and at the same time start exerting her leadership qualities with ease and a minimum of tension. The satisfaction that she might find in group activities may help her to clarify her outlook on "people," which is heavily matured with mixed emotions.*

Her statement, "People are the *main* forces on almost anyone's life, and I am to be no exception," seems to be indicative of her determination for some sort of equality. This same feeling of inadequacy is expressed when she reasons why it is important to meet people, "Because after leaving home, I will have no one to hide behind from this world of people." This counselor wonders just how much Sharon included herself when she commented, "I feel that the 'little people' should be treated as everyone, also." She will probably respond better to encouragement than to disapproval.

3. *Sharon needs to be made more aware of the various opportunities and occupations in which she can employ her talents, as well as to the important part that high school subjects play in the development of her potentialities, even the courses that she does not find "necessary."*

Sharon's goal in life, working in a special home for the mentally retarded, is highly people-oriented. She is so intent upon this ambition, which began when her father was ill, that she would like to finish high school early so that she would be able "to get college over with sooner" and thereby reach her goal. This drive has even centered in her present high school program, where she would like to drop choir and physical education because these subjects are not needed for college entrance.

Sharon stated that she is scheduled to take typing during the next school year. Is it possible that she would be able to take one semester of typing and then practice (with suitable exercises) at home and gain enough knowledge for her personal use? The school time might be better spent on additional subjects or advanced courses.

4. *Sharon's interest for English should be stimulated in order to help her overcome her present weaknesses. She should do intensive work in eliminating anything that might limit her potentialities for future success. These steps might be considered.*

   (a) She should be encouraged to expand her scope of reading interests and could be given some help in selecting books.

Although she says she spends approximately eight hours each week reading out-of-school assignments, she should devote more time to reading books rather than newspaper and magazines alone. A guided reading program in other areas would also be helpful.

   (b) She should be required to use the dictionary frequently for spelling and to keep a list of spelling words that cause her difficulty. In an essay written at the Guidance Laboratory, she misspelled the following words: entrance, urge, encourage, too.

Sophomore Year Information

1. *Is there any change in your family situation since we last saw you?* No.
2. *What courses are you taking this year? (List them and give best estimate of marks.)*

Chemistry — B	History — A
Typing — B	Latin II — B
English — A	Geometry — A

3. *How many study halls per week do you have?* Two.
4. *If you could spend all your time on one of your current subjects, which one would it be? Why?* Chemistry. Because it will be the hardest during the year and you do more in that class.
5. *Second choice? Why?* Typing. Because one should learn to type, and it's a course in which not a day should be missed.
6. *If one subject were to be dropped from your current high school program, which would it be? Why?* Latin. Because I could take first year Spanish, French, or German instead.
7. *Second choice? Why?* Gym. Because it could be made up any other year because it involves no homework.
8. *Do you have enough time to complete your assignments in school?* No.
9. *How much time, on the average, do you spend in doing school work each night?* 2–3 hours.

10. *In what group activities—school, church, or community—do you partici-pate?* Church Youth Group, Pep Club, AFS, Job's Daughters, Latin Club.
11. *Any offices?* Recorder in Job's.
12. *What do you do when there is nothing that you have to do?* Read or bake.
13. *Any activities in which you would like to participate but can't?* Skiing.
14. *Why choose them?* Because during the winter everyone is always out skiing.
15. *Why can't you participate?* I don't know how, and none of my friends will take the time to teach me.
16. *What courses are you planning to take in your third year?*

Physics	History
Algebra II	Gym
English	Choir

17. *What courses during your fourth year?*

Trigonometry	Gym
English	Science Course
History	Work Experience

18. *Is there any subject in particular you are looking forward to taking in your next years in school? Why?* Senior English and Trigonometry. Because the teachers are great.
19. *Given the opportunity to finish high school in two years instead of three by doing extra work, would you take it?* Yes. *Why or why not?* Because I like the kids in that class and I want to go away to college.
20. *Would you like to be in classes composed only of better-than-average students?* No.
21. *Why or why not?* Because lots of the smarter kids are drags.
22. *What real advantages are there in being a better-than-average student?* You'll have a better chance for scholarships and getting jobs.
23. *What disadvantages?* Some of the other kids dislike you for it.
24. *If I were to ask your friends what kind of a person you are, what do you think they would say?* They'd all say something different, but you'd get something nice from Helen.
25. *What qualities would they like most about you?* I'm pretty loyal to my friends, and I like to do about the same as they do.
26. *What occupation are you considering most as a career?* Teacher.
27. *Why are you considering it?* Because there's a demand for teachers and I could get a job.

28. *What other occupations have you considered during this past year?* Pharmacist, secretary.
29. *What has your father said about your plans for your future?* He asks what I want to but isn't going to force me to decide.
30. *What has your mother said about your plans for your future?* About the same as my dad.
31. *If things worked out just the way you wanted, what would you like to be doing 10 years from now?* Working or running a home.
32. *If you had any three wishes, what would they be?* To have a part-time job, to have a different personality, and to go to another school where the kids aren't such gossips.

Sophomore Counselor Report

1. All of Sharon's teachers, counselors, as well as other members of the faculty are in a position to help her gain the self-confidence, security, and acceptance that she is striving for. She needs a chance to express herself, to develop leadership, and to be able to talk over with someone any new ideas that she may develop.

The faculty should be commended on the fine progress it has made in helping Sharon gain self-confidence, security, and acceptance. Her attitudes toward herself, her family, and the school have changed greatly over the past year. Activities, such as being a teaching assistant in her physical eduation class and helping at the school during the summer vacation, have given her a chance to make use of her leadership ability and to feel accepted.

Since she has lived in seven different locations during her life, Sharon has a broader outlook on life than many of her peers. She feels restricted by their attitudes toward her but is learning to live with "the group's" viewpoints and still be an individual. Even though much progress has been observed during the year, Sharon still needs a great deal of understanding from those around her.

2. Some provision should be made for nonjournalism students to help with the production of the school newspaper.

Sharon is taking a full academic schedule and probably will not take a formal journalism course during high school. She would like to participate in the school newspaper but is not allowed to because she is not taking journalism. Could some provision be made for Sharon, and other students like Sharon, to take part in the production of the school newspaper?

3. The time spent in taking a second semester of typing this year might be better spent in some other activity.

Sharon enjoys typing and could learn the fundamentals during the first semester and increase her speed and accuracy during the second semester by self-study. She said that her father was going to buy her a typewriter.

The extra period a day could be spent in an activity such as a laboratory assistant, library assistant, or advanced study. It is felt that time spent in an enrichment activity would be of greater value than another semester of typing.

4.   *Sharon should take five academic subjects during her junior and senior years.*

The courses planned for the junior and senior year are only tentative at this stage, but Sharon seems to shy away from taking five academic courses. She includes courses in science, mathematics, social studies, and English for each of these years.

The addition of a fifth subject, such as a modern foreign language, would be of greater benefit than spending an hour a day in study hall.

Because of frequent moves and illness in her family, Sharon has had to make many adjustments. Presently, she is gaining a sense of security but is on guard against another move. Her father who is employed by the Federal Bureau of Investigation told her that the family wouldn't move until Sharon was graduated from high school, but she seemed to be in constant psychological preparation for another move.

Now, her biggest concern is with her peer groups. She is vacillating between two cliques and trying to maintain some cohesiveness with both groups. Sharon would like to innovate many changes in the attitudes and activities of her peers, but she is stopped by social pressure.

As far as the future is concerned, Sharon believes the beginning of her sophomore year in high school is too early to make definite decisions. She appears to be looking at the future realistically but often lacks enough information.

She is considering the possibility of applying to an eastern girl's college. Status and social prestige appear to be factors which are influencing this thought. Other institutions of high learning are also under possible consideration. Both parents are conscious of Sharon's higher education aspirations and are knowledgeable in giving assistance and gaining necessary information.

Junior Year Information

1.   *What courses are you taking this year? (List them and give an estimate of marks.)*

Mathematics — A   English — A

Physics — B+   Journalism — A

History — A

2.   *How many study halls per week do you have?* Seven.
3.   *How many hours of homework do you do on an average evening?* 1 to 1 1/2.
4.   *Any problems about getting your homework done?* No.
5.   *If you could spend all your time on one of your current subjects, which one would it be? Why?* Physics. I find it the most interesting, and one must work day by day to keep up with it.
6.   *Second choice? Why?* Journalism. It is probably the most fun of my classes.
7.   *If one subject were to be dropped from your current high school program, which one would it be? Why?* Algebra II. The teacher is boring and acts like he doesn't enjoy teaching us.
8.   *Second choice? Why?* History. The teacher is so easy and it's about the fourth time I've gone over the material.

9. *List the courses you plan to take during your senior year.*

English

French I

History

Bookkeeping

Senior Science or Physiology

10. *What do you plan to do the year after high school graduation?* Go to college.
11. *What has your father said about your plans for the future?* He wants me to go to college.
12. *What has your mother said about your plans for the future?* She wants me to go to college.
13. *What occupation are you considering most as a career?* I'm not really sure because I'd like to look into all chances.
14. *Why?* I keep changing my mind.
15. *What other occupations have you considered during the past year?* Some ideas are: dietician, because I love to cook; lawyer, because it interests me; school psychologist, because I would enjoy working in a school.
16. *List school, church,*   *Offices held in*
    community activities   *such activities*

    Job's Daughters   Reporter

    Pep Club

    Youth Group at Church

    Future Teachers

    School Paper Staff

    American Field Service

17. *What do you do when there is nothing that you have to do?* Cook or read.
18. *If you have a part-time job, what do you actually do on it?* During the summer I did some work at the high school office, running ditto machine, and so forth.
19. *Is there anything about your health that prevents you from doing anything you would like to do?* I have a shoulder that gets all messed up when I work with my hands for any length of time.
20. *If I were to ask your friends what kind of person you are, how do you think they would describe you?* Sharon would say something nice, because she's that kind of girl and my best friend; I don't know what the others would say.
21. *What real advantages are there in being a better-than-average student?* You don't have to study so hard.
22. *What disadvantages?* Kids are always wanting you to cheat for them.

23. *Does any person expect too much from you? Comment.* Sometimes I think my mother does: I work at home and I'm in a lot of other stuff for her, yet I just can't seem to make her proud of me.
24. *Does any person expect too little from you?* I think this might be Mom, too. Because when I try for something that means a lot to *me,* she just doesn't back me up like she should.
25. *If you could change your school in any way, what changes would you make?* Take the junior high away; the kids are always underfoot. Sometimes I wish my mom wasn't always there, too.
26. *If you had three wishes, what would they be?* Get a full scholarship to some neat school, live somewhere other than here, have a half-way normal home life.
27. *To whom in your school have you gone when you wanted to talk over your plans and your problems? Name.* There's no one at school I'm able to talk to. *Position.*

The kids have never really "taken me in" since I moved here. Sharon is about the only one who doesn't care if I do something wrong. She tones me down, and I seem to pep her up. The others seem to want me to be just perfect at all times, never to falter. And they keep teasing me about the way I walk. It did used to be different, but I trained myself to walk straight, yet they still tease and then get mad at me if I ignore them. I can't win.

Junior Counselor Report

1. *The possibilities of attending a summer workshop in journalism or the dramatic arts should be investigated.*

Sharon indicated that she would like to attend some type of summer school between her junior and senior years. She would like this to be an educational experience, and also the opportunity to be on her own for a few weeks. Summer workshops offered for high school students on college campuses was a suggestion she received enthusiastically.

Of the several types of programs explained, Sharon appeared especially interested in journalism and speech workshops. She also liked the idea of living in a college dormitory with other high school girls for two weeks. This would give her the chance to study something she enjoys and experience being relatively independent.

Information about special programs for next summer are not yet available. Brochures and booklets explaining the particulars are usually ready for distribution early in the second semester. In the past, the state college has offered excellent programs in drama and theater arts, and the state university has held a journalism workshop, These are only two of the many programs that may be available to Sharon next summer.

2. *Sharon appears to need some adult figure to whom she can express her thoughts, ideas, frustrations, and energy. She will probably need some mentor who can lend support but will not offer judgments.*

Sharon said, "There is no one at school I'm able to talk to." This situation appears to be predicated on two situations.

First, Sharon manifests a tremendous amount of physical and psychological energy.

This energy channels itself into many diverse activities. The long list of, school, church, and community activities in which she participates tends to confirm the breadth and diversity of her interests. Organized activities do not seem to channel all of her energy which then appears in such behavior as rapid speech patterns, expression of many thoughts and ideas, and general exuberance. When talking with adults, her general vitality may quickly change the direction of conversation. As yet, Sharon reports finding few poeple in the school who are willing to just listen to her thoughts about the daily ups and downs of life.

A second situation which may be connected to Sharon's interest in finding someone to talk to is the appointment of her mother's friend as one of the school's counselors. Sharon said she would not be comfortable talking to the school counselors because they might report the conversations back to her mother. Sharon went on to indicate that even though the counselors probably wouldn't inform her mother, she just would not be comfortable with them.

One adult who may be in a situation to listen to Sharon's thoughts is the physics teacher. The small class size and Sharon's interest in the subject may establish the teacher as someone to whom she can talk.

3. *Speech, theater, and journalism are Sharon's favorite avocational activities. Could the teachers associated with these activities provide Sharon with some information concerning the possible opportunities in these fields?*

As far as the future is concerned, Sharon feels it is still too early to make any decisions. She has so many interests that it is difficult for her to eliminate any. Presently, speech, theater, and journalism activities are her favorites. Since these are her favorites, it may be valuable to obtain more information about possible career opportunities in these areas. Sharon expressed great interest in acting, for example, but she does not want to be an actress because of the instability involved. There are many openings in the theater besides being a "star." Realistic information may help her capitalize on her avocational interests as well as provide the stimulus to investigate other fields.

During Sharon's first two years in high school, the school staff has helped her gain self confidence, security, and develop leadership. The faculty should be commended for the individual attention afforded this student and other students. One area in which the staff may be of further assistance to Sharon is understanding. Suggestion No. 2 presents some ideas for consideration on this matter.

Beyond having someone to talk to, Sharon does not feel accepted by her peers. "The kids have never really taken me in since I moved there." She still seems to vacillate between several clicks trying to maintain cohesiveness within each but in essence finds few intimate relationships. She has a broader outlook on life than many of her contemporaries, and only one other girl in her class wants to make something of herself. According to Sharon, the rest of the peers, and especially a group dubbed the "eels," consider positions such as proprietorship of a bar successful. Sharon's apparently quite open degradation of other student's aspirations is not a factor which facilitates cohesive relationships.

Conformity to peer pressures is not necessarily an advantageous goal, but having a better understanding of why group pressures are applied may be advantageous. Sharon's outward reaction to peer pressures for conforming behavior is "I don't care." This may be only a manifestation of a situation she does not comprehend. Teachers and staff members are in a position to help her understand the situations. The adult staff can probably view the adolescent structure from a broader perspective than the students. Communicating a knowledge of the situation and indicating awareness of the daily patterns of behavior may help Sharon understand and gain more satisfaction from her peer relationships.

Guide to the Senior Year Interview

1. *Any interesting experiences since your last visit with us?* Since my last visit I have attended Badger Girls State and a drama institute in Milwaukee.

Review of Family Situation:

(This review is necessary for scholarship and admission application)

2–3. *Father's occupation? (Be as specific as you can about location and activity and what he does on his job.)* My father is employed by the Federal Bureau of Investigation.

4. *Mother's occupation?* Teacher.

5. *What does she do on her job if she works outside the home?*

6. *Names of older brothers and sisters. (Give their occupations if employed. If they are in school or college, give the grade or year.)* Penny—First grade teacher; Phillip—freshman in college.

7. *Names and ages of younger brothers and sisters.* None.

Review of School Record (Grades 9–12):

8. *Number of English courses taken and now taking. Give names of English courses if the names differ from the usual English 1, 2, 3, and 4. Circle honors courses.* English 1–2–3–4, Journalism, Library Practicum, Speech, Drama, Humanities

9. *Looking back at all the English you have had in high school, what comments would you make? (Try to think of the subject field itself, not about teachers.)* The courses should be coordinated in the style of grammar that should be taught. Each year the teacher uses a different approach and form.

10. *Would you choose an occupation in which high performance in English was the main requirement?* Yes. *Why or why not?* I enjoy English in the form of drama.

11. *Names of mathematics courses taken and now taking. Underline honors courses.* Algebra I, Geometry, Algebra II, and Trigonometry.

12. *Looking back at all the mathematics you have had in high school, what comments would you make? (Try to think of the subject field, not about the teachers.)* I was switched midstream from regular mathematics to modern; I think all students should get either one or the other.

13. *Would you choose an occupation in which high performance in mathematics was the main requirement?* Yes. *Why or why not?* I feel I've accomplished a lot after doing work in mathematics.

14. *Names of science courses taken and now taking. Underline honors courses.* Biology, Chemistry, Physics, PSSC.

15. *Looking back at all the science you have had in high school, what comments would you make? (Think of the subjects, not the teachers.)* The science department at _____ should offer more in laboratory work.

16. *Would you choose an occupation in which high performance in science*

was the main requirement? No. *Why or why not?* I don't feel that I know enough about science.

17. *Names of social studies (include history) courses taken and now taking. Underline honors courses.* Civics, World History, U.S. History, American Problems.
18. *Looking back at all the social studies you have had in high school, what comments would you make? (Think of subject field, not the teachers.)* The courses should vary more. We usually get the same material year after year.
19. *Would you choose an occupation in which high performance in social studies was the main requirement?* No. *Why or why not?* I don't enjoy it that much.
20. *Names of foreign languages taken and now taking. Underline honors courses.* Latin I and II.
21. *Looking back at all the foreign languages you have had in high school, what comments would you make? (Think of the subjects, not the teachers.)* The course has since then been dropped, but it was more memorizing than learning.
22. *Would you choose an occupation in which high performance in foreign languages was the main requirement?* No. *Why or why not?* I didn't learn anything.
23. *Other subjects taken (list them with number of units of each):* Home Economics—1, Choir—1, Physical Education—4.
24. *Looking back at these subjects, what comments would you make? (Think of the subjects, not the teachers.)* The Physical Education courses should be revised.
25. *Would you choose an occupation in which good scholarship in Home Economics was the main requirement?* Yes. *Why or why not?* Because I enjoy working in the course.

Review of School, Community, and Other Activities:

26. *Activities in which you participated*	27. *Number of years:*	28. *Offices held:*
Jobs Daughters	5	Recorder, 1st mess 4
Church Choir	2	
AFS	4	
Future Teachers of America	2	Historian
Pep Club	4	

29. *List any special honors or activities.* Chosen to attend Girls' State. Attended drama clinic at Milwaukee.
30. *Looking back at these activities, what comments would you make?* They are ordinary clubs, none of which are as active as they should be.

31. *Has participation in any of the activities influenced your choice of an occupation?* Yes. *If so, tell which one and how it has influenced you.* The drama clinic has given a firm support to my hope of working in that field.
32. *About how many hours per week of nonrequired reading do you do?* Three.

Plans for the Future:

33. *What do you plan to do next year?* Go to college.
34. *What steps have you taken toward your plan?* Taken or signed up for required tests. Narrowed down choice of schools.
35. *What occupation are you planning to enter?* Drama or computer science.
36. *Why did you choose that one?* I enjoy the drama, but I like the computer science and it would be practical.
37. *What other occupations are you considering?* Home Economics major.
38. *Why did you choose them?* I like doing the sewing, cooking, and so forth, that goes with this. I feel I've accomplished something when I do this type of work.
39. *Does your mother agree with your educational plans?* Yes.
40. *Does your mother agree with your vocational plans?*
41. *Any comments on the two questions above?* She agrees, but she doesn't really confirm either choice of vocation.
42. *Does your father agree with your educational plans?* Yes.
43. *Does your father agree with your vocational plans?* Yes.
44. *Any comments on the two questions above?* Yes. He hasn't commented on a choice either.
45. *Who, if anyone, helped you to make up your mind about the place you have considered for post-high school training?* My mother and friends.

General Review:

46. *Is there anything about your health that keeps you from doing what you would like to do?* No.
47. *What special problems have you met because you have been a better-than-average student?* Teachers expect a lot from you, but if you try to give them extra, they won't take it. Students are jealous.
48. *What special problems have you met because you were chosen to come to the laboratory?* It's hard to explain to other students why you come, without giving them the wrong idea.
49. *Are there any matters about your education or future plans that we should discuss during our interview?* Helping to decide what field of study would be the best for me.

Senior School Report

In the time allotted, write about your high school experiences (Grades 9–12). The three questions below are guides but in the last one you are free to write whatever comes to mind.

1. *Looking back at your high school experiences, suggest ways in which high school might have been made more valuable?* The whole outlook of the teachers could have been made more inviting. It isn't supposed to be party-time every day, but most of the teachers seem to have a grudge against the students for coming.
2. *How could your experiences have been made more interesting?* If the teachers had shown enthusiasm for teaching, the students would have joined in and the whole process would have been more fulfilling for everyone. The subjects offered were not difficult, and the teachers made no effort to put forth anymore than they had to.
3. *We would like to have any comments you would like to make about your school experiences over the last four years. Use the space in any way you wish. Write on back of this sheet if you need more room.* The emphasis is placed on test scores and not on the student's work, attitude, and so on. I think that this is the wrong approach to learning. In our school 7–12 grades are literally crammed into one high school. Not only is it rough on the students both younger and older, it messes up a lot of activities. No accelerated classes are offered.

Senior Counselor Report

1. Sharon's interest in drama and the dramatic arts should be stimulated to help her develop personally and to utilize her enthusiasm for performing for the benefit of others. Embodied in the explanation below are several plausible activities. Are there more appropriate ones you can think of?

Sharon has expressed an interest in acting and drama for the past two years. School plays and summer stock have given her several chances to perform. Speech and drama classes, forensics, and a drama institute at the State University have all added to her knowledge and improved the quality of her work. Even after these experiences, Sharon is frequently chided when she expresses an interest in pursuing a career in drama. Apparently most adults think she should seek what they call a "more practical" occupation. This attitude had also been expressed by her peers. For example, while on a campus visit at the university, one of her classmates asked whom she would see on the professor visit. Sharon informed him that it would be a professor of speech and drama. He responded with "Can't you think of someone better to see?" Sharon feels as if pressure is being applied to conform to a scientific society. Might it not be better to encourage rather than discourage any possible artistic talent she may have?

Since Sharon is interested in learning more about the theater and doing more acting, could her interests be put to use? Before casting the next school play, she might help the director block out the actor's movements or possibly work out the blocking on her own. This might give her some idea of the preliminary planning that goes into a production. Some additional alternatives might include performing at local elementary schools. A children's play might be produced or dramatic readings of children's stories could be given for the lower elementary grades. Hopefully, those who have observed Sharon's dramatic performances and know the local situation can suggest additional ways to encourage her.

2.   *Whenever possible, could some type of honors or accelerated classes*
        be provided for those students most capable of profiting from the
        experience?

During the senior year, we ask students to report on their high school experiences.
Many of the high performing mentioned something about the lack of honors classes.
Sharon probably stated the case as succinctly as anyone. She wrote: No accelerated
classes are offered to more advanced students. The teachers try to go at a middle pace
—too fast for the slow learners and too slow for the fast learners. Some teachers shift
one way or the other, always cheating at least one group of students.

Over the years, Sharon's counseling reports have noted a steady improvement in her
peer relations. Social pressures are still causing her some difficulty (as reported in suggestion No. 1), but she now seems to cope with the situation easily.

CASE NO. 9 Emmy
(Grades 5 and 6)

After her husband died prematurely, Emmy's mother increasingly turned her attentions to her only daughter. Emmy's school pattern was fairly accommodating, but her peer relationships were marginal and she developed few outside interests. Finally, Emmy got so she did not want to leave her mother to go to school, and the earlier somatization pattern became more dominant.

Many children come from homes in which one parent is deceased or the parents are separated or divorced. Emmy's father died five years ago; after an adjustment period, her mother returned to college and became certified for public school teaching. There was little enough time to meet academic requirements and be a responsible mother, so Emmy and her mother spent much of their available time together. Few school activities and classmates seemed important to Emmy, and she never felt strongly inclined to get involved in projects outside of the mother-daughter relationship or family home. They both seemed to need this relationship.

CASE STUDY MATERIALS ON EMMY

Emmy was referred by the Director of Special Education for a psychological evaluation. Emmy has been having trouble adjusting to the school program

254

and has recently been transferred to the building where her mother is employed.

School Referral Report (Completed by the Sixth Grade Teacher, April 1971)

Period of time child has attended this school. Aug. 29, 1965 to present. (Transferred to Smith Grade School as of Apr. 19, 1971.)

Present grade level. 6.

Grades repeated. None. *At what grade level should this child be?* 6.

Academic adjustment:

Grade Marks

Subject	Present mark	Indicates improvement or deterioration	Comments
Reading	C+	Improvement	Loves to read.
Language	B	Improvement	
Arithmetic	C+	Improvement	Does have some difficulty with certain problems.
Spelling	A	Improvement	
Science	B	Improvement	
Social Studies	C+	Improvement	

Attendance record. Recently child has been absent so much that recent grades were affected. Attendence record for Grade 1—Absent 11 days; Grade 2—Absent 4 days; Grade 3—Absent 1½ days; Grade 4—Absent 4 days; Grade 5—Absent 0; Grade 6—thus far 15½ days.

Special academic interests (please list). Loves to read.

Special academic difficulties. Has difficulty in arithmetic at times; is very concerned in doing a good job and is deeply troubled if she doesn't understand problems in arithmetic.

Classroom participation. Has been good until recently; doesn't like to participate in Physical Education but is always eager to recite in front of the class.

Testing Program (Achievement, Intelligence, Reading, and so forth):

Name of test	Date given	Grade level when given	Grade	Scores status	Pupil score	Administrator
Lorge Thorndike A	3-14-66	1	1.6	IQ 115		Mrs. Moore
Metropolitan				Cl.Med.		
(Reading) A	5-3-66	1	1.8	2.1	2.4	Mrs. Moore
Metropolitan				Cl.Med.		
(Arithmetic) A	5-4-66	1	1.8	2.3	1.6	Mrs. Moore
Metropolitan				Cl.Med.		
(Reading) B	5-1-67	2	2.8	3.4	3.3	Mr. Miller
Metropolitan				Cl.Med.		
(Spelling) B	5-1-67	2	2.8	3.1	3.6	Mr. Miller
Metropolitan				Cl. Med.		
(Arithmetic) B	5-1-67	2	2.8	3.5	3.6	Mr. Miller
Iowa Tests				Composite		
of Basic Skills 3.68		3		4.1		Mrs. Shaw
Iowa Tests				Composite		
of Basic Skills 3.69		4		6.6		Mr. Smith
Iowa Tests				Composite		
of Basic Skills 3.70		5		5.9		Mr. Jones
Lorge Thorndike				Verbal IQ		
ID	9-28-70	6		117		
				Nonverbal		
				100		
				DIQ		
				109		Mrs. Gray

Social adjustment:

Describe this child's relationship with peers. Her peers seem to like her; however, she is just a member of a group, not a leader in her peer group; is disturbed when peers do not overly "flock" to her; has feeling of complete rejection of peers; has feeling everyone is against her; feels inferior with certain peer group; does not fit into clique and is hurt because she is not accepted.

How does this child participate in groups? Always was willing to be in a group. Complete withdrawal starting April 1. Constantly cries while with peers; feels more comfortable by herself; remained at school in a room by herself; would cry if brought back to the room.

What roles does she usually assume (leader, follower, passive, aggressive, and so on)? Follower; would like to be leader; however clique that child wants to enter doesn't accept her. Feels rejected socially; complete withdrawal from peers.

What is the child's response to authority? Accepts authority; always obeys.

What is this child's general physical appearance? Good; a little overweight —is very self-conscious and feels everyone is making fun of her chubbiness.

Are any particular health problems apparent? (Describe) None—this is an only child.

What is the relationship between the school and this child's parents? Father deceased; mother aware of child's problem; concerned about child; is willing to seek help outside of immediate town. Mother is teacher.

Other comments. Child constantly cries in school—started April 1. Feels rejected by peers. Doesn't want to come to school. Says no one likes her. Is transferred to another school—completely new environment as of April 17, 1971.

> Signed
> Grade 6 Teacher
> Mark Twain Grade School
> April 17, 1971

Parent Information Report (Completed by the Mother, April 21, 1971)

Referral information:

Please state in some detail why this child is being referred for an evaluation. Describe what problems are present at home, at school, in the community. Emily is showing increasing reluctance to attend any social group without me. Her fear has resulted in crying spells, pleading, upset stomach, and frequent bowel movements. She has missed choir practice, communicant's class, special services in which she was to sing with a youth choir, and is miserable at 4-H parties—left the last rally before it really started. I am not aware of any home problems other than her moodiness and reluctance to have me go anywhere without her. Two weeks ago she stayed home five days with a cold. The following Monday she begged me to let her stay home. I refused. That week of three school days, she had crying spells at school—said she did not want to be in the classroom.

Has this child ever been examined or received treatment for this problem before? No.

Type of neighborhood where home is located (rural, small town, city). Small town neighborhood but outside city limits.

Is home rented or owned? Owned.   *Number of rooms.* 4.

Amount of total family annual income. (My husband died five years ago at age 29. He was a college-educated electronics engineer.)

_____ Less than $4000.   _____ $4000 to $6000
__X_ $6000 to $8000.   _____ More than $8000.

Describe briefly the family's social contacts and activities. I was previously active in church youth organizations and Girl Scouts—now I am busy teaching and working toward a master's degree. Emily has always been active in youth groups at my insistence. Now, however, she would like to drop out of everything.

Family's religious affiliation. Lutheran.

Is this child sociable or does she prefer to be alone? She is very sociable when around adults and small groups of friends—however, she does spend a lot of time alone (with me at home).

How does this child get along with: Mother. Demands a lot of attention —often moody—complaining.   *Brothers and sisters.* None.

How does this child behave in adult company? Depending on who the adults are, with older acquaintances she is friendly and talkative—with my close friends she is rude, demanding her own way over what others want.

How does this child get along with friends his own age? Depending on who the friends are, she is usually cooperative and generous, does not like to be teased.

With whom does this child prefer to be? Mother.

Developmental history:

Birth. Full-term.

Unusual birth circumstances. Not on records. *Explain:* Doctor told me (when I asked him the reason for the excess of stitches I had) that Emmy had turned immediately prior to birth—her heartbeat had slowed and they were concerned for her and gave her some extra physical help being born. I was "put to sleep" upon request as I entered hard labor and was unconscious during Emmy's birth.

Illness or difficulties following birth. Convulsions. *Explain:* Emmy began having convulsions at about 6 weeks. These occurred maybe every 3–6 months. Increased at two years. Doctor prescribed phenobarbital which she took for at least 1½ years, during which time the seizures increased in frequency and severity resembling Grand Mal attacks. She was weaned from the phenobarbital in 1963 and since that time has had seizures every 6 to 8 months. (Sometimes the span is greater.) She has not been treated medically for this disorder since. During early treatment she had skull X rays (1962). Following auto accidents (1966 and 1968), she had skull X rays. In 1970, following examination of lump on the back of her neck, she had upper spine X rays. No irregularities were shown.

Early development. All normal or early. Bladder control normal during daytime, poor during sleep until age six.

Describe any severe illness or injuries, difficulties or irregularities in early development. Reluctant to take bottle—would fall asleep after sucking a few times; reluctant to take food even after she could feed herself—had a very poor appetite until about seven years old (and was anemic). She had a very severe case of measles in 1965. She was ill about 14 days. Doctor was not at all concerned.

Interests and Activites:

What are this child's main interests? Reading, playing with her dolls, playing with the cats, watching television, changing furniture and things in her room around.

What recreational activities are enjoyed most? Movies—an occasional fair.

Are there work responsibilites? Yes. What kind? Making her bed, keeping her room clean, drying dishes, sometimes cleaning the living room, sometimes feeding the cats, sometimes taking out trash.

Attitude toward work. Usually complains—takes her a long time to get started, task is often interrupted by some other interests so that completion of task is often delayed an hour or so.

> Mother's signature
> April 21, 1971

Psychological Report

Parent Interview

Emmy was accompanied by her mother to the Pupil Personnel Offices for consultation with the psychologist. She began by reporting that she was teaching first grade in a Title I Project with most of the children coming from low social economic homes and most frequently with no fathers in the homes. This was her first teaching job; prior to the current school year, she was a student at a nearby university. The client's husband has been deceased about five years as was indicated in the family background history. He was killed in the recent war. Apparently following the untimely death of her husband, she began her college career in earnest, first completing two years of training in a local junior college and then finishing her bachelor's degree with an emphasis in elementary education.

The initial discussion very quickly led into her concerns about her daughter's refusal to attend school. The mother has very strong feelings that Emmy should not be forced into school attendance at this time, because she suspects her daughter is epileptic. She feels that by pressuring her daughter to any considerable extent, convulsions will result. At this point in the dialogue, the mother said that one of the main problems in school is that her daughter simply does not want to be near other children. Emmy is able to associate satisfactorily only with very close friends or family, in the mother's opinion.

At the first of the current calendar year, the mother had resolved to keep her daughter active in other social activities, including school participation. It was at this point, of course, that she broadened the discussion base of the adjustment problems of her daughter. The surfacing maladaptive patterning would eventually include almost all aspects of the family and neighborhood encounters. In paraphrasing her daughter's statements, the mother said, "Nobody likes me." Her approach with Emmy has been one of rational explanation to try to persuade her daughter to affiliate with other children and to participate in play activities. Under these conditions the daughter intitially attempts to conform to the mother's expectations, but soon begins to "whimper," with the eventual result of the mother's giving in to the daughter's requests of nonparticipation. The mother's empathic sensitivity here is remarkable.

At this point, the mother again shifted back to specific school problems and stated that for a long time Emmy had refused to take the bus to school. Thus the mother takes the daughter to school and most often picks the daughter up immediately after school. She has almost no tolerance for her mother's tardiness. About a month ago, Emmy had a moderately severe case of the flu and was unable to go to school for a week. The mother observed that when her daughter was ill, she seemed to be sick during the school day but was not so disabled for home activities in the evening and on the week ends. When the mother attempted to deal with her daughter about this inconsistency, Emmy would "work herself into a fit." During these spells, Emmy begins with a severe crying spell and eventually becomes so upset that she does, indeed, seem to become ill. When forced to attend school during the following several weeks, Emmy had crying spells and her fears that the other children were looking at her were now confirmed because she was becoming such a nuisance in the classroom that they were, indeed, attracted by her unusual behavior. The accommodating teacher then decided to let Emmy stay out of the classroom to do her lessons. This seemed to reduce the child's tension and also allowed her to maintain a marginal degree of participation in the school program. Since the mother is a school teacher, with cooperation from school officials, Emmy was transferred about two weeks later to the building where her mother is teaching. The mother thought this would help "reduce Emmy's anxiety and insecurity." She added that it was another case of her daughter's begging and pleading with her until she gave into the suggestion. Emmy now has school privileges in an adjacent vacant room next to the mother's first grade room. This arrangement was facilitated by the Director of Special Education.

At this point in the interview, the mother began revealing more of the behavioral pattern descriptive of her daughter in the family constellation. She believes these problems go back to the time when Emmy first began walking and talking. This child has always demanded a great deal of loving. The mother has always tried to get her daughter interested in other people, but this effort has been a source of constant frustration. Even when Emmy was enrolled in nursery school, she evidently let her mother know that she very strongly disliked this activity. She fussed with her mother about being exactly on time when she called for her at the nursery school building, even at this early date. Another chronic difficulty has been the child's strong feelings of never wanting to go to bed at night and trying to figure out ways to stay up later in the companionship of her mother. The mother reported there had been no babysitters for her daughter up to age six, except for occasional assistance from a maternal grandmother.

Obviously, separation from the daughter was considerably difficult for the mother, too, as she very strongly indicated that she "hated to leave her." Evidently she fears she would not be adequately responsible for her daughter if she were not there to take care of the child herself. Likewise, Emmy does not want to share her mother with other people; in most instances, she is in the constant companionship of her mother. The mother conveys feelings of guilt about leaving the child with just about anyone under most circumstances. Thus their activities included a wide range of associations while going out to eat, attending movies, shopping, going to zoos, going on picnics, taking hikes, doing the laundry together, and so forth. Since her husband is deceased and she occasionally dates, this has meant that in almost all instances the men would not only take the mother out, but also her daughter. She stated, smilingly, that they saw a lot of children's movies together.

The mother appeared to be increasingly aware of, and concerned about, her daughter's pattern of adjustment both in the home and in the school community. She feels that more is now expected socially of her daughter by other people; she feels Emmy acts more like a preschooler than a preadolescent. The mother then indicated she simply does not know how to help her daughter be a more effective person in school and with her peers. The sense of protectiveness was again brought out by stating that other children use her daughter and take advantage of her. She related several instances about bringing other children into the home setting to share Emmy's toys in play experiences, but that there simply has been no reciprocity. Rather than see the problem her daughter is having in developing effective relationships with age peers, the mother interpreted the situation as a problem of the other children's being inconsiderate to her daughter. Another example reported was that other children teased Emmy about her father's death. This unfairness and also other situations would upset her daughter, who gets upset very easily.

Throughout this discussion, the mother was unable to attribute any of Emmy's adjustment problems to the patterning of the mother-daughter or her child-rearing procedures. When I talked with her on a second occasion, I had an opportunity to pursue in more detail her interpretation of the presumed diagnosed convulsive disorder. She described Emmy's behavior as a kind of rageful crying with loss of breath, followed by "passing out." In explaining the behavior, the mother was able to indicate that her daughter did not actually fall to the floor or on any occasion injure herself; but rather she crumpled to the floor and, in fact, in such a way that the mother would reach out and help Emmy as she collapsed. To a considerable degree, the mother associates her daughter's convulsive behavior with a "strange expression on her face." Once in the prone position, Emmy would become tense and look as if she were suffocating. There were some movements described as "jerking," followed in a short period by Emmy's waking up "surprised" and "confused." Following the so-called seizure, the child would not sleep and would recover rapidly. Emmy has not taken medication for this disorder for seven years. During the time of medication, Emmy was prescribed phenobarbital, during which time the number of "seizures" increased dramatically to as often as four times a day. After 10 months of intermittent medication, the mother voluntarily discontinued use of further medical consultation.

Test results

Emmy was seen briefly for testing with the following tests administered: BMGT, D-A-P, and TAT (selected cards). At the time of the examination, Emmy was described as a clean-appearing, slightly heavy, preadolescent girl. Grooming and hygiene appeared to be well above average and there were no apparent cosmetic problems. She was cooperative during the interview and was able to discuss to a limited extent her problems in school and her need for studying away from the other children. Outwardly, she appeared to be not unusual in terms of her appearance and physical development. As indicated earlier, she seems to be able to relate well with adults, and this was characteristic of her during the testing session.

In response to the perceptual motor tasks, the student did not demonstrate any substantive impairment, thus suggesting there was no organic or neurological involvement in the perceptual motor processes. In a technical sense, planning and organization were adequate on the BMGT. During this aspect of the examination, she seemed mildly distracted by some irrelevant background stimulus material and sought information from the examiner as to the correctness and appropriateness of her responses. In general, she appeared to be slow and cautious in her work. Her drawing of a person was the front view figure of a female who looked remarkably like her own mother. The drawing did not present conceptual problems for the client and the feminine figure included much detail of clothing and human features.

The following themes were developed by Emily to the TAT:

Card No. 1 presents the picture of a boy sitting at a table on which has been placed a violin and several sheets of paper.

Can't tell what it is. The boy might be blind. (Pause.) The boy is looking at a book or picture. He is reading a mystery book. (Pause.) Just reading it. Can't think of anything else. (Pause.) He is sitting at home and his parents have gone to the store. He is scared. The room is dark. (Pause.) He hears some noise. He is very scared. He keeps reading. Finally his mother and dad come home. He goes to bed.

Card No. 2 is a farm scene with a young lady in the foreground carrying books, with a man in the fields plowing with a horse in the background and on the left side of the picture an older woman stands leaning against a tree.

This could be a girl in the olden days. Living on a plantation or farm. She is going to school and looking at the slaves. They are fixing up the farm. (Pause.) She is watching the slaves. The plantation owners are beating the slaves. She takes her books and goes to school. (Inquiry—"Tell me more.") She doesn't like the idea of people having slaves. This makes her very sad. (Inquiry.) In school she has lots of friends, but all of her friends don't feel the way she does about slavery. They don't worry about slaves. (Inquiry.)

Card No. 3G shows a woman standing in a doorway looking down and perhaps dejected.

This girl could be lame. She lives in an institution and has to stay in one room by herself. They think she is crazy and stuff. There is a room nearby that nobody is supposed to go in. She hears weird noises and goes down the hall—but doesn't go in. But one night she enters the room and gets scared. She runs back to her own room. (Pause.) (Inquiry.) She has no parents. She lives in the institution in a room by herself. She doesn't like people; they are mean to her. Sometimes she does things that they don't like her to. She says what others say not to do. She does what others say not to do.

Card No. 4 presents a mature man and a woman with the woman reaching out for the man apparently looking in another direction.

This looks like maybe these people work in a restaurant. The man is mad because somebody didn't pay him. The woman is trying to hold him back. (Pause.) She doesn't want him to kill a man or something. (Inquiry.) He kills the other guy.

CASE NO. 10 Calvin
(Grades 5 through 8)

Most teachers can name a half-dozen students who should be achieving at grade level but do not seem to apply themselves. They are variously labeled "lazy," "underachieving," and "disinterested." Calvin does not perform well in the classroom, and has a long history of being a "daydreamer" and "immature." Many psychological, social, familial, and physical factors seem related to his classroom pattern.

Calvin's mother sees her son in her own image and has a long history of being emotionally disturbed. Recognition of the problems within the family unit has resulted in the mother's seeking assistance at the local mental health clinic. In the meantime, however, Calvin makes minimal use of his educational opportunities at school. He seems to fade out in the classroom, while daydreaming has become a substitute for actual achievement. Without supervision, his interests turn inward and his motivations diminish. How much his problems are caused by neurological dysfunctioning and emotional immaturity is difficult to ferret out. What educational programs should be developed remain an equally challenging concern.

264

CASE STUDY MATERIALS ON CALVIN

Calvin is now a twelve-year-old, sixth grade student with an extended history of marginal educational adjustment in the elementary school program. His mother made many contacts with school personnel, and the family has had contact with the local mental health clinic. Educational planning has been difficult. Related information is available from the last two years.

Parent Interview (with Mental Health Clinic Social Worker, Winter 1969)

The mother described Calvin's development as unremarkable up to the age of about four. At that time he developed severe stomach pains, which persisted for about five years. During the last several years abdominal problems have been less of a bother. Examination by the family doctor did not reveal a physical cause for these pains, and the mother interpreted the doctor's findings to be that the cause was "nerves."

Calvin attended a parochial school during the first and second grades. During the first year, his grades were "A's" and "B's," while his grades during the second year were uniformly "C's". His mother seems to attribute this drop in grades to his second grade teacher but hinted that Calvin's learning capacity might have been less that year. During Calvin's first year of school, either she or her husband would spend at least three hours tutoring Calvin every night. They were quite satisfied with his scholastic performance during that year. However, during the second year, Calvin seemed to have more difficulty learning, and the parents became slightly impatient with his learning difficulties. He transferred to a public school in the third grade and has remained there until now. During the third and fourth grades, his parents still attempted to tutor him, but the father became increasingly frustrated with Calvin's inability to retain material and seems to have eventually "thrown up his hands" in disgust. During these years, Calvin's interactions with his father were primarily in this type of situation. Recently, the father has begun to work with Calvin in building model airplanes, but his relationship with Calvin still remains limited.

Calvin's emotional involvement seems almost totally with the mother. She described herself as having a quick temper, as being very impatient with Calvin, and frequently punishing him for relatively minor transgressions. She says she often knows she is hurting Calvin and behaves impulsively in their relationship, although she states she does not know why. She stated that her husband and relatives have often told her she is "too hard" on Calvin and that she could give him more leeway. She sees some merit in their ideas but, nevertheless, seems to be afraid of what he "might do" if she allowed him more freedom. She also stated that she believes Calvin is very much like herself; in many situations in which she punishes him, he behaves as she herself would behave. In her words, he should "do as I say, not as I do."

Although the mother evidences great concern over Calvin's welfare and has devoted a great deal of attention to him, the quality of their interaction is essentially hostile. She seems to be overcontrolling in the relationship and has a great deal invested in Calvin's school success. She has a high level of aspiration for him. Her description of Calvin's behavior leads one to believe that, except for occasional outbursts, Calvin expresses hostility toward her indirectly, in a passive-aggressive manner.

Calvin appears to be rather friendly and well-mannered with others. His mother stated that she would not describe either Calvin, herself, or the father as "warm" people and stated that there is only minimal overt demonstration of love and affection.

The mother seems to have some insight into the irrational aspects of her relationship with her son and of how they foster each other's hostility. She seems to have enough strength to deal with this with professional help. She seems genuinely motivated to understand and change her relationship with her son. It is probable that Calvin's behavior in the school situation is symptomatic of his familial relationships.

Both parents seem to have tried everything they could and have been continually frustrated by their attempts at improving Calvin's academic performance. The parents seem to have an adequate relationship and seem genuinely concerned about Calvin, yet their continued frustration seems to have led to an impasse. Thus the mother, at least, seemed to be quite open to professional intervention.

Medical Report, Winter 1969

Clinical evaluation. All categories checked as "normal."

What residual, if any, from past illness or injury seems to be presently affecting this person? None.

Please give any additional information or comment about this person that you believe would be helpful in our evaluation of him. Complete checkup and blood work normal.

(Physician's signature)

Notes on an interview with the mother (by the School Counselor, Spring 1969)

This interview took place in the living room of the family's fashionable home. The mother's opening statement was, "If Calvin has problems, I am probably the cause of them." She has had diabetes since age 22, and admits that she does not stay on her diet until she is forced to do so. The diabetes affects her in many ways, she says. It makes her tired, irritable, and very short-tempered. Therefore, she easily loses patience with Calvin. She kept repeating over and over, "No wonder he acts the way he does, the way I scream and throw things all the time."

In reviewing Calvin's developmental and health history, the mother reported having serious health problems during her pregnancy. Calvin was born a few weeks prematurely. The doctor tried to induce labor, failed, and sent her home. Three days later natural labor began and the doctor, using forceps, delivered Calvin. Calvin was filled with fluid, a result of his mother's diabetes; he was very red in color and was placed in an incubator. At age three he had a severe ear infection and inflamed tonsils, which resulted in a tonsillectomy performed at that time. At age five he had measles and chickenpox simultaneously, accompanied by very high fever. Also at age five, he developed severe stomach pains accompanied by cold sweat. The doctor told the mother that these pains were comparable to an adult's migraine headache. About age 9 the pains diminished and have presented no problems to date.

It was mentioned that in the past two years Calvin has fallen out of bed twice and has been caught sleepwalking twice.

He has what his mother called an "aroma about him." She stated that even after a bath and shampoo, his body and scalp have an unpleasant odor.

Calvin is called "stupid" by his classmates, and his mother says that "everybody knows he is the lowest in his class." She further explained that Calvin can build from kits model airplanes, ships, and cars. He plays chess, cards, and pool, and has his own pool table.

Before moving to the present town six years ago, Calvin saw very little of his father, who was at home only on weekends because of his work. He and his mother were very close during those years. For the past six years, the father has not traveled but the mother stated that the two do not see much of each other. The father helps with homework sometimes, and plays chess and pool with him occasionally.

The family sought help for some of their problems from the Mental Health Clinic earlier this year and are now waiting for their application to be processed.

School Report (by Classroom Teacher, Spring 1969)

Present grade level. Fifth.
Grades repeated. None. *At what grade level should this child be?* Fifth.

Academic adjustment:

Subject	Present mark
Spelling	P
Arithmetic	P
Social Studies	P
Reading	S
Science	S

Attendance record. Very good—missed only one day in 67, one day in 68, and so far this year he has missed only one day.

Special academic interests (please list): He shows some interest in art.

Special academic difficulties. Calvin is unable to keep up with his fellow students.

Classroom participation. He very seldom volunteers to participate in any classroom activities.

Testing program:

Name of test	Date given	Grade level when given	Scores	Administrator
Kuhlmann-Anderson	11/17/65	Second	IQ, 110	
California Short Form Test of Mental Maturity	9/20/67	Fourth	IQ, 99	Teacher
Iowa Test of Basic Skills	10/68	Fifth	Composite 4.3	Teacher
Weekly-Reader Silent Reading Test	1/19/69	Fifth	16-Poor	Teacher

Social adjustment:

Describe this child's relationship with peers. Calvin seems to get along well with peers, but because of his immaturity they don't seem to treat him as an equal.

How does this child participate in groups? He does not contribute.

What roles does he usually assume (leader, follower, passive, aggressive, and so forth)? Passive.

What is the child's response to authority? He does show respect, but because of his immature actions he is somewhat of a behavior problem.

What is this child's general physical appearance? Good.

Are any particular health problems apparent? (Describe). No.

(Teacher's signature)
(Principal's signature)

School Psychological Report (Spring 1969)

Calvin is presently a fifth grader at the public school. The teacher reports that his behavior is immature and he has a short attention span. He seems to be lacking in any desire to learn or a willingness to try. Calvin hardly ever demonstrates any competitive spirit, only varying degrees of indifference. He does not demonstrate those interests that are normally expected of a fifth grade child. He has been given special help in school but shows little responsiveness. Conferences have been held with his parents, and they appear to be concerned about his lack of motivation. Calvin attends school regularly, and his grades are fair. He has poor grades in arithmetic and social studies.

Previous tests:

10–66	Iowa Basic Skills
	GP 3.7
10–67	Iowa Basic Skills
	GP 3.5
10–68	Iowa Basic Skills
	GP 4.3

Current tests:

Wechsler Intelligence Scale for Children
  Verbal Scale   IQ 100
  Performance Scale   IQ 114
  Full Scale   IQ 107

Wide Range Achievement Test
  Reading   GP 6.1
  Arithmetic   GP 5.0

Peabody Picture Vocabulary Test
  MA 11–7   IQ 102

Bender Visual-Motor Gestalt Test

Draw-A-Person Test

Incomplete Sentence Blank (Rotter)

Observations:

The psychological examination was conducted in the nurse's room at Calvin's school. He was a friendly and outgoing child, exhibiting verbal spontaneity and cooperation. He did not appear lazy or disinterested to the examiner, and he attacked the test items with vigor and enthusiasm. It is interesting to note that perhaps the one-to-one relationship stimulated Calvin's interest because the examiner did not observe the signs of disinterest or lack of enthusiasm cited with reference to Calvin's performance in the classroom. He is a nice looking child, well dressed, neat and clean. He did have a very slight odor, which did not appear to be body odor due to uncleanliness, but as mentioned by the parent, an odor that is simply a part of Calvin's person whether he is clean or not. Calvin told the examiner that he had had some tests last month at the Mental Health Clinic like the ones that he was being administered. He stated that he enjoyed going there for the tests and that he was having fun doing the examination items.

Interpretation of test results:

Calvin, an eleven-year, seven-month-old boy, has achieved an overall level of intellectual functioning which falls within the average range. His performance skills are somewhat better than his verbal skills, and a 14-point verbal-performance discrepancy is evidenced in favor of the performance scale. Calvin's performance skills fall within the bright-normal range. There is a moderate degree of scaled score scatter evidenced on the WISC, which tends to indicate the presence of emotionality. Calvin's poor scores on the WISC were in the areas of Information, Arithmetic, and Picture Completion. This profile is not indicative of any specific learning disability, but it is felt that training in the area of arithmetic skills may be necessary.

Verbal tests	Raw score	Scaled score	Performance tests	Raw score	Scaled score
Information	13	9	Picture completion	9	7
Comprehension	14	10	Picture arrangement	30	10
Arithmetic	8	7	Block design	38	13
Similarities	13	12	Object assembly	32	18
Vocabulary	41	12	Coding	48	12
Digit slan	10	10			

Calvin's performance on the *WRAT* indicates that he is reading at the 6.1 level which is commensurate with his mental age and is doing arithmetic at the 5.0 level which indicates underachievement of nearly one year, again pointing out the deficiency and need for help in the area of arithmetic.

His performance on the BMGT was good, indicating no obvious signs of visual-motor impairment. Projective indications include some signs of passive aggressive behavior, inadequate self-concept and self-image, and an overall attitude of inferiority.

Discussion:

Special class placement need not be considered for Calvin at the present time, since his achievement is reasonably commensurate with his present grade level. Calvin's intellectual skills show evidence of the possibility of above-average potential; consequently, it seems imperative that this child receive some special help in the area of guidance and remediation in arithmetic. Calvin will be referred to the guidance personnel for personal counseling and educational planning.

Calvin's teacher should attempt to find areas in which Calvin shows some interest, and she should work from these areas toward helping him become more interested in school in general. This child shows exceptional ability in some manipulation performance areas. He also showed a high-interest level in these areas. The teacher might try to get Calvin interested in puzzles, mechanical drawing, or putting things together mechanically.

His special ability appears to be art and he seems to have some interest here also. Calvin told the examiner that he liked to read, so maybe he could read some books on art and drawing and obtain some materials with which he can work in this area.

The parents should take Calvin for a complete phsyical examination for the purpose of determining whether any of his physical symptoms may be organically based.

Signature
School psychologist

One Year Later

Report from a Medical Neurologist (to the Family Physician, Spring 1970)

Dear Dr. _____:

Calvin was seen Feb. 13, 1970 and is a 12-year-old boy who has had a clear-cut problem of poor achievement in school and episodes of petit mal type of disturbances of consciousness. The mother is diabetic. The patient was premature and had excessive edema at birth, but weighed 6 pounds 14 ounces and spent 3 days in an incubator. The mother states that this child has been slow in all areas of development, has been poor in developing motor coordination, and has been progressively not doing well since the first grade.

The past history indicates the mother had another baby three years after the birth of Calvin, and this child died a few days after birth. There are no other children. A family history of epilepsy is denied.

The EEG is marked paroxysmal dysrhythmia, nonfocal consistent with a convulsive disorder.

Examination reveals a 12-year-old boy 4'10" in height and weighing 95 pounds. He is somewhat undersized and developed for his age. Reflexes and motor function are normal, no sensory losses. The cranial nerves are intact. The optic fundi are negative.

The findings in this patient, the history, and EEG are entirely consistent with organic brain damage with a petit mal convulsive disturbance. The brain damage is manifested by the patient's being a poor achiever. I would suggest Paradione, 5 grs., twice a day.

I think this patient would be considerably helped with a complete psychological profile. Since it is obvious this patient will need special educational help in addition to anticonvulsant therapy. I think all facilities should be investigated in regard to the maximum program that can be set up for him. We will be glad to cooperate in any way we can.

Signature
Medical neurologist

Special Staffing at the Public School (Spring 1970)

A staffing was held at the public school with the school principal, a mental health clinic psychologist and the current classroom teacher to discuss new information reported by the medical neurologist.

In reviewing Calvin's school performance during the 1969–1970 school year, a number of clinic, educationally related problems were reported by school personnel: poor performance in academic areas, poor attention to subject matter, little interest in anything, and almost no sense of academic or social interchange. Calvin was described as an agreeable boy, with several friends and no behavior problem in the school setting. Evidently, his mother pressures him and is upset with his educational retardation.

Calvin is now in the sixth grade but has evidenced another year of minimal educational progress. At 13 years, 0 months of age, he is one of the oldest boys in the class. He is in the lowest reading group, and his group test in reading was a year *lower* in 1970 than in 1969. Functionally, his educational level appears to be in the fourth grade range. Calvin's mother has employed a private tutor during the last six months to help her son to make educational gains.

There is now medical evidence of organic impairment which would indicate Calvin's eligibility for educational procedures for children with neurological impairment. In addition, educational retardation is marked, and there is information of personality trait disturbance and passive-dependent characteristics.

Special Education Department

School Psychology Report (Spring 1970)

Clinical impressions

Calvin is a nice-looking boy, normal-appearing in every respect. He is right-handed, freckled-faced, does not appear unduly clumsy. His tactile or touch sensitivity seemed to be quite good. There does appear to be some visual anomaly. He is unable to converge his eyes to near point; however, after several attempts, he did seem to achieve some convergence, indicating some possibility that corrective exercises might lead to ability in this area. His fine control of extrocular muscles (eye movement) is good. This is a skill that is very important in reading. At one point, he put so much pressure on the pencil that he broke the pencil (not the point). He looked disconcerted for a moment, then smiled. The KVST was administered with the only anomaly being a doubtful result on test three (Lateral Posture Far Point), and an alternation on test two (Vertical

Posture Far Point). There is some evidence that he is alternately suppressing one eye. The Spache Binocular Reading Test was administered, and it is found that he is reading 46 percent with the right eye, 57 percent with the left eye. Thus he is occasionally suppressing vision in the right eye, however, to an insignificant degree.

An effort was made to administer the WADT, however, the results were so consistently bad that the test was abandoned after item number 27. This subject could not possibly be communicating as well as he does with an auditory discrimination disability of this magnitude. It is possible that he either has a hearing problem or is evincing an emotional type response.

The results of the WRAT indicate that he is reading at grade level 7.7, spelling 4.6, and doing arithmetic at 5.7. Actual grade placement is 6.9.

The D-A-P protocol indicates some overworking at the level of the shoulders and the upper trunk. The stance is one that indicates that the subject is not willing to project himself into the environment; that is, it is a type of withdrawing response. There is a rather pronounced general asymmetry, favoring the right side. The left side is distorted, dimmer, generally weaker.

The Hand Test indicates that this is a markedly disturbed individual. He is completely lacking in affection responses, an indication that other people have not proved to be emotionally need-reducing to him. That is, he has not been emotionally reinforced by people. The high percentage of fail responses is characteristic of organics. It represents organic deterioration. The relatively high interpersonal responses, although largely negative, do represent an effort to cling to reality. This is a disturbed individual but not a psychotic one. The acting-out ratio is in the direction of withdrawal, rather than acting out (3/2). There are no high maladjustment responses that could override the natural tendency to withdraw and drive an individual to an acting-out pattern; thus it is postulated that this child will not likely become an acting-out person, but that his aggression will be expressed passively. However, the ratio is not overpowering.

Parent interviews with the school psychologist (summer 1970)

The mother reports that recently Calvin has twice engaged in physically aggressive behavior. Each time he attacked his closest friend, in each instance after provocation. He stated that he really wanted to hurt him. The mother is a little disturbed at this abrupt change in the boy in the last seven days. Since he evinced very low probability of such behavior at the last testing session, a change has obviously occurred. It appears that instinctual drives may be breaking through his defenses. The boy may be displacing his latent hostility toward his mother onto the peer. The reason for the new method of expressing aggression is not clear. It may be that the medication he is taking is reducing his anxiety to the level that he is able to express aggression outwardly without the previous threat. It may also be that since some effort was made to reduce the mother's guilt, she is responding to him in a different way. At any rate, it appears that his passivity is breaking up and that he may adopt a more integrative defense than repression.

One month later: Calvin's mother called and requested an interview. She stated that it is becoming more difficult for her to suppress her hostility toward Calvin. She stated that she is constantly finding fault and screaming at him and that their conflict is almost continuous. She said that she feels empty, devoid of affect, and generally describes a depressive syndrome. She said that she feels she has intropunitive tendencies and states that the scars on her face are self-inflicted. She has to overcome constant fear that her hostility will overflow into actual overt aggression, which it sometimes does. She said that there has been recent evidence that she cannot trust people, that she is suspicious and hostile toward most people. She would like for Calvin to leave home and be placed in a private school, but she is afraid that the separation would be traumatic for him. She evidences excessive guilt feelings centered around Calvin and is not able to cope with them. She was advised to enter a diagnostic hospital in a setting completely removed from her home and receive a complete physiological and psychiatric diagnostic workup. Since she is a serious and uncontrolled diabetic, many of her symptoms might be attributed to a physical reason. She states that she had not had a diabetic consultation for five years. As a minimal alternative, it was recommended that she see her family physician and receive counseling on a local basis.

Another month later: At a preschool conference with the director of the special education district, two school psychologists and the parents of Calvin, it was decided that placement in a regular but decelerated class would be optimal.

CASE NOS. 11 AND 12 on Family Counseling, Sue (Grade 6) and Gene (Grade 7)

Sue and Gene are a boy and girl who have had difficulty in getting along in their family situation. The reader is asked to consider factors beyond typical academic settings that may seem fruitful for working with the children and their family.

Individuals function as members of units, and the unit that most frequently comes to the attention of pupil personnel workers is the family. Frequently, work with one member of the family will indicate the need to work with the larger group; at times group approaches can be a great deal more expedient than individual approaches.

The materials presented below are, however, of the individual type. Two children in the family were referred by their mother for evaluation. Each of these series of reports takes a close look at the individual involved, but each also notes that a look at the larger family unit and its individual members would be profitable. When reading these materials and answering questions that follow, the reader should keep the group approach in mind.

THE FAMILY UNIT

At the time the attached materials were collected, the parents had been divorced. The father, a 37-year-old electrician, was still living in the same midwestern city that had been the original family location. The mother, a 33-year-old housewife, and the children had remained in the same city during the parents' first year of separation. The separation and the need for greater financial resources in the years to come helped crystallize the mother's decision to return to school. She enrolled in a two-year vocational training program in dental hygiene and moved the family several hundred miles away from their community into a student housing complex. The children are: Gene, age 13 in the seventh grade; Sue, age 11 in the sixth grade; Omar, age 8 in the second grade; and Paul, age 5 in kindergarten.They began school in the new surroundings, and the case study data start in the spring of the year after the move when the mother referred first Sue and then Gene.

CASE MATERIALS ON SUE

Reason for Referral

Sue was referred by her mother because of a sleeping problem. During the past months, Sue has had difficulty in getting to sleep at night. The problem has increased since December to the point where the mother felt it advisable to bring Sue for evaluation.

Interview with the Grandmother

Since Sue's mother could not come to the first interview, her maternal grandmother came in the mother's place and proved to be a helpful informant, although her point of view did not always agree with her daughter's. The main problems discussed by the grandmother were: (1) the situation with the father, (2) disciplining the children, (3) and Sue's difficulty in getting to sleep. She also mentioned her recent, "partial nervous breakdown." She is staying with her daughter until she recovers from mononucleosis.

According to the grandmother, Sue's father is a very selfish man who tries to buy the children's love. She feels he uses his visitation rights to show his authority, not because he wants to be with them. The marriage appears to have been on a shaky foundation for quite a while, as the father had brought the mother and the children to the maternal grandparents several times and "dumped" them there. The mother had tried to get him to accept professional help, but he refused. He had violent temper tantrums of which the mother was afraid. Eventually he left his wife and family, and the mother went back to school at a junior college and is now training as a dental hygienist.

The mother had six pregnancies in 13 years of marriage and "almost died" when the last child was born. The father had surgery so as not to have more children and "will not have more children" in his second marriage.

The grandmother described discipline problems as arising from the father's laxness with the children when they visit him and from the inability of their baby-sitters to control them at home. She described behavior such as eating popcorn in bed, staying out too late in the evening, and wrestling in the house as instances of discipline problems. She has made it clear to the children that she expects them to do what she wants, and they caught on quickly as to what was expected.

The grandmother stated that Sue has had too much responsibility for her age, especially in caring for Paul, the youngest child. She thought that mother and daughter have leaned on each other, that Sue needs a friend to play with and study with. Sue's sleeping problem consists of restlessness—getting out of bed and wandering before she settles down to sleep. The grandmother told her she had to go to bed and relax, and Sue obeyed. She wondered if the fact that Sue had not started menstruating was a factor in her restlessness at night. The grandmother also indicated that she thought her daughter was overconcerned about Sue.

A "partial nervous breakdown" appears to have been more serious than the grandmother was willing to admit. She thought "people were against her" and developed some unusual suspicions. She "accepts" now that some of the things she thought happened during her breakdown did not happen; she just imagined them.

Interview with the Mother

Sue's mother is an attractive young woman who seemed to be trying hard to handle her problems in a mature way. She confirmed that her mother had a serious emotional disturbance from which she is recovering. The mother said that helping her and the children is good for her mother, since she then feels useful and necessary. In regard to the discipline problems, the mother said, smiling, that her mother is not used to boys but she can keep them in order. Discipline does not appear to be a problem with the mother, nor did she describe problems with the baby-sitters.

There was concern about problems arising from the divorce and its effect upon the children. Visitation by the father has been a problem. The children had visited the father at Thanksgiving and Christmas and he had asked for them at Easter also. The children did not want to go for the whole vacation but just for two or three days. The father said, "If you don't come for the whole time, don't come at all." He has threatened not to send the money for the children and to take the mother to court.

A situation involving Gene, the oldest boy, that concerns the mother was described. The father, who has an electrical business, has offered a summer job to this 13-year-old-boy as a helper for $35 a week. The mother does not wish the boy to be with the father all summer because he will not be given adequate parental supervision. Gene is tempted by the money. Gene offers a further problem in that he is dedicated to sports and resents having to spend time on his paper route.

Sue has had a sleeping problem for years. She is conscientious and helps around the house very much. Last summer, when the family moved, she was comparatively friendless but now she has made friends at school.

The mother described Sue as having headaches and stomach aches at first when her father came to visit. Now she has a feeling that Sue thinks that men are no good. Last fall the girl saw a man beating up his wife and was so scared that for a while she would not sleep without the light on. The mother said with a smile that she herself feels that men are no good, since she sees so much of men leaving their families in worse condition even than hers.

The mother described herself as having been a very dependent person who is learning at last to be self-reliant. She was frightened at first at the thought of going back to school; now she seems eager to complete her training and start working in the dental laboratory at hours that will coincide with those of her children at school.

According to the grandmother, the mother is dating a 30-year-old man, who believes in discipline and is in school at the university.

Interview with Sue

At the beginning of the interview, Sue appeared rather quiet and shy. She seemed uneasy and responded with very brief answers to general questions concerning how she liked school, what she did in school, and what type of things she liked to do. In order to help establish rapport, the examiner, after talking with Sue for about 10 minutes, administered the HTP. Although she stated that she could not draw very well, Sue seemed to enjoy the drawing and responded with smiles to the examiner's praise of her drawings. After drawing, Sue appeared more relaxed (her hands and feet were less active) however, at no point in the interview did she initiate conversation. Sue was cooperative throughout the interview, but almost all of her answers were brief and without emotion.

Sue stated that she enjoyed school and liked most of the other children in her class. She said that she studied a good deal and liked to read, but that she was not very good in arithmetic. She has several girl friends at school who live near her. When asked what type of things they did together she said, "We ride our bicycles and go to the park and just talk." When asked what they talked about, Sue said after a long pause "just things." It was generally difficult to get her to talk at length about anything. When talking of her family, she did not mention her father; when asked how many people were in her family, she said, "Five, my mother, my three brothers, and me. Sue stated that she helped her mother a good deal with houseworking, and particularly in taking care of her youngest brother Paul, who is not yet in school. She seemed especially close to Paul and said she liked taking care of him, playing with him, and taking him to the park. She said that her mother was very busy and gave the examiner the impression that she felt it was her duty to help her mother as much as possible, as she is the only girl in the family. At times, she said, her brothers pick on her and they fight, but generally they get along pretty well together.

Sue did not mention her difficulty in getting to sleep at night, and the examiner did not want to force that topic. When the testing was concluded, the examiner asked Sue about her father by mentioning that he did not live with her family. She seemed somewhat relieved that the examiner knew that the father was living away from the family. Her face lit up, and she said spontaneously, "He called us last night and is coming to see us this weekend." This was literally the only time during the interview that Sue was spontaneous and volunteered information without questioning. When asked if she liked her father to visit, she said, "yes," somewhat unenthusiastically. When asked how she liked living here, Sue said that it was a pretty big place and that she liked living where they lived before best. There everyone knew everyone else, and then the whole family was together. She said that it was difficult changing schools when she moved here, but that she has made some friends here now. When she said that she has a paper route, the tone of her voice hinted that she didn't particularly enjoy it. When asked if it gave her some spending money, she said, "No, it goes to buy clothes for school."

Generally, throughout the interview, Sue appeared to become more at ease but not to a great degree. She was hesitant to say anything negative concerning any topic and did not talk spontaneously without questioning.

Test Observations

Sue's quiet manner prevailed throughout the testing. She was cooperative, attentive, and followed directions extremely well, yet she often had to be prompted by the examiner for a response. Her TAT stories were very short and uninformative, and would have been shorter without urging from the examiner. After giving a one-or two-sentence response, Sue would sit in silence. After four or five cards, it was obvious that Sue was not enjoying the task. She became uneasy and was moving her feet a great deal. The examiner terminated the TAT and went on to the Roger's P.A. Inventory. On the PAI, Sue took her time and thought about each question before answering. Several times, she asked the examiner to clarify a question for her. After Sue had finished the PAI, the examiner administered an abbreviated form of the Stanford-Binet. The examiner felt that Sue was uneasy during much of the testing and that it would be good to end the session with a task that she would enjoy. Sue was more responsive when administered the Stanford-Binet. She appeared to put all her energy into each subtest, showed good concentration on tasks above her mental age, and seldom needed urging to response. She seemed to enjoy the challenge of the items and left the test room with a smile.

Interview with Sue's Teacher

Several days after the evaluation, the examiner talked with Sue's teacher by phone. She stated, "I have only good things to say about Sue." She was a pleasure to have in the classroom; she was doing very well in school; she was well-liked by her classmates and had many friends. She said that Sue could be both a good leader and a good follower, but that she tended to be a leader. Sue is mature in her interactions with the children in her class and is very considerate of others. She said that Sue had talked with her previously concerning her visit, particularly about the possibility that she was different or that something was wrong with her. The teacher reassured Sue; however, she said that Sue was somewhat fearful of the visit and also that other children in the class might find out about it. She said that Sue told no one in the class, except her, about going. It is possible that Sue's fear of her visit to the clinic was in part responsible for her apparent shyness and hesitancy to initate conversation with the examiner.

Test Summary and Conclusions

In general, Sue appeared to be quiet, mature, and somewhat restricted for a girl of 11. She was unspontaneous throughout the interview and most of the testing. She was cooperative, yet would not initiate conversation. Results of the Rogers PAI and the interview indicate that Sue may feel a great deal of responsibility for her family, both by helping her mother and feeling the financial strains on the family. It is possible that this responsibility and pressure may contribute to her restricted manner and, possibly, her sleeping problem. However, the view of Sue as being very quiet and unspontaneous is contradictory to the report of her teacher concerning her school behavior. Sue's hesitancy to talk during the interview and testing may partially be a function of her worry of being different and her fear of the trip to the clinic. Results of the PAI and HTP indicate that Sue may have a feeling of inadequacy, and it is fairly evident that she unrealistically downgrades herself with respect to her looks and intelligence, as she is an attractive girl and in the high-average range of intellectual functioning, according to this assessment (IQ: 112, Stanford-Binet). The HTP also indicates the possibility that Sue may not be having her affectional needs met at home and looks to her school environment for satisfaction; however, the validity of the HTP as an instrument for personality assessment is questionable and the above interpretation is weak without supporting information.

From the PAI and interview, it is evident that although Sue is separated from her father, she includes him in her thoughts and feelings. This may be a possible source of conflict for her.

If Sue is seen in counseling, a male counselor would perhaps be preferable, in that at home she lacks a mature male figure.

Recommendations

The mother will be seen for several interviews before the end of the term to give this mother some support in handling her problems. Some reassurance may be needed for the mother, who seems overconcerned regarding the likelihood that mental illness may occur in other members of her family. Other areas troubling her are likely to be her insecurity regarding her own ability and strength, possible guilt about imposing on Sue, and fear of losing the children to the father's blandishments. It seems likely that she will eventually use the clinic resources for herself primarily.

Gene, Sue's brother, has been referred for a diagnostic evaluation.

Sue has been referred to a male counselor, with the understanding that the mother will come regularly for counseling as well. At present, she is seen as more in need of help than Sue.

Referral Information on Sue

Please state in some detail why this child is being referred for an evaluation. Describe what problems are present at home, at school, and in the community. Parents are divorced—mainly adjustment problems

When did the problems described above first begin? Has trouble getting to sleep. Has had this problem off and on for 3 to 4 years. Has gotten progressively worse in December 1969.

Home and family history:

Parents of child.

____Married _X_Divorced ____Separated ____Parent(s) Deceased

Type of neighborhood where home is located (rural, small town, city). Family housing for married students.

Is home rented or owned? Rented.   *Number of rooms.* 3 bedrooms.

Amount of total family annual income. Child support
        __X_Less than $4000.   _____$4000 to $6000.
        _____$6000 to $8000.   _____more than $8000.

Describe briefly the family's social contacts and activities.

Is this child sociable or does he prefer to be alone? Sociable.

How does this child get along with: Mother.   Yes.   *Father.*   ?

Brothers and sisters. Somewhat.

How does this child behave in adult company? Very well.

How does this child get along with friends his own age? Very well.

Interest and activities:

What are this child's main interests? Music, studies.

What recreational activities are enjoyed most? Skating, cheerleading.

Are there work responsibilities? Yes *What kind?* Some housework.

Attitude toward work. Very responsible. Acquires responsibility on her own.

This form completed by. Mother.

Second Interview with the Mother

A followup interview after the evaluation was arranged because of the likelihood that psychotherapy could not be arranged until the summer session at the earliest.

She seemed less concerned about Gene than was the case at the first interview but still desirous of an evaluation of him. The impression remains of a very concerned mother with many growing strengths. However, she is very senstive about being divorced; she is also bitter toward her former husband and resentful that he does not provide enough money to meet the needs of the children comfortably. She seems to see them as definitely underpriviledged. It is very likely that these feelings have been communicated to the children in spite of her statements that she does not wish to alienate the children from their father.

The mother made a comparison between Sue and Gene in the way in which they approach their father. Sue asks him for what she wants and sees that she gets it; Gene will not ask for this kind of help.

She has referred often to the children's need for security, as well as her own, and seems to feel that she is providing it increasingly for them. She has expressed optimism about the future when she finishes her training.

School Report on Sue

Period of time child has attended this school. 5 months.

Grades repeated: None. *At what grave level should this child be?*

Grade Marks

Subject	Present mark	Indicates improvement or deterioration (comment)
Mathematics	B+	These are typical grades
Social Studies	A	Sue is very conscientious
Science	A—	about her school work.
Reading	A	
All others	A— average	

Attendance record. Good—9 days absent this year as of March 2.
Special academic interests (please list). Biological science, ancient history.

Attendance record. Good—9 days absent this year as of March 2.
Special academic interests (please list). Biological science, ancient history.
Special academic difficulties. None.

Classroom participation. Very good.

Testing:

Name of test	Date given	Grade level when given	Scores	Administrator

Past school records not received
No tests given during 1969–1970.

Social adjustments. Describe this child's relationship with peers: Very good, Sue seems a good friend of many. She is thoughtful and kind and well accepted by different groups.

How does this child participate in groups? Sue takes an active part. She leads often but also allows others to share leadership.

What roles does he usually assume (leader, follower, passive, agressive,and so forth)? Leader, but not aggressive.

What is the child's response to authority? Good. No discipline is ever required. Very helpful and concerned at home also.

What is this child's general physicap appearance? Very attractive.

Are any particular health problems apparent? (Describe). None.

Family contact:
Please discuss briefly any problems (social or academic) that have been ob-served in this child's siblings. No problems. Both boys are active, well accepted by peers and successful in school.

What is the relationship between the school and this child's parents? The mother requested we see if Sue could be tested. Relationship is a loving and concerned one. Sue is doing much of the housework, unasked. She gets so involved in hobbies and friends, and does her schoolwork so thoroughly she seems to get overly tired and nervous. She often has much trouble sleeping. Her mother says she had the same problem as a child. Mother is either getting a divorce or has received a divorce. Sue talks of past schools but never mentions her father.

Signed, Sue's sixth grade teacher

CASE MATERIALS ON GENE

Reason for Referral

Gene was referred by his mother for the following reasons: Gene skipped school one day. He has been sleeping more than usual. He has a bitter attitude and he has a grouchy disposition at times.

Background Information

According to information available at the time of the evaluation, Gene is the oldest of four children living with his natural mother. The parents were divorced several years ago, and the father remains in a northern city where he is self-employed as an electrician. The mother is currently enrolled in school, majoring in dental hygiene. Two of the younger children attend school, and the next oldest child, Sue, has also been referred by her mother for psychological services. According to other information provided by the mother, the family income is less than $4000 a year, and as I talked with her later, she indicated her husband has been very negligent in his financial support of the children since the divorce. She describes Gene as sociable with his own age group, as having an average relationship with his mother but as having a poor relationship with his father. He gets along very well in adult company and ordinarily gets along well with his brothers and sisters, though at times they fuss. At the present time, the health history is negative. Gene has an active interest in sports including baseball, basketball, and football. She describes his attitude toward work as only one of toleration, but he has a regular paper route.

Testing

Wechsler Intelligence Scale for Children
Verbal IQ (prorated)	–104
Performance IQ (prorated)	– 86
Full Scale IQ	– 95

Wide Range Achievement Test
    Reading Grade Equivalent   – 8.7
Bender Motor-Gestalt Test
Draw-a-Person
Thematic Apperception Test (selected cards)
Rorschach Test
Consultative interview: Mother.

Test Results and Observations

Gene was a 12-year, 11-month-old boy, who arrived for the psychological evaluation unaccompanied by his mother. She was interviewed later the same day in the late afternoon at a time when she was available from her training program. Gene would be described as a rather small boy for his age who is more boyish in appearance than adolescent with secondary characteristics. He has sandy hair and freckles and gives the appearance of being well nourished and healthy. There was a noticeable scratch on his nose and he stated he has sustained the slight injury while playing baseball. His dress was average, as was his grooming. There were no apparent speech difficulties, although he often speaks rather softly. I would describe him as generally cooperative during the evaluation, although he does not express himself effectively very readily in his speech and communication. He seemed to work more eagerly on tasks that required his drawing of designs and on the human figure drawing. Concentration appeared to diminish later in the examination, although not to a point where it impaired the evaluative process. His wishes were to become a professional ball player and be of sufficient stature to be named to the Hall of Fame. I would describe Gene as a mildly passive boy but perhaps rather controlling in his general manner. He stated that he has a regular paper route which both he and his sister work on. From his report, the money which they earn is used to pay for their clothing. This was verified later by the mother during my interview with her.

The results of the WISC indicate that Gene has normal intelligence when his work was compared with the norms for his age group. Both of the areas of testing were rather widely scattered, with his general performance level noticeably higher on the verbal subtests. The low subtests reflected problems of comprehension of social requirements, and he obtained a lower score on the performance subtest of picture completion because he appeared to work rather slowly and was handicapped by the time requirements of the test. His work on the WRAT indicated reading skills well within his grade placement for the coming academic year. This finding would coincide with that reported by the teacher and would be reflective of his fairly consistent achievement in his school program. Perceptual motor tasks would be described as being completed quite satisfactorily on the Bender Test and his work was done with considerable care and accuracy. His drawing of a person presented the front view of a male, elaborately detailed with dress and facial features. Gene's response to projective tests would indicate no gross distortions in his perception of reality. However, his development of his perceptions within his own unique view of the world indicates generally some strong and angry feelings which he tends to harbor and which are evidently expressed in more passive, aggressive ways. His themes were characterized by child-mother conflict, a sense of isolation from peers and loneliness, and a lack of basic finances. Relationships are viewed as conflicting.

The mother was casually and appropriately dressed in summer wear at the time of the parent interview. It was apparent almost immediately and throughout the consultation that she is under a great deal of pressure, including the fact that she harbors many feelings about her marrige and has current reality problems of limited financial resources and academic and social pressures. She appears to need supportive work and feedback on the degree to which she is being effective in dealing with her children. She indicated her husband sees the children about once a month when he comes to town to spend time with them on a weekend. The children spend alternate holidays with the two separated parents. The mother has been active in the Parents without Partners Group and plans to attend the national meeting in Texas this summer. She has developed a restrictive social life but is generally very much confined to expending her time and energy with her family and completing her school requirements. At times during the interview, she was tearful and gives the impression of trying to pull her life back into a reasonable form with herself as the major resource. I talked with her about having a conference with a counselor from the Division of Vocational Rehabilitation to see if they might be able to provide some financial assistance for her.

Recommendations

Results of the psychological evaluation of Gene would indicate that this 12-year-old boy has developed some patterns of behavior which are not particularly adaptive, noticably within the family unit. I would recommend the following diagnosis: personality trait disturbance, passive aggressive personality, passive dependent type, mild; normal intelligence. The mother indicates a need for communication about her child-rearing practices of Gene and the other children in the family. I would recommend establishing regular (weekly) counseling services for her. It is my impression that the mother needs assistance in planning activities for her children and in getting feedback on the procedures she employs in dealing with the children. I think equally important in terms of planning on this case would be to provide therapy services in order for her to come to more effective terms with her own personal needs and the negative factors in her marriage relationship.

Referral Information on Gene

Only those items which differed from the form the mother completed on Sue are included.

Please state in some detail why this child is being referred for an evaluation. Describe what problems are present at home, at school, in the community.

April 1970: Suddenly slept more than usual.
Skipped school one day.
Has bitter attitude—grouchy disposition at times.

When did the problems described above first begin? Not completed.

Is this child sociable or does he prefer to be alone? Sociable with own age group.

How does this child get along with. Mother. Average. Father. Poor.

Brothers and sisters. Fuss sometimes; very well other times.

How does this child behave in adult company? Very well.

How does this child get along with friends his own age? Very well.

With whom does this child prefer to be? Own age group.

Interests and Activities:

What are this child's main interests? Sports—baseball, basketball, football.

What recreational activities are enjoyed most? Sports—swimming.

Are there work responsibilities? Yes. *What kind?* Paper route.

Attitude toward work. Doesn't like it. Tolerates it.

School Report on Gene

Period of time child has attended this school. One year.

Present grade level. 7.

Grades repeated. None.

Grade Marks

Subject	Present mark
Reading	C+
Mathematics	C+
Language	C
Social Studies	B
Science	C

Attendance record. Missed 16 days last year.

Special academic interests. Social studies.

Special academic difficulties. Gene seems to lack interest in most school work.

Testing program (Achievement, Intelligence, Reading, and so forth):

Name of test	Date given	Grade level when given	Scores
Macginitie Reading	Sept. 24, 1969	7.1	Vocabulary, 8.3 Comprehension 6.7
	May 14	7.9	Vocabulary 9.2 Comprehension 8.2

Social adjustment:

Describe this child's relationship with peers. Gene gets along well with most boys and girls his age. However, it was reported to school authorities that Gene hated to come to school because some of the boys have been teasing him about working.

How does this child participate in groups? Gene is quiet and does not demand attention.

What roles does he usually assume (leader, follower, passive, aggressive, etc.)? Follower.

What is the child's response to authority? Most of the time he is respectful and gives attention. Sometimes his attention wanders and he doesn't comprehend what is being said to him.

Are any particular health problems apparent? None.

Family contact: Does this child have any siblings attending this same school?

Name	Age	Grade level
Sue	11	Sixth
Omar	8	Second

What is the relationship between the school and this child's parents? Very little contact.

Signed
Gene's seventh grade teacher

EPILOGUE TO THE FAMILY COUNSELING CASE

An epilogue to the cases of Sue and Gene follows. This outcome is not the only acceptable means of handling this family; it simply represents the professional decision made.

Sometime after the original contacts described in the case materials, the mother was seen by one of the authors. This first interview added little more than what was already covered in these materials. However, it was decided during the interview that the next meeting would involve the whole family, with the exception of Paul, the youngest. These resulting sessions proved to be very productive.

In the first of these group sessions, the mother sat back and allowed the interviewer to interact with the children. It soon became apparent that Omar, the third child, was in some ways the family leader, or if not its leader, the manipulator of the others. He appeared to be very bright and could quickly think up ways to manipulate Gene and Sue when they were given parent surrogate responsibilities. This was part of the major problem for the mother because in the evenings when she had to study, the commotion in the house bothered her and Omar could usually prevent Gene and Sue from carrying out their responsibilities. Each of the family members, including the five year old, who was soon included in the sessions, realized what each sibling was doing and, in many cases, why they were doing it. Once this was out in the open, there was an attempt to talk things out, but this did not seem to change things much. There were too many ingrained patterns that were difficult to alter. For example, Omar saw Gene, a very good seventh grade athlete, as his idol. Consequently, Omar was always trying to get into Gene's games or get him to wrestle. Both boys got satisfaction from this and did not change their behavior, even though they realized that it was disruptive in the small apartment. Because the talking therapy did not seem to be bringing about rapid change, another approach was tried.

At first, with the children, in order to get their approval, and later, with just the mother, a behavior modification system was developed. The children were given points for doing everyday tasks like brushing their teeth after meals (an important aspect for their mother who was training to be a dental hygienist), getting to meals on time, and going to bed on time. These points were traded in for pleasures the children wanted, like going to the grade school basketball games or getting to choose a particular television program. As this program developed, it was interesting to note that Omar, the disrupter, was the strongest proponent of the system and that Sue, the mother surrogate, was at first the most fearful of not getting to do some of the things she wanted. In two weeks time, the system was established, with very happy results for the mother, and at least acceptable results for the children.

When the behavior modification program was in full force at home, the mother came in without the children for one more session to go over the program again. After this session it was five months until she was seen again. This contact was an accidental meeting at which she reported that she was surprised at how easy it had been to work things out in her family. She had only kept up the program for about eight weeks and then found it no longer necessary. The family unit was getting along well and, hopefully, still is.